SECRETS YOU KEEP
FROM YOURSELF

Also by Dan Neuharth, Ph.D.

If You Had Controlling Parents:
How to Make Peace with Your Past
and Take Your Place in the World

SECRETS
YOU KEEP FROM
YOURSELF

How to Stop Sabotaging
Your Happiness

Dan Neuharth, Ph.D.

St. Martin's Press ♨ New York

www.stmartins.com

Library of Congress Cataloging-in-Publication Data

Neuharth, Dan.
    Secrets you keep from yourself : how to stop sabotaging your happiness / Dan Neuharth.—1st U.S. ed.
        p. cm.
    ISBN 0-312-31247-4
    1. Self-defeating behavior. 2. Self-actualization (Psychology). I. Title.
BF637.S37N48 2004
158.1—dc22

                                                                    2003020525

First Edition: March 2004

1   3   5   7   9   10   8   6   4   2

For Alexandra, who keeps no secrets

CONTENTS

TO THE READER

This book is written for a general audience and is intended to help in understanding and coping with common problems of everyday life. It is not intended to be a substitute for psychotherapy or other health care services.

If you are experiencing any of the following . . .

- Unusual or persistent stress, anxiety, or depression

- An unaddressed chemical dependency or similar addiction

- An untreated serious medical problem or mental illness

- A physically or sexually abusive living situation

. . . then your first step in taking care of yourself is to get professional help as soon as possible. Resources for finding professional help and emotional support can be found on the author's Web site: www.SecretsWeKeep.com.

The personal stories in this book are drawn from interviews with individuals ranging in age from nineteen to seventy-eight. Names and identifying characteristics have been altered to honor the confidentiality of those interviewed.

DO YOU STOP YOURSELF SHORT
OF HAPPINESS AND FULFILLMENT?

There are three great mysteries of nature: Air to the bird, water to the fish, and man to himself.

—HINDU PROVERB

How to be more fulfilled is not a mystery. Exercise regularly. Face, rather than avoid, your problems. Help others. Have goals that matter to you. Love and be loved. Accept yourself. And there are many other such relatively straightforward paths to reducing your stress and becoming happier and healthier.

The mystery is why we don't always follow the best path.

We are undeniably complex beings. Our impulses can kidnap us. Our thoughts can mislead us. Our behaviors can mystify us. Our emotions know no reason. Part of human complexity is our innate ability to create the unimaginably good as well as to mislead, distract, or outsmart ourselves and undermine our own happiness.

We all do things on occasion that aren't in our best interests. Our *What-was-I-thinking?* moments are often harmless, even humorous. Yet many actions and oversights don't make sense. Have you ever wondered why you did something that wasn't good for you? Why you stopped yourself short of having what you wanted? Why, even when you knew the best course to take and were capable of pursuing it, you didn't take it?

We each possess uncharted inner provinces, home to anxieties and desires that steer our behavior like unseen hands. Has it ever seemed to you as though an essential part of you looked the other way while some rogue aspect took over? Whatever takes over can use what it knows about you to sweet-talk, distract, or overpower you in counterproductive ways. Curiously, at times it may seem as though part of you wants this undermining aspect to succeed.

When you take stock of such challenges as unfulfilling relationships, emotional turmoil, unhealthy habits, or career petrification, an integral factor may be that you are keeping secrets from yourself. The definition of secret is "something hidden from knowledge or view" or "using hidden aims or methods." You have probably experienced the frustration when a mate, friend, colleague, or customer deceives you or withholds part of the truth. It can hobble you and weaken the relationship. Yet we do the same to ourselves.

Take a moment and think of a time when you got in your own way. My point isn't to assign blame or kindle guilt; most of us already feel too much inappropriate guilt. The point, rather, is that if you examine the times you've unnecessarily complicated your life, you may see patterns of behavior that are at odds with who you know yourself to be and who you aspire to become. A friend who recently entered therapy shared with painful candor the insight that changed his life: "It's not the other people and situations in my life that have been making me miserable. It's me that has been making me miserable."

Perhaps you can recall one or more situations in which you consciously or unconsciously:

- Pursued short-term gain at the cost of long-term pain

- Cruised through important situations on autopilot

- Pressured yourself without letup, paying a price with your health

- Overlooked, minimized, or rationalized serious problems that you needed to face

- Ate, drank, or spent too much, then felt bad about yourself

- Ignored your intuition or experience and got hurt

- Gave yourself to those who did not cherish you, then lost self-esteem

- Waited too long or quit too soon, forfeiting your hopes and needs

- Denied yourself victory or pleasure after working hard to attain them

- Stoked unrealistic expectations, ensuring an inevitable letdown

Such lapses can cost dearly: your deepest yearnings abandoned; dearly held relationships and opportunities lost; health, energy, and time misspent; peace and contentment ransomed to a cycle of guilt and regret. The cost of self-sabotage registers in your mind, body, and heart. Your mental life may twirl in confusion or wither from harsh self-criticism. Your body may ache from addictions, stress, or injuries. Your heart may beat to anxiety, frustration, or depression.

With enough time and repetition, lapses like these become enduring patterns that may go unnoticed for years until punctured by a disquieting moment of truth. When you disclaim your deepest yearnings or inner wisdom, you imprison an essential part of yourself. This can happen quickly, ushered along by what seem at the time like compelling reasons, and keep you from the life you were meant to live. Perhaps you awake one day and recognize that you have spent years focusing on success, approval, or the rules, but have given scant attention to what matters most to you: intimate connections, inner peace, family, or contributing to others, for example. Perhaps in a candid moment you tally the damage from thousands of hours listening to a self-critical monologue and failing to give yourself votes of confidence when needed most. Or perhaps a friend's innocent comment shakes your denial and you realize that you have remained in a marriage that long ago stopped providing you with nurturance and has left you living with a mountain of grief and loneliness. Even a single, dire self-inflicted loss can significantly alter your life for the worse.

Some of life's deepest pain comes from living with a lie. When things don't turn out as you had hoped, it is easier to reconcile your disappointment when you know that you did all you could have done on your behalf. But when things go awry, and you sense that you helped derail your goals, you face the next challenge with a dirty slate instead of a fresh one.

"An unexamined life is not worth living," Socrates said. Becoming more self-aware does not mean that you will always get what you want. It does mean, however, that you are more likely to face disappointments without the added angst of wondering whether you had a hand in your own suffering.

To be sure, we cannot foresee the future, and we all have occasional errors in judgment. Yet if you've ever recalled times when you let your life drift, sold yourself short, or looked the other way, you may have wondered, "What was I doing all that time?" More importantly, it raises the more disquieting question: "How can I know for sure whether I'm acting in my best interests even now?"

Please understand me, I am not saying that you cause all of your problems. There are plenty of injustices and tragedies in the world that you had nothing to do with yet which bring you suffering. You are *not* responsible for pain that others inflict upon you. Nor am I referring to honest mistakes. We all make mistakes. Making mistakes is how we learn and grow.

Rather, it is simply a risk of human nature that we sometimes unwittingly hold back or go too far, often bringing upon ourselves the very pain we'd sought to avoid. As Wittgenstein wrote, "Nothing is so difficult as not deceiving oneself."

Getting in your own way is not uncommon. You probably see it in others pretty clearly and even know what they could have done to prevent it. But it is more difficult to see your own missteps, and it isn't always clear how to remedy them.

We keep secrets from ourselves because we seek to avoid emotional losses. Life can bring tremendous emotional loss. Tragedies befall us and treasures elude us for reasons beyond our control. We experience fear, disappointment, hurt, grief, and anger. We lose our loved ones, our good health, and, ultimately, our lives. Along the way we may lose hope, inner peace, and balance. Many of these are the necessary losses inherent in being alive, as Judith Viorst wrote in *Necessary Losses*. But what about *unnecessary* losses? How many of your losses in life are avoidable? Which losses do you, at least in part, bring upon yourself? The irony is that some of our attempts to avoid loss accelerate or magnify the very losses we had hoped to avoid.

Rita Mae Brown defined insanity as "doing the same thing over and over but expecting a different result each time." I can't tell you how often I've said to psychotherapy clients, *You're speaking as though you feel that your life is something to be endured.* Clients often respond just as I did when I was first asked this by my therapist years ago: *You mean it's not?*

Though rationally you know that we're not here just to endure, it can feel like it when your primary focus is avoiding emotional loss. You attend, consciously and unconsciously, to fears rather than desires. You risk leading, as Thoreau wrote, a life of "quiet desperation."

Many of us have accomplished what we thought would make us happy only to find happiness insufficient or fleeting. Are you *almost* happy, visiting the neighborhood of happiness, peace, and fulfillment but rarely moving in to stay? The problem is not that we don't set goals, work hard, or accomplish great things. The problem is that we undermine ourselves by means of various forms of denial.

Denial is a powerful force in personal psychology. Denial can make you feel unable to stop yourself even when you know you should. Perhaps you can recall a time when you found yourself at the *I-know-I-*

shouldn't-but-what-the-hell brink and stepped over. Maybe you were frustrated in a heated discussion so you opted to get personal. Maybe by the third spoonful of chocolate fudge ice cream you felt unable to halt your spiral to the bottom of the pint. Perhaps you allowed flirting with a subordinate at work to get out of hand.

At other times denial plays the opposite tune, and you can't get started. Perhaps you're puzzled by mounting tension between you and a friend, but you keep skirting the subject. Or perhaps someone is smoking in a no-smoking zone, talking during a movie, or making thinly disguised racist comments at a party. You may be livid but feel unable to say anything, so you stuff your feelings.

Being captain of your soul can require negotiating around extremes. For example, at one extreme you may overidealize situations or people, constructing unrealistic assumptions and expectations that will house only disappointment. At the other extreme you may undervalue yourself or others, selling yourself short or critically judging others. You may overreact to everyday situations, or feel defensive around the people closest to you. Or you may box yourself in with excessive procrastination, fantasizing, approval-seeking, or watching mental reruns.

Our self-inflicted losses and the denial that facilitates them are difficult topics to tackle. How do you focus on motivations, feelings, and actions that part of you doesn't want to see? It can be unsettling to recognize that you've acted for reasons other than you thought, particularly when the consequences were painful. When another person harms you, the object of your anger is external. But outsmart yourself, trip yourself up, or do the "same old, same-old," even though it hasn't worked for years, and who but you is responsible? My psychotherapy clients often express abundant grief over, and few easy explanations for, their self-sabotage.

Yet as uncomfortable or difficult as it may be to recognize and overcome your denial and counterproductive actions, doing so is within your reach. I'm here to tell you that denial and self-sabotage are not signs of weakness or anything to hide or feel guilty about. If you sometimes miss the boat, "step in it," or trip yourself up, you are not flawed, bad, or dysfunctional. You are human. Self-defeating behavior is a habit reinforced by biology, culture, and your individual upbringing and development. Like any habit, it can be unlearned. Disciplines from psychology to biology to economics have established a surprising truth: There is a predictable science to denial and self-sabotage. Understand that science, and you can master both the art and science of decoding the secrets you keep from yourself so that they can work *for* you rather than against you. Learning to recognize and negotiate around potentially counterproductive situations is part of life's work. Rather than being failures, your self-defeats are messages sent from within you. When you take these messages to heart, you gain more conscious use of your life.

Keeping secrets from yourself, just as keeping secrets from anyone you love, is akin to trying to keep a beach ball submerged. It requires constant energy. When you explore your secrets, you free tremendous energy. Unlike situations in which external circumstances or other people get in your way, you wield tremendous influence when it comes to your awareness and will. The key to overcoming counterproductive patterns lies not in ignoring them or feeling bad about them but in understanding how and why they happen so that you can change them. Unrecognized liabilities can reign in your life like an unseen virus. Once you see counterproductive patterns, you can heal them.

This book is designed to help you:

1. Reduce your unnecessary losses and the suffering that comes with them.

2. Increase your self-awareness and authenticity, and let go of the suffering that comes from not being yourself.

What I ask of you is an openness to look inward, reflect, and be honest with yourself about what you observe. When you "know thyself" in the full sense of Diogenes' words, you open the path to "thine own self be true" in every sense of Shakespeare's phrase. We'll explore what gets in the way of knowing and being true to yourself. We'll discover what obstructs your life's flow and how you can allow your life to flow optimally. Along the way, we'll explore six questions at the heart of being yourself:

- **Who are you at your best, and what makes you lose touch with your best self?**
  Part One will explore the nature and payoffs of self-sabotage, payoffs that can make acting in your worst interests appear to be your best choice.

- **How can you more readily recognize and overcome unhealthy habits and overreactions?**
  Part Two will show you several early-warning signs of denial and self-sabotage so that you can seek healthier outcomes.

- **What are the keys to overcoming fear?**
  Part Three will explore how your personal "Defense Department" can keep you living behind a facade or shutting down emotionally. Understanding this process can enhance your emotional authenticity.

- **How can you achieve greater balance and self-acceptance?**
  Part Four will help you recognize and harness the power of your deepest strengths, values, and desires, including some that you may have overlooked or forgotten.

- **How can you best triumph over adversity?**
  Part Five will offer tools to help when you feel stuck or overwhelmed. You'll learn how to take control by defining any problem, no matter how difficult or long-standing, so that it can best be solved.

- **How can you live each day based on what really matters to you?**
  The final part of the book will offer seven principles to take forward into your daily life to foster serenity and fulfillment.

Each of us has regrets, what-ifs, and if-onlys. Hindsight can be a useful source of learning, especially if you don't use it to beat yourself up, and hindsight is always clearer than foresight. But what if you could substantially sharpen your foresight and increase your awareness of potentially self-defeating situations, particularly in areas that matter most to you? What if you could harness willpower that you may not know that you have and act in your best interests even when tempted otherwise? What if you could make peace with lingering guilt or regret over past self-defeats?

You could change the course of your life.

Let's get started.

PART ONE

◆

The Secrets We Keep

The discovery of a deceiving principle, a lying activity within us, can furnish an absolutely new view of all conscious life.

—JACQUES RIVIÈRE

This book will address the three components to reducing your unnecessary losses and increasing your happiness and fulfillment:

1. Recognizing when you are at risk for self-inflicted losses (Parts One and Two)

2. Understanding the self-undermining influences in your life and learning how to transcend them (Part Three)

3. Motivating yourself to choose the healthiest paths (Parts Four and Five)

1

WHO ARE YOU WHEN
YOU'RE NOT BEING YOURSELF?

*We are so used to disguising ourselves from others that we end up
disguising ourselves from ourselves.*

—FRANÇOIS DE LA ROUCHEFOUCAULD,
DUC DE LA ROUCHEFOUCAULD

We want to know and be known for our very best. One way we identify
this is to look for the best in others. You probably have known rare individuals who seem to craft their lives moment-by-moment with deliberate, positive actions. People like Morrie Schwartz of *Tuesdays with Morrie*,
Mitch Albom's book about the seventy-eight-year-old former sociology
professor who met his terminal illness with inspiring dignity and grace.
How do people like Morrie live exceptional lives? What can we learn
from such people about cultivating the exceptional in ourselves?

Perhaps you feel at your best when you "follow your bliss," as Joseph
Campbell wrote. Who or what within you recognizes your bliss and
leads you to it? Pause for a moment and recall a time when you felt
deeply content. Perhaps you experienced an epiphany about your life's
goals, felt at peace with the world, or intuitively knew the right choice
in difficult circumstances. Think of your most intimate relationship or
closest friendship, and recall an exceptionally satisfying moment. Perhaps you felt deeply connected, seen, and heard. What was the source
of these moments? What made them end? How might you create them
more often?

The answers on how to cultivate and express the exceptional within
you are found to a large extent in how you define yourself. You have the
ability to define who you are at any moment. For example, surveys have
reported that:

- 25 percent of high school students rated themselves in the top 1
  percent in leadership ability

- 80 percent of drivers rated themselves as better than average

- 83 percent of college students thought themselves more generous than other people

- 94 percent of university professors ranked themselves better than average at their jobs

- 85 percent of people rate their own manners as good or excellent, but only 23 percent give the same marks to others

- Individual investors at one conference confidently predicted, on average, that their own retirement savings would be twice the average size of the savings of all other investors in attendance

Flattering self-definitions like these are benign. Self-images exist on a continuum from helpful to harmful. You can view yourself as small or big, dumb or smart, unworthy or worthy, loser or winner. When you define yourself as small, dumb, unworthy, or a loser—even when you do so without awareness and are none of these—your attitudes, emotions, and actions move in accordance with this negative self-view. You can mentally negate years of love or work with a single thought. You can look at a twenty-year marriage and see only what is missing. You can look at a career of overcoming challenges and contributing to others and think, "So what?" Of course, the goodness in your marriage isn't actually lost and your career accomplishments don't actually vanish. But when you feel small, it is as though what you do counts for nothing.

The vast array of ways we define ourselves without knowing we're doing so is astounding. A fleeting first impression, when acted upon, sets in motion one course of events and excludes a universe of possible others. A doubt, once you run with it, can dictate your actions and moods. You might take a moment and recall a time when you lost an opportunity, a cherished connection, financial wealth, or happiness because you were behaving in accord with a negative self-image. *Simply because of a definition.*

You've probably seen this happen to loved ones. At times, they may have chosen to quit, even when you knew they could have kept going and succeeded. At other times, they may have chosen to believe in themselves, perhaps with your help, and kept going instead.

The irony is that every time you undermine yourself with a negative or inaccurate self-image, you provide evidence of your extraordinary power. You possess an innate ability to make a convincing case for your worth, or the lack of it. You can foster your dreams as well as neglect them. You can act from self-confidence or be overtaken by worry or guilt. Most important of all, you have the ability to forget who chose one self-image over another.

How Self-deception Works

How can you deceive yourself? It seems a contradiction in terms. One analogy for how self-deception works, offered by philosophy scholar Herbert Fingarette, is to that of falling asleep. Each night you go to bed and eventually sleep overtakes you. When you awaken, you may recall what your last thoughts were prior to falling asleep, or remember your first dream of the night, but it is impossible to remember the *exact moment* you fell asleep. In this shift from awake to asleep, even though you are the one doing it, sleep descends upon you.

Self-deception is similar. Just as we are unaware of what is happening at the moment of falling asleep, we are unaware of the moment we enter into self-deception. Denial, like falling asleep, is experienced as happening *to* you. If you're aware of falling asleep, you're not yet asleep. When you see your denial at work, you're no longer fully in denial.

During sleep, magical events happen. You dream. Your attention is selective. You may stir at the sound of your infant crying, but pay no attention to city sirens or country crickets. Similarly, with self-deception, you see what you want and ignore what's in plain sight. Self-deception lives in a world of alternate realities based on "what-if" or "if-only" premises. Social psychology researchers call this phenomenon *counterfactual thinking*. It is, quite literally, thinking and perceiving contrary to the facts.

Counterfactualizing has benefits, or we wouldn't do it. It can give feelings of mastery, explain mysterious or upsetting events, and soothe or console by allowing you to shift blame or justify your own or others' actions. But your alternate realities may also drop roadblocks in your path.

When I began researching this book and told others that I was investigating how and why people subtly mislead themselves and unwittingly sabotage their dreams and plans, the most common response I received was, "Oh, I know someone like that." Self-sabotaging behavior is often easier to see in others than in ourselves. When we view others' self-sabotage or lack of self-awareness, we often rubberneck as if passing a car wreck. It's distressing to see but fascinating to watch. We can't believe what they're doing. We're glad it's not us. We'd shudder to think of ourselves as similarly clueless, inept, or self-destructive. We wonder why they can't see it. We may try to warn them but it often seems as if they can't or won't listen.

For example, perhaps you've noticed friends, family, neighbors, or coworkers who:

- Repeatedly enter into inappropriate romantic relationships, each time vowing that this one will be different

- Spend more time fantasizing about improbable financial windfalls, like winning the lottery, than working

- Overbook and overpromise so often that you no longer trust what they say

- Work hard to lose twenty pounds through various diets, then quickly regain the lost weight and then some

- Dwell on regrets or resentments and can't seem to move on

- Endlessly take care of others' needs ahead of their own but, in a candid moment, tell you how unappreciated they feel

- Procrastinate by submitting a job application late after hours of hard work, only to find the job filled

- Make major decisions without considering the consequences

- Automatically shun advice or a helping hand

- Ignore a romantic partner's mistreatment, or stay in an unhealthy relationship even after deciding to leave

- Overspend wildly, but get a steady stream of new credit card applications

- Yearn to have children, but choose potential mates who clearly signal they aren't interested in being a parent

Everybody Keeps Secrets

Self-sabotaging denial is universal even among the famous and powerful. Two presidents faced impeachment after sabotaging themselves. Richard Nixon tried to cover up Watergate. Bill Clinton tried to cover up the Monica Lewinsky affair. Despite each man's strengths and accomplishments, their presidencies descended into embarrassment not only because they tried to keep secrets from the public, but because they kept secrets from themselves.

Nixon audiotaped the Oval Office, then proceeded to repeatedly break the law and incriminate himself with the tapes running. What was he thinking? In wanting a record for posterity, he tied his own noose. Call it denial, a tragic flaw, or karma, Nixon engineered his march to the brink of impeachment and subsequent resignation.

Clinton had an affair, but steadfastly denied it to a grand jury, friends, and the public. Then he admitted it. How could a man so intelligent use such poor judgment in his personal behavior, lie about it, then fail to take into account the damage that would ensue when his lie was exposed?

Both Nixon and Clinton were in denial. Despite the immense power and responsibility of the office, the men who have been president and the women and men who will be president are just like you and me. They mislead, distract, and undermine themselves.

What drives this phenomenon that has brought down presidents, kings, and the rich and powerful? Self-defeating denial has the power to hurt you and those you love in ways large and small. Most of us put a premium on not hurting others. Yet we hurt ourselves with a vast array of self-defeating behaviors.

One reason it can be difficult always to act in your best interests is that behavior occurs along a continuum of awareness. At one end, you have little or no awareness of your actions or their negative consequences until afterward. At the opposite end, you know full well that what you're doing isn't in your best interests, but you do it anyway. In between, your awareness may be diffuse, for example an inkling or vague concern. It may be fleeting—a mental warning that passes quickly. You may know what to do but can't summon the motivation to act. Or you have competing motivations and can't choose.

The following table illustrates this continuum.

Continuum of Awareness						
	Less aware	<	<	>	>	More aware
What you do	Fail to recognize counter-productive behavior until it's too late	Recognize the potential for self-sabotage but get distracted	Recognize the potential for self-sabotage but become confused or ambivalent	Recognize the potential for self-sabotage but justify, dismiss, or misjudge the situation	Recognize the potential for self-sabotage but feel unable to act any other way	Recognize the potential for self-sabotage but don't want to act any other way

No matter where you find yourself on the continuum of awareness, denial plays a role. When you have no clue that you're getting in your way, your denial is total. You have little chance of avoiding unnecessary losses and no choice about the outcome. At best, you get lucky. Yet even when it seems as though you see the complete picture, something may be overlooked. Denial clouds your ability to see what you are doing, why you're doing it, and the negative consequences. As with the moment of falling asleep, something goes unwitnessed. It may be something you're distracting yourself from, pretending about, or bringing selective inattention to. Perhaps you lack a full recognition of the risks. Perhaps you silently abandon your values.

Counterproductive efforts to sidestep loss:

1. Tend to be reactive rather than chosen

2. Are more likely to arise when you don't see all your options

The remedy for both is greater self-awareness.

Self-deception Takes Many Forms

Our secrets can be difficult to spot because they take so many forms. One of the most subtle ways of undermining ourselves is what social scientists sometimes term "self-handicapping."

Steven, now a distinguished and able engineer, nearly failed his licensing exam. He initially answered the multiple-choice test on scrap paper rather than on the exam sheet. He finished with a half hour to spare and began reviewing his answers, after which he intended to transfer the answers to the official scanner-ready sheet. The next thing he knew, the exam proctor announced, "Time is up, pencils down." Steven stared in shock at his empty answer sheet alongside his answers on scrap paper.

A sympathetic proctor allowed him to fill in the answer sheet under the proctor's scrutiny, and an appeal to the licensing board eventually allowed his score, which was significantly higher than average, to count.

During the test, Steven felt that he was acting with good intentions. He wanted to be as certain of his answers as possible and hand in a pristine answer sheet without erasures or smudges. Afterward, his near-miss shook him. "I still don't know what I was thinking. If I were going to be all psychological about it, I suspect that my trial-run answer sheet might have to do with being nervous about making a final commitment to each answer," Steven says.

Why would Steven fear commitments? One possibility is that he feared the blow to his self-esteem that a failure would trigger. Another possibility is that self-handicapping like Steven's can be an indirect way of protesting against authority when we feel we cannot directly or openly say no. In addition, self-handicapping covertly carries the potential to turn daunting situations into no-lose enterprises. If you put obstacles in your way and still triumph, your victory is all that much greater. Should you fail, you have ready-made explanations to excuse or mitigate your loss.

There's nothing sinister or premeditated in self-handicapping. It happens when you haven't yet brought sufficient awareness to recognize and understand your counterproductive patterns.

Judy, a smart and competent attorney, nearly missed her shot at law school because she forgot to accept an offer of admission by the deadline. She was in her senior year of college and routinely met deadlines for her term papers and tests. She even submitted her law school financial aid package paperwork on time. But at 8 P.M. on May 15 she realized that she'd missed the law school's May 15 deadline for accepting admission offers. Only after a breakneck trip to a large city post office 100 miles away was Judy able to get her acceptance form postmarked before midnight to secure her admission to law school.

Sometimes self-handicapping like Judy's is an attempt to resolve the dissonance between promising circumstances and a poor self-image. Judy grew up doubting her worth and abilities. In high school she wasn't part of the "in crowd" and didn't feel particularly attractive. Although Judy ranked twenty-third in a class of 350, in her way of thinking she was undeserving of being in the same league with the very top students. Yet here she was applying to be a lawyer, a career that would surpass most of her classmates, which seemed at odds with her downcast self-image. In the clandestine calculations of Judy's unconscious, forgetting the law school deadline may have been a way to take pressure off herself.

From a logical viewpoint, it is obvious that, rather than easing Judy's stress, missing the deadline would actually create more stress. But the logic of self-defeat follows its own rules. Perhaps some part of Judy, home to her feeling undeserving, couldn't allow her symbolically to enter law school through the front door, so it orchestrated a last-minute backdoor entry.

Both Steven and Judy had no awareness of their near-misses until it was nearly too late. When you handicap yourself as Steven or Judy did, it's as though an inner trickster nimbly detours you, laying down camouflage or distractions that fog your normal awareness. The muffled warning shouts of your best self are noticed only in retrospect.

Other forms of getting in your own way are less subtle.

Roy, a stockbroker, cannot think of a single area of his life he could describe as "laid back." His lengthy workday to-do lists are matched by his lists of household chores for his days off. He cannot recall the last time he had five minutes with nothing to do. "I tell people that I'm not just a type A personality, I'm a type A-plus personality," Roy says. Yet Roy assigns himself a failing grade when it comes to attending to his wife and two children. His wife has learned that trying to initiate spontaneous romantic or family activities can be a lost cause. His daughter must make appointments with Roy two days in advance to get help with her homework.

Roy's modus operandi is quite different from Steven's and Judy's. Instead of lacking awareness about what he is doing in the moment, Roy sees the problem but believes that he cannot behave any other way. He feels a slave to his obsessive, hard-driving style.

Feeling unable to change can be a deal brokered by part of the unconscious mind. For example, saying that you are unable to change a bad habit can be a polite way of expressing a less palatable truth: that you don't want to change. Roy may derive benefits from ordering his world so rigidly. Any potential appeal of easing up may be dwarfed by the dangers that he perceives would ensue from living more spontaneously. He may be so unaccustomed to unstructured downtime that he fears that having nothing to do would threaten his stability and sense of self.

Another reason we sometimes feel unable to change an unhealthy habit or lifestyle is that the habit is powered by deep, self-defeating beliefs like *I don't deserve to have it all.* We each construct our identity in childhood, unwittingly striking bargains before we understand their implications. We may conclude that happiness is a mysterious experience over which we have little influence. In Roy's case, he may believe deep down that he can be happy in love or happy in work, but not both.

Celine, fifty-four, is her own worst critic. When she stands in front of a mirror, she sees crow's feet, bad posture, and a disappointingly matronly appearance. "Sometimes when I look into the mirror I feel like a criminal in a police lineup," Celine says. She is judgmental of her actions, even second-guessing her idle chit-chat at parties and worrying that she comes across as lacking intelligence.

Just as Roy feels overwhelmed by his driven style, Celine feels overpowered by negative self-judgments. She knows that her self-criticism isn't healthy but feels unable to hold a balanced view of herself. Simply contemplating the possibility of a more positive self-image summons an internal mental "giant or ogre," as she calls it, that towers menacingly until Celine retreats to her self-critical norm.

Diminishing yourself, however painful its side effects, can have the benefit of reducing your own and others' expectations of you. If you aren't all that great, it makes sense not to tackle big challenges. Tearing yourself down keeps a psychic status quo. Sometimes excessive self-deprecation is a pattern learned in your family. Celine remembers her mother as a nonstop worrier. "She would just go on automatic and think out loud, voicing her worries about every little thing. It was like she would open a vein and bleed worry," Celine says.

Whereas Roy feels hostage to an internal overachiever, Celine feels under the thumb of an inner ogre. Both are demons of their own creation. It's not that Roy's compulsiveness or Celine's self-doubts are not real—they are all too real. These patterns take a toll. They can't simply be wished away. The irony is that both Roy and Celine feel inferior to a part of themselves.

You may not have an inner critic as dramatic as Celine's, but you may undermine yourself without knowing it. How often do you withhold from yourself the benefit of the doubt? How often do you deprive yourself of positive experiences?

Self-definitions can also bedevil intimate relationships. With unconscious hypocrisy, we sometimes undercut our closest connections but live as though someone else is responsible.

Harold, thirty-three, and Maggie, thirty-two, have been married for three years. When Maggie's cat Tipper died at age sixteen, Maggie was teary for days. Tipper and Maggie had been together since Maggie was a junior in high school. Harold was initially gentle and supportive, but shifted his demeanor by the third day of Maggie's mourning. He told her that continuing to talk tearfully about Tipper would only make things worse. He suggested Maggie consider getting a kitten to replace Tipper.

Harold and Maggie struggle with a dynamic familiar to many couples: opposite emotional styles. "Maggie's the emotional one in our marriage. I'm the logical one," Harold says. When Maggie expresses difficult emotions, Harold feels compelled to offer solutions. "When someone close to me is upset, I feel as though I have to fix it," Harold says.

Maggie doesn't want Harold to "fix it." She wants him to listen, so she can feel a connection with him. When he offers solutions, she feels misunderstood and pressured. She then dismisses or ignores Harold's suggestions. In turn, Harold feels confused and put off.

Harold tends to not show emotions easily, partly as a result of his formal, upper-crust British upbringing. Although Harold is largely unaware of it, Maggie's emotionality stirs up all manner of feelings in him. By focusing on Maggie's problems, Harold avoids facing his own frighteningly strong emotions. Underlying his fix-it response is a belief, held mostly out of Harold's awareness and thus unquestioned, that strong feelings could destroy him. With his mind working overtime to find logical solutions to Maggie's problems, Harold has little time or motivation to get in touch with his emotional needs and desires.

For her part, Maggie has backed into a reactive posture, ever more upset about Harold's intellectualized approach. "I love my husband, but when he goes into problem-solving mode with my feelings, it's pretty damn hard to remember why I love him," Maggie says.

On the continuum of awareness of potentially counterproductive behavior, Harold is somewhere between Steven's and Judy's lack of awareness, and Roy's and Celine's full awareness. Harold has fleeting recognitions that he does not act wisely, but most of the time he blames Maggie or distracts himself from the true cause of his anxiety.

Harold could break up his counterproductive dance by paying more attention to his motives, feelings, and beliefs. He could realize that it is not Maggie's feelings but rather his own fears of emotional overload that scare him. He could then choose to deal with his feelings—or not—but either way he would not be blaming Maggie.

Maggie could remind herself that even though Harold may do things she doesn't like, she has the choice to not take his actions personally. She could remind herself that his conscious intent is to be helpful.

Unnecessary Complications

The common thread is that Steven, Judy, Roy, Celine, Harold, and Maggie are unnecessarily complicating their lives. No one other than Steven and Judy caused them to flirt with career disaster. No one outside of Roy or Celine maintains their compulsive, self-depriving patterns. No one but Harold is responsible for his fix-it manner, just as no one but Maggie is responsible for how she reacts to it.

Acknowledging when you undermine yourself can be unsettling. Self-inflicted losses hurt just as much as life's necessary losses but carry an added pain: you have no one to point to but yourself. We don't always wish to know our motives or see the consequences of our actions, particularly when our motives feel dishonorable or the consequences hurt us and those close to us. It can be a challenge to acknowledge behaviors that trigger sorrow, embarrassment, or shame. You may worry that peering into your darker corners will open a Pandora's box. You have to live with yourself, after all, and each of us has his or her own comfort level for confronting unpleasant realities.

In addition, an innate dilemma of self-awareness is how you can possibly be aware of what you are hiding from yourself. In the movie *Awakenings*, Robert De Niro plays a patient in a psychiatric hospital who emerges from a years-long catatonic state after being given an experimental drug. The more he awakens, the more he wants to do, see, and be, much to the alarm of some of the hospital's staff. In one scene, a defensive hospital administrator confronts De Niro by saying, "Are you aware of how much unconscious hostility you are exhibiting?"

De Niro answers calmly, "If it's unconscious, how could I possibly be aware of it?"

Nevertheless, there are clues to motivations and feelings that live outside your conscious awareness. Have you ever noticed a symphony of symptoms tuning up when you are face to face with a daunting task? For example, you may suddenly feel tired or hungry, have a headache, or feel a strong need to exercise. Pleasant or mindless distractions like reading the latest *People* magazine or vacuuming the kitchen floor may beckon convincingly. As you contemplate starting a difficult task, you may feel resentful, confused, indecisive, or doubtful of your abilities. Perhaps you feel a compelling need to make a better to-do list before starting.

Any of these may be instances of denial hijacking your mind, body, or heart. Self-sabotaging denial is often a cement mixed of selective inattention and rationalization. Each time we skip exercising, avoid flossing, or overeat, we make a concrete decision to do so. We tend to do it so smoothly, however, that we rarely experience making deliberate choices. The same can be true for more significant lapses, like postponing saving for retirement or ignoring medical conditions.

At times denial can help you cope. For example, deciding to not think about something stressful, or ignoring someone who is annoying you. In addition, some facts of life—the extent of suffering in the world, for example—might lead to despair or emotional paralysis if dwelled upon relentlessly.

The key is learning how to distinguish adaptive or benign denial from counterproductive, risky denial. Counterproductive denial leads you to overlook or dismiss information that could make your life better. Risky denial hides potential dangers from you. One remedy for counterproductive, risky denial is to examine how you relate to yourself.

Your relationship with yourself is unlike any other relationship you have. You stand with yourself at every moment of your life. No one bears witness to your every success, defeat, pain, and pleasure as you do. Other loved ones may accompany you in body and spirit for a majority of your life, yet their witnessing is imperfect and incomplete.

Your feelings and thoughts about yourself are every bit as complex and powerful as those you have about other significant people in your life. When you are perplexed or in turmoil about your relationship with a mate, child, parent, sibling, or friend, it can be difficult to ignore. Yet when you are puzzled by or at odds with yourself, it may be easier to look the other way.

In your relationships with others, contact and intimacy, no matter how rich or healthy, may bring doubts or an urge to distance, merge, or control. You don't tell others everything you are thinking, feeling, or doing. But how do you keep these from yourself? Where do you go to take a vacation from a 24/7 lifelong companion?

If a marriage is stale or smothering, some people seek help, end the relationship, or escape through affairs. But how do you "cheat" on yourself? How do you reject, fight, love, disdain, and make peace with yourself? Is it any wonder that we get bored, play games, fantasize, look the other way, or space out? We need the breathing room. Though many of us struggle with intimacy and judgments of others, true self-acceptance may be one of the most difficult tasks we face.

Fortunately, you don't have to uncover every self-deception—nor could you—and your remedies don't have to be perfect. Your best ally in overcoming harmful denial is its architect: you. It is within your relationship with yourself that a significant portion of the quality of your life is determined. You have within you all the raw materials you need to increase your self-awareness and reduce your unnecessary losses. Knowledge is power. Even a small increase in self-awareness goes a long way.

Creating "Wake-up" Calls

You possess the ability to awaken and start anew psychologically and emotionally at any time. As Jean Houston wrote, "We all have the extraordinary coded within us, waiting to be released." You might take a moment and recall a time when you "woke up." Perhaps you realized that you had lost course, fallen for an illusion, or hidden behind a pretense. Remember how it felt to awaken? Perhaps you felt awed, a bit disoriented, or more energetic. You engineered these moments of clarity.

One way to release the extraordinary within you is to recognize and learn from the times when you operate from less than your best self. Even a trivial instance of counterproductive behavior can teach you as much as the most costly example. All self-inflicted losses share certain principles. Recognizing those principles even in the smallest situation can help you choose a healthier course in future instances when you have a great deal at stake.

The key to creating personal wake-up calls is to recognize how you put yourself to sleep. The following exercise can help.

If You'd Like to Go Deeper: Identifying Your Customary Approaches to Challenges

This exercise can stimulate your thinking about how you tend to approach various kinds of challenges. The more clearly you identify your unique style, the more effectively you can prepare for any potential pitfalls that are inherent in your characteristic approach.

The following eight questions will ask you to generalize. Try to pick the answer that *best* describes your tendency in that situation, even if none of the answers completely fits for you. There are no right or wrong answers.

1. When I get overwhelmed by a difficult task, it is *most* likely to occur when I am . . .

    ■ Trying to get started on the task

    ■ Somewhere in the middle of the task

    ■ Trying to finish the task

2. When I don't pursue my desires, it is *most* likely because . . .

    ■ I'm unsure about or unaware of my true desires

    ■ I feel undeserving of, or unable to achieve, my desires

    ■ I'm too busy, overwhelmed, or distracted

3. When I get stuck, the *most* difficult part for me tends to be . . .

    ■ Admitting that I'm stuck

    ■ Knowing what to do about it

    ■ Taking steps to get unstuck

4. When it comes to my emotions, it is *most* difficult for me to . . .

    ■ Know what I am feeling

    ■ Express what I am feeling

    ■ Accept what I am feeling

5. Among the following emotions, I *least* like to feel . . .

▪ Anger

▪ Sadness

▪ Fear

6. Among the following emotions, I am *most* distressed when I feel . . .

▪ Lonely

▪ Unworthy

▪ Out of control

7. Among the following aspects of myself, I tend to pay the *least* attention to my . . .

▪ Mental life (i.e., attitudes, self-talk, thinking patterns, introspection)

▪ Physical life (i.e., bodily sensations and needs, physical appearance, health)

▪ Emotional life (i.e., moods, feelings, intuitions)

8. When my thoughts drift from the here-and-now, I am *most* likely to be thinking about . . .

▪ The future

▪ The past

▪ Someplace else I'd rather be at the moment

Interpreting Your Answers

Review your answers and then look at the following descriptions of how each coping style might manifest in self-sabotaging ways. Remember, none of the choices is bad or wrong. Every way of coping with difficult or uncomfortable situations has advantages and disadvantages. Self-sabotage tends to result from choices made without awareness. By becoming more aware of your unique coping style, you can more readily anticipate potential self-sabotaging situations and be prepared if they arise.

Q1: Being Overwhelmed by Difficult Tasks

At one time or another, all of us have frozen in the face of a challenge. What is important is how readily you recognize the situation and find ways to extricate yourself.

How being overwhelmed may manifest

If your greatest resistance tends to be at the *start* of tasks, you may notice that you tend to think of worst-case scenarios or exaggerate expected difficulties. You may delay getting started by doing a host of less-difficult, less-necessary tasks. You may avoid putting yourself in situations that involve frequent change, instead favoring situations with a steady routine. Perhaps you seek longer-term projects that you can do at your own pace, rather than shorter-term projects that require frequent adjustments and innovation.

If you tend to bog down in the *middle* of challenges, you may notice that what once seemed important, even vital, becomes questionable. You may lose touch with your initial motivation or begin finding fault with the project itself. You may rationalize your lack of desire or progress, perhaps blaming others or external circumstances. You may become increasingly distracted, miss deadlines, or fall behind the pace. You may unconsciously do things that let your momentum drop. For example, skipping regular reviews with other people or scheduling important incentives too soon or too late in the project, thus leaving yourself with few tangible rewards during the long middle stretch.

If you tend to run out of steam just as you approach the *finish* line, you may tend to start new projects before finishing existing ones. New projects can seem fresh and exciting and draw your attention away from completing the old task. Perhaps failing to finish allows you to escape the judgment or final review of others. In social situations, you may avoid emotionally charged good-byes. For example, if you or someone you care about is moving on, you may promise to say a final good-bye before you part, yet somehow never do.

(Part Five will show you powerful tools for shaking off feeling overwhelmed at any stage of a challenge.)

Q2: Failing to Pursue Your Desires

Identifying when and why you forfeit your desires is an important part of zeroing in on self-sabotaging behavior. If fear is the stick, desire is the carrot. Desire can be as powerful a motivator as fear, if not more so.

How failing to pursue your desires may manifest

If you don't pursue your desires primarily because you don't know what you want, perhaps you haven't given yourself permission to wish or desire. You may have become used to not getting what you want. As a result, perhaps you no longer bother to think about your desires, much less try to achieve them. You may need to clarify your longings. (Possible ways to do this include reading books like *What Color Is Your Parachute?*, consulting a counselor, talking with a trusted friend, or making a list of the happiest times of your life and then identifying which desires were fulfilled on those occasions.)

If you feel undeserving of or unable to achieve your desires, perhaps you hold inaccurate views of yourself and the world. You may give others the benefit of the doubt but sell yourself short. You may follow a low-risk, low-reward approach, aiming low rather than pursuing what you really desire. You may notice negative self-assessments like *I'm not strong enough* or *I'll never be ready.* Such thinking patterns can arise from a history of being criticized or repeatedly being disappointed.

If you are too busy or distracted to pursue your desires, perhaps you've lost sight of what matters most in your life. This can happen all too easily in a busy life, because having too much on your plate may offer benefits. Overactivity can give you a socially acceptable method of avoiding risks. For example, if you desire something but have strong fears of falling short, your crammed schedule makes it easy to put off your desire and, thus, avoid a potential failure.

(Part Four will show you several ways to articulate and promote your greatest desires.)

Q3: Getting Stuck

We all bog down at times. When you don't recognize that you're stuck, or you cannot move forward, the underlying issue may be a fear of being criticized.

How getting stuck may manifest

If your Achilles' heel in difficult situations tends to be admitting that you're stuck, you may tend to deny problems, cling to wishful thinking or unrealistic expectations, or become defensive in the face of questions or criticism. Perhaps you view getting stuck as a sign of weakness or incompetence, so you are reluctant to admit it when you get bogged down. By avoiding recognizing a problem, you may unconsciously hope to avoid rejection, disappointment, or feeling like a failure.

If you generally recognize when you're stuck but are unsure how to free yourself, you may tend to second-guess every solution you come up with. You may shy away from asking for help. When you do ask for help, you may "yes, but" others' suggestions. You may overlook your past successes and lessons learned in similar situations.

If you know how to move forward but just can't do it, you may be in the grip of a harsh inner critic. Feeling paralyzed, you may lose sight of any incentives and motivation for moving forward. This paralysis may manifest as attitudes like *I can't, I don't want to,* and *It won't matter what I do.* In such a downward spiral you may forget a simple truth: sometimes you have to "just do it" even when you don't feel like it. Once you get started, your energy may increase as your resistance evaporates.

(Part Three will show you how to overcome denial and resistance that can keep you stuck.)

Q4: Dealing with Your Emotions

Each of us has dozens of emotions every day, yet awareness of feelings varies from person to person. Having difficulty knowing, expressing, or accepting your emotions may reflect fears of losing control.

How difficulties with your emotions may manifest

If you find it difficult to *know* what you are feeling, you may have a habit of isolating or distracting yourself during emotionally charged situations. You may act out your feelings in counterproductive ways without even knowing it. This may result from growing up in an emotionally dysfunctional family in which emotions were rarely expressed or expressed irresponsibly. As a result, you may have come to view feelings as foreign territory.

If you recognize your feelings but find it hard to express them, you may hold a conscious or unconscious belief that expressing certain emotions will harm you or others. Or you may fear that you won't be able to control yourself once you start expressing a difficult emotion.

You may tend to seek the perfect way of saying what you are feeling, but rarely find it.

If you have difficulty accepting your feelings, you may view emotions as "things" that are somehow separate from you. Perhaps you think that some feelings are "wrong." Yet by not accepting your emotional self, you deprive yourself of vital clues that could help you recognize and recover from self-sabotage.

(Part Three will help you understand and more readily express your emotions.)

Q5: Least-favored Emotions

Anger, sadness, and fear are the "Big Three"—the most troublesome emotions for many people. These raw, primal emotions touch our core.

How avoiding anger, sadness, or fear may manifest

If you struggle most with *anger*, you may hold that emotion in for too long and then explode out of proportion to the situation at hand. You may even vigorously deny that you are angry. You have probably noticed another person wearing a forced smile, even when it was obvious that he or she was fuming. Difficulty with anger may also reflect a discomfort with asserting yourself. You may view anger as an illegitimate or dangerous emotion. It is easy to forget that anger, like all emotions, is innately natural and healthy. Anger is a sign of a real or perceived violation of your rights or needs. As such, it can motivate you to protect your legitimate rights.

If you struggle with *sadness*, you may postpone grieving life's necessary losses. When sadness arises, you may distract yourself with activity, leave, or instead feel other emotions like boredom or irritability. You may avoid talking about situations that make you feel sad. You may downplay or even stop having expectations, hoping to avoid the disappointment from unfulfilled expectations. It is easy to forget that sadness is a natural response to emotional loss. Expressing sadness, while sometimes painful, can be profoundly cleansing.

If you deny or ignore *fear*, you may stick to tried-and-true activities, put great stock in superstitions, or follow habits that make you feel protected. It is easy to forget that fear, like anger and sadness, is an innate, helpful emotion. Healthy fear is a warning sign of danger.

(Parts Three and Four will help you distinguish between healthy and unhealthy responses to fear and other emotions.)

Q6: Distressing Emotions

Feeling lonely, flawed, or out of control can be distressing because all three tend to trigger a sense of being fundamentally bad or wrong as a person.

How reactions to distressing emotions may manifest

Feeling excessive *loneliness* may spark negative and inaccurate self-assessments, which can hasten a downward spiral in anybody's mood. This is one reason we seek to connect and be active. Yet if you will do anything to avoid feeling lonely, you may be tempted to settle for unsatisfying relationships. You may also neglect the opportunity to get to know and accept yourself.

If you will do anything to avoid feeling *flawed*, you may be hypersensitive when you feel criticized or judged. You may work especially hard, perhaps to the point of unhealthy perfectionism. You may be tempted to seek validation from external sources such as money, power, or beauty.

If you will do anything to avoid feeling *out of control*, you may compensate by becoming overly controlling of yourself or others. You may seek situations where you alone are in charge of the outcome, preferring not to be subject to a superior's rules or scrutiny. Before trying something new, you may insist on knowing all the details. You may feel anxious or overwhelmed more easily than you would like.

(Part Four will help you recognize and promote your internal strength and flexibility in the face of difficult experiences.)

Q7: Least-attended-to Aspects of Yourself

We each attend to our minds, bodies, and hearts in varying degrees. There is no "right" way to be, but ignoring your mental, physical, or emotional life can lead to self-sabotaging oversights and excesses.

How least-attended-to aspects of yourself may manifest

If you tend to ignore or overlook your *mental* life, you may notice that you are easily distracted or have difficulty concentrating. You may get confused easily or feel indecisive. You may feel less competent or intelligent than others and, as a result, give short shrift to valuable mental functions such as planning ahead, putting words to your experience, and making meaning of events.

If you tend to ignore your *physical* life, you may notice that you have difficulty being "in the now." You may feel one step removed from your surroundings. You may pursue goals without regard to physical limitations or needs, thereby risking health problems.

If you tend to pay little attention to your *emotional* life, you may notice that you intellectualize feelings or overanalyze people and events. You may find it difficult to be spontaneous or to respond to the feelings of others. You may try to "think away" uncomfortable feelings. The problem is that denied emotions may eventually resurface as physical aches and pains or mental rumination.

(Part Four will show how to achieve optimal mind, body, and heart fitness.)

Q8: Drifting Thoughts

Nothing is inherently wrong with a tendency to focus on the past, future, or some other place you'd rather be. But any of these outlooks can be self-defeating if used too often or to escape reality.

How drifting thoughts may manifest

Looking to the *past* can help you make sense of events, learn from mistakes, and plan for the future. Yet if you dwell too much in the past, you may notice that much of your joy in life comes from *reliving* rather than living events. You may avoid challenges or fail to plan for the future. You may replay regrets, thus bringing old pain into the present. You may idealize past high points so much that you assume that your best days are behind you. You may find yourself mentally rewriting past events with more pleasing endings. This may serve as a way to distract yourself from current-day anxieties or pressing problems.

Focusing on the *future* can help you anticipate opportunities and avoid dangers. Yet too much of a forward focus may mean that you always look to the next activity and neglect to take any satisfaction from jobs well done. Living too much in the future, just like living too much in the past, may be a way to avoid feelings of anxiety from existing challenges or problems.

Focusing on *someplace else* you'd rather be can spark your imagination and offer new perspectives. Yet it may be a form of escapism. Fantasizing about another place may compensate for feeling a lack of control in your current situation. Too much drifting from the here-and-now can have you living in "daylight wastings time."

(Part Four will help you balance the past, present, and future in your daily outlook.)

2

A LITMUS TEST
FOR SELF-SABOTAGE

The easiest person to deceive is one's own self.

—EDWARD BULWER-LYTTON

Self-inflicted losses are characterized by one (or more) of four behaviors:

- Misleading
- Distracting
- Overreacting
- Abandoning

Misleading: When you mislead yourself, you put yourself in the dark and forget who turned out the lights. You rationalize, oversimplify, distort, or overlook crucial information.

Think of Lucille Ball's character in the TV show *I Love Lucy*. Lucy was always trying to find a shortcut. When her efforts led to problems, she'd scramble to cover up her gaffes. As we watched, we knew it was a matter of time before her actions were discovered by her husband, Ricky. Whether you rooted for Lucy to get away with it or you couldn't wait for her to get caught, *I Love Lucy* was the nation's most-watched TV show for years, because we could see part of ourselves in Lucy's missteps.

The problem with misleading yourself is that when you're in the dark, risky choices and harmful behaviors can appear to be reasonable, healthy paths.

Distracting: When you distract yourself, a part of you gives over to escapist urges by seeking solace in activities like fantasizing, shopping, eating, or procrastinating. The goal is to avoid unpleasantries by substituting a pleasant diversion.

Think of Dagwood Bumstead in the comic strip *Blondie*. Dagwood lived for his towering sandwiches, weekend naps, and extra winks on workday mornings. His single-minded pursuit of distraction left his wife, Blondie, to play mother as well as mate, hunting him down from couch to bathtub to neighbor's house, reminding him to finish household chores.

Self-distraction offers immediate relief by taking your focus off what is uncomfortable. As long as you stay with the diversion, the reduction of bad feelings reinforces your belief in the wisdom of your distraction.

Overreacting: When you overreact, you become overpowered from within. One or more feelings, thoughts, or activities seem paramount and your self-restraint or confidence washes away. You may blow your top, act without thinking, or become paralyzed by your fears.

Think boxer Mike Tyson. Or, at the opposite extreme, Chicken Little. When you feel small, having big feelings can give you a sense of power and justify behavior you might otherwise never do.

Abandoning: When you abandon yourself, you partially or fully "check out." Your priority is avoidance or escape. As opposed to self-distraction, which moves toward what feels good, abandoning is primarily a move away from what feels bad. Self-abandonment is risk-reduction. You space out, hedge your bets, or put distance between you and a threat. You may perpetually convince yourself that you have more important people, places, or things to see, be, or pursue. You may forfeit your rights, needs, and healthy boundaries by becoming overly dependent on others. You may deprive yourself of comfort, resources, or positive experiences. Meanwhile, you cede countless moments of "now." The perceived payoff: It's harder for danger to hit a moving target.

Think of TV sitcom "space cadet" characters like Phoebe on *Friends* or Chrissy on *Three's Company*. Or think of the stereotypical commitment-phobe.

The following table illustrates these four elements of self-sabotage.

The Elements of Self-sabotage	
	Examples
Misleading	• Ignoring or forgetting key lessons from past experience • Oversimplifying a complicated or important situation • Thinking in all-or-nothing, black-and-white terms • Talking yourself into a dangerous situation or out of a beneficial one • Stoking unrealistic expectations • Excessively rationalizing or justifying
Distracting	• Overindulging in escapist activities like overeating, shopping, TV viewing, playing on the computer, or drinking • Fantasizing or daydreaming at inappropriate times • Stalling or procrastinating to your detriment • Substituting pleasant time-wasters for unpleasant but needed chores
Overreacting	• Fixating on the trivial • Acting impulsively in important or complicated situations • Pursuing short-term gratification despite long-term costs • Feeling paralyzed when you need to act • Criticizing or threatening others without provocation • Frightening yourself with worst-case thinking • Self-loathing • Overly pressuring yourself • Rebelling no matter what the cost
Abandoning	• Trying half-heartedly or giving up too often • Spacing out at key moments • Running away from situations you need to face • Automatically avoiding commitments • Denying yourself support, comfort, or pleasure • Becoming overly dependent or ignoring your needs and boundaries

When you recognize that you are misleading, distracting, overreacting, or abandoning yourself in unhealthy ways, you can choose healthier behaviors. For example:

Misleading

Liz, a thirty-eight-year-old business consultant, worked with a client, Brent, for several months on improving his productivity and reliability. Brent had a pattern of failing to meet his promised quotas and either ignoring the situation or trying to hide his shortfalls. In addition, his personal spending habits were out of control and he was in debt.

Liz genuinely liked Brent and was heartened as he seemed to take the coaching sessions to heart and began turning his work situation around. Because of this, Liz agreed to postpone payment of the bulk of her consulting fee until Brent was earning more money.

Eventually Brent was offered a lucrative job in another city. He promised to pay Liz before leaving but did not. After Liz heard nothing for two weeks, she phoned Brent, who promised he would get an advance on his salary and pay his $1,100 debt within a week. Since then, despite several phone messages and E-mails, Liz has heard nothing.

Liz feels disappointed, hurt, and a bit foolish for agreeing to postpone payment of her fees. Only in retrospect has she gained clarity on why she ignored the early-warning signs. "He seemed so earnest that it never occurred to me he would skip out on his commitment," Liz says. She didn't want to accept that someone whom she liked could be so disingenuous. She wanted to believe that Brent would honor and respect her as she had done for him.

"Agreeing to extend credit to a guy with a pattern of flaking out wasn't a smart move. It certainly wasn't in my interests, and it played into his negative patterns. My job is to work with people to break their bad patterns, and somehow I lost sight of that," she says.

The point is not that Liz is a "sap" or that she is to blame for Brent's irresponsibility. Nor should Liz necessarily feel foolish, although her reaction is understandable. She made her choice based on love of her work and trust in others. It can be difficult to know when trust in others is misplaced. We can all be forgiven for looking for the best rather than the worst in others.

Nonetheless, by misleading herself, Liz paid a financial and emotional price. Had she fully weighed the implications of letting someone with a track record of financial irresponsibility slide on paying her fees, she might have taken a more hard-nosed approach. If she had, it's likely Brent would have either paid his bill or sought another consultant, thus saving Liz the heartache. "I now know that he was paying other bills while we were working together, so I suspect he had the money to pay me," Liz says ruefully.

In understanding her motives and recognizing the costs, Liz opens the door to choosing healthier courses in the future.

Distracting

Henri, a twenty-six-year-old sales associate, learned that he had finished the quarter third in sales among twenty-eight associates. His sales were only a few dollars shy of the first-and second-place associates. However, only the top two sellers each quarter win a trip to Hawaii as a reward.

Henri headed for Krispy Kreme. Four doughnuts later—two glazed devil's food, one maple glazed, and one fudge-iced with sprinkles—Henri returned to the office. On two of the next four days, he left work early to attend movie matinees. "I felt compelled to get away from work even though I risked making a bad impression," he says.

Henri is no slacker. He routinely works fourteen-hour days. Whether he is distracting himself with comfort food or working overtime to finish a project, there is a driven quality to his experience. "I have to have it, whatever it is. I don't so much choose it as feel compelled to get it," he says.

Henri feels compelled to eat, leave work early, or overwork because he's avoiding something. Henri has periodic feelings of emptiness, which he developed while growing up with alcoholic parents. The emptiness frightens and depresses him. Although he doesn't always make the connection, his "must-have" pursuits distract him from the emptiness inside, if only temporarily.

Henri has two recognitions that he can carry forward from this incident:

1. *His compelling self-distractions are a sign that he may be feeling empty or depressed.* Doughnuts and movies are, at best, short-term solutions to emptiness and depression. More helpful would be to recognize the reappearance of this familiar emptiness and deal with it directly. He might seek to understand what in his environment is leading to these feelings so he can address the situation. He might seek help.

2. *He has options besides distracting himself with doughnuts, movies, or overwork.* When Henri learned that he had finished third, he might have taken comfort in being ahead of twenty-five other sales people, many of whom had more experience than he. He might have sought out his supervisor to discuss how he could improve his sales for the next quarter. He might have found a trusted friend and talked about his disappointment. Or he might have waited until after the work day to reward himself with a stress-reducing, enjoyable activity like taking a long walk or bike ride.

Overreacting

Sheena and her boyfriend of four years moved in together, something both of them wanted and had planned for months. Within two days of living together Sheena felt anxious, teary, and had difficulty sleeping. She began thinking that living together was a horrible mistake. "I couldn't understand it. Roberto and I had felt ecstatic about living together. Why would I freak out when I got what I wanted?" she says.

Sometimes when we get what we want, fear of loss steals our happiness. Fortunately, Sheena tried to make sense of her feelings. She realized that even though she wanted the intimacy of living with Roberto, the move-in had triggered her fears of losing autonomy. The source of her emotional turmoil dated to her upbringing and past relationships. Sheena feared she'd feel trapped and controlled by Roberto as she had been by her parents and a previous boyfriend. She also realized that her overreactions to the move-in had a hidden payoff in that they slowed her entry into the uncharted territory of happiness—territory that Sheena longs for but fears would feel out of control. Recognizing that the source of her feelings lay in earlier situations allowed Sheena to regain her perspective and reassure herself that her relationship with Roberto was much healthier than earlier relationships.

Abandoning

Dennis, a forty-year-old hair stylist, recently sought therapy. "I feel uncertain about so much in my work and personal life," he says. Dennis has mixed feelings about the salon in which he works, even though he is the top stylist and the salon owner has offered to match any salary offer Dennis gets. He is also uncertain about whether his five-month-long relationship with his lover, Gregg, has a future.

As Dennis began working in therapy, he realized that for much of his life he's held a "not-it" worldview. "It's like whatever job or relationship I have is never good enough," he says. "My lovers are never 'The One.' The job never pays enough. I'm always thinking that a different job or a new lover would be better. I even get disappointed on vacations because the resort or the sights rarely measure up to my expectations."

Dennis's recognition of his pervasive "not-this, not-now, not-enough" worldview is a healthy step. Without this insight, he would likely continue to assume that external circumstances are the source of his dissatisfaction—a viewpoint that, when carried to the extreme, abdicates personal power and responsibility. By recognizing the role that his perceptions, judgments, hopes, and fears play in his reactions, Dennis can step back into his life and reclaim his power to have an impact on what troubles him. In seeing the mental "atmosphere" in which he lives, Dennis opens the way to assess his job, lover, and other activities more accurately. From there, he can either appreciate what he has or make changes.

Self-awareness Tool #1: When in Doubt, Apply the Litmus Test

This book incorporates many of the main points into tools for growth and awareness that you may find useful in your daily life. This is the first such self-awareness tool.

Take a moment to recall a recent situation that didn't turn out as you'd hoped or expected, at least partly because of your actions. Identify specifically what you did that was counterproductive. Do you notice any form of misleading, distracting, overreacting, or abandoning playing a role? You may want to refer to the table on page 34.

For example: You went dancing instead of finishing the now-overdue work project (distracting), or you assumed that your partner's stony silence around you for three straight days after you'd had an argument was because of her job pressures (misleading).

You can use this litmus test any time you find yourself in a frustrating or confusing situation. Try to recall what you had been thinking, doing, and feeling just before things went off course. See if you can pinpoint an "uh-oh" moment: the instant, however subtle or fleeting, that you had an inkling of discomfort, worry, concern, or a recognition that you didn't like where circumstances or your feelings or thoughts were headed. Recall what you did next. Do you notice any of the four behaviors?

Ask yourself how your detour may be benefitting you as well as what it might be costing you. If the costs are higher than the benefits, think of at least two ways you might handle the situation better.

3

WHY WE GET IN OUR OWN WAY

Rationalizations . . . are more important than sex. . . . Have you ever gone a week without a rationalization?

—Jeff Goldblum in *The Big Chill*

In the simplest sense, human behavior is driven by two aims: getting the "good stuff" and avoiding the "bad stuff." Each of us has our favorite good stuff: love, pleasure, helping others, peace, comfort, material wealth, raising children, fulfillment—whatever experiences, relationships, qualities, and possessions we most desire. Bad stuff can be summed up in one word: Loss. We don't want to lose good stuff. We seek to avoid emotional, psychological, and physical pain and loss.

Although we are capable of great courage, optimism, and intelligent risk-taking, we are loss-avoiders by nature. Consider:

• On a physiological level, nature fosters loss-avoidance by hardwiring us with a fight-or-flight response. When we perceive that our survival is threatened, this powerful response kicks in, overwhelming all other considerations.

In addition, traumatic incidents appear to be imprinted in our brains differently than other events. Memories of traumatic loss get priority on our nerve highways, offering us ready reminders when we sense something similar to the original trauma. For example, someone whose house caught fire in the past might react strongly to the unexpected smell of smoke even from a barbeque or fireplace.

• On an economic level, fear often governs our financial decisions more than dollars and sense. "Losing money feels twice as bad as making money feels good," economist Richard Thaler said. That's why many investors hold on to money-losing investments even when they would ultimately make more by cashing in for a better investment. That's why we finance vacations on credit cards even when we have the money in savings. We mentally tend to wince more at the prospect of an immediate drop in our savings balance than at the dramatically more expensive vacation we purchase over time with credit card interest.

Our aversion to economic loss leads us to value the same commodity in different ways. For example, the overdue twenty-dollar debt from a coworker may spark far more internal energy than the overdue twenty dollars you owe your brother-in-law. Your internal valuation of gain versus loss is also why when you win a hundred-dollar slot-machine jackpot you're likely to treat that money more cavalierly than the hundred dollars in hard-earned money you carried into the casino.

• On a behavioral level, we weigh *now* much differently from *later*. We are often more likely to choose a small pleasure now despite significant pain later rather than face a small amount of pain right away even if it would head off significant pain in the future, according to several studies. That's why procrastination is as likely to become extinct as the cockroach. When you think about starting a big task, your anticipation of the burdensome "oomph" needed to get going is tangible. On the other hand, put off starting and you taste immediate relief. In the moment, immediate relief seems worth more than future pain even if your eventual pain is multiplied for not tackling a task now.

• On an emotional level, sensing that we might lose that which we hold most dearly can stir the heart and rile the body. One emotion above all others—fear—functions like the U.S. Marines. Fear is designed to protect us from harm and avoid losses by magnifying threats and elevating their risks above all else. Fear isn't designed to instill perspective, it is designed to make us change perspective and pay attention to a potential loss. This is both the power and danger of fear.

• On a psychological level, we struggle with loss and gain, particularly when it comes to self-image. One reason we get in our own way is that we don't fully accept ourselves. It is human nature to hide or oust aspects of yourself of which you are ashamed, such as small-mindedness or lack of compassion. Practicing such selective self-acceptance, however, invariably leads you to overlook or deny not only unwanted aspects but the best parts of you. As a result, you may naturally settle for less, not let others to see who you really are, or pursue short-sighted, self-undermining strategies. The remedy is to accept, even embrace, both your unwanted and best parts.

• On an existential level, the tacit knowledge of our own mortality, perhaps the ultimate loss, can play a role in shaping life and relationship choices. Whereas children and young adults tend eagerly to welcome their birthdays as adding to their life credentials, by our thirties, forties, or fifties the birthday experience undergoes a sea change for some. Researchers have found that instead of measuring our lives in years added since birth we tend to begin measuring it in years left. This shift can trigger midlife reevaluations of relationships, accomplishments, and goals.

We don't always make the connection between the fear of loss and our thoughts, actions, and feelings. Emotional loss is inherent in all that we avoid, protest, dread, fight, and deny. In my experience, a feared or actual loss is at the core of virtually every unpleasant emotion, thought, or experience we face.

Think of any emotion you resist and look for the loss connected with it. Embarrassment brings loss of face. Anxiety brings loss of confidence. Guilt brings loss of self-esteem. Regret brings loss of contentment. Depression brings loss of hope. Boredom brings loss of vitality. Anger follows a perceived loss of safety or rights.

When you don't recognize the presence of a real or feared loss, your reactions may confuse you. You may dismiss, deny, or ignore your feelings. You may displace your feelings onto others. You may assume you are just bored, then fail to spot such deeper issues as fear, grief, or anger as well as the situations causing them. You may believe your rationalizations. When you assume that you're simply tired or annoyed when in fact you've tapped into grief or wrath, you build a wall between you and your heart.

You may be wondering, then, if we are such natural loss-avoiders, how it is that we do things that increase our losses.

Counterproductive behavior starts out just like successful behavior. It attempts to solve a conflict. For example: You want a new car but can't afford it. Chocolate fudge cake tastes delicious but isn't necessarily good for you. Hitting the snooze button would feel good but being late wouldn't. You're attracted to someone, but he or she is happily married.

You consciously solve such conflicts many times a day. You also solve many conflicts without knowing it. These unconscious solutions may later mystify or shock you. You wonder, "What was I thinking?" Looking back, you may discover that you weren't thinking, at least not clearly or realistically. You may have been distracted, spaced out, or fixated on other thoughts, feelings, or events. Even so, there's often a method to your madness.

Misguided Loss-avoidance

Man wishes to be happy even when he so lives as to make happiness impossible.

—St. Augustine

Self-defeating behaviors spring from overzealous or misguided efforts to avoid emotional losses. In these cases, we consciously or unconsciously try to solve dilemmas:

1. With no loss whatsoever

2. Based on an unrealistic assessment of likely losses; and/or

3. By substituting chosen losses for dreaded ones

Like it or not, it is impossible to solve conflicts with absolutely no loss. Though you may find good or even optimal solutions, in a conflict, by definition, something has to give even if what is lost is your fears or illusions. For example:

- You want to lose weight but love chocolate. If you forego the chocolate and maintain your diet, what do you do with your unmet cravings? Perhaps you go for immediate gratification and eat the chocolate, then rationalize ("It's only a small box of chocolates").

- You desire sizzling romance but don't have an appropriate partner. When you hunger for romance, how do you cope with your loneliness until you meet your mate? Perhaps you pursue an unavailable or inappropriate lover, finding distraction from your loneliness while deceiving yourself as to the eventual outcome ("He'll leave his wife for me," "She has special qualities that others don't see").

- You want a more rewarding career but are afraid of failing. If you aim high in your career, how do you soothe your fears while climbing the ladder? Perhaps you fantasize about what it will feel like to succeed but you procrastinate starting, thus postponing failure and, unfortunately, success as well.

Loss is painful. It is natural to want to avoid or minimize losses. I'm not suggesting that you should actively recruit emotional losses or welcome them when they appear. What I am suggesting is that if you avoid feeling life's losses by misleading or distracting yourself, even when done with no awareness, you purchase an expensive detour. If you'll do anything to avoid feeling out of control or deprived, you may ransom spontaneity, grace, and generosity along with their countless unanticipated benefits. When loss-avoidance or loss-substitution become your dominant motivation, you narrow your emotional range. Your heart wants and needs to be heard.

If you let yourself feel such difficult emotions as grief or emptiness, these feelings, like all feelings, will eventually move on. Your efforts to resist authentic sadness can hurt more and take longer than the sadness itself.

Renee says that she is dying to "give over to love." In several intimate relationships so far, however, she has felt unable to give over. As strongly as she wants to surrender to love, she resists doing so. Her resistance feels outside of her control.

Renee's dilemma is shared by many on the road to intimacy. We experience a stalemate: our desire for closeness matches our resistance to closeness. Feeling stuck, we may seek recourse through actions that unwittingly prolong the stalemate. For example, perhaps we stay with a partner, but hide a part of ourselves away to a lock-box fantasy of a someday love. Perhaps we substitute blame for pain, and find a culprit in ourselves or our partner. When the prospect of intimacy seems frightening, perhaps we short-circuit intimate connections. Taking a romantic vacation but fighting all the while is a good example.

Self-awareness Tool #2:
Look for the Loss

Think for a moment of an unpleasant feeling or problem you recently faced. Can you identify a feared or actual loss? Or the next time you feel stuck, unhappy, or confused, ask yourself, "What emotional losses do I most fear or want to avoid in this situation?"

In either case, identify any feared emotional loss that may be driving your attitudes and actions. For example, are you taking control because that will best solve the problem at hand, or is your urge to control primarily designed to keep you from feeling helpless, inferior, or uncertain? Are you postponing a decision because you honestly need more information, or doing so primarily out of a fantasy that the problem will go away or that somebody else will solve it for you? When you explore what you're avoiding and acknowledge the payoffs and costs, you view your counterfactualizing in a more realistic light.

The Benefits of Self-sabotage

Though it's not possible to avoid all loss, we still try. The reason: Self-sabotage offers benefits. Procrastination, for example, actually does postpone loss and can give a feeling of control over the pace of events. Rationalizations give emotional breathing room. Fantasies brighten the routine. Distractions bring nifty respite. Even self-destructive rebellion can give emotional intensity or a feeling of purpose.

Albert, a twenty-six-year-old software programmer, has been promised company stock options and a raise, but neither has materialized. He wants to speak with his boss about the problem but keeps putting it off. In addition, he dreams of entering graduate school and earning a doctorate but postpones applying. "Sometimes I see myself thirty years from now, still thinking about graduate school, still waiting for a raise. What worries me is that I can't seem to motivate myself to do anything about it," Albert says.

Albert is clear that there's a problem: He isn't getting the compensation he was promised and he isn't moving ahead in his career. He is less certain about why it is so hard for him to do something about it.

It's understandable that Albert, like many of us, might dread the prospect of a confrontation with the boss even though he feels that he is in the right. It's also understandable that taking a big step like entering a doctoral program might feel daunting. Even so, Albert's holding pattern serves protective functions of which he is gradually becoming aware. By not talking to his boss, Albert avoids the potential pain of rejection that would come if his boss were to deny or stonewall his raise and stock options. Albert also sidesteps the potential chagrin of discovering that perhaps he has been financially taken advantage of by his employer.

By not applying to graduate school, he postpones finding out whether he will be accepted and whether he can earn a doctorate. He also avoids facing the emptiness that might ensue if he were to begin graduate school and find it no more fulfilling than his job.

Albert's case illustrates why self-defeating patterns can persist so stubbornly. Day after day, Albert unwittingly skews his mental arithmetic so that the risks of taking action appear to outweigh the costs of doing nothing. Over time the inertia of Albert's inaction makes it progressively more difficult to act.

As it stands now, Albert feels like a clueless procrastinator. If he were to identify and thoroughly understand the costs of his avoidances and the reasons underlying them, he might increase his motivation to act. Were he to acknowledge the powerful fears standing in his way, he'd have the chance to face them head on. Were Albert to confront his boss, seek career counseling, or investigate graduate schools, he'd risk discomfort, but at least he'd have the opportunity to take charge of his life.

Sandra, twenty-six, feels hurt and upset when her boyfriend, Trey, is late for dates and doesn't apologize. She has discussed the problem with female friends but has yet to raise the issue with Trey. She wonders whether he is late with other people or late only to meet her. If he's globally late, Sandra would feel less disrespected than if Trey is late only to see her. But without raising the subject, she can't know. She hesitates out of concern that she might be making too much of a minor issue. Meanwhile, her frustration increases.

By not raising the issue with Trey, Sandra gains several benefits.

1. She avoids the discomfort of a confrontation.

2. She avoids the potential pain of finding out that perhaps Trey does not cherish her.

3. She avoids facing her anger, which she worries might feel out of control or lead her to say things that she will regret.

4. She avoids facing the uncomfortable, deeper issue of whether she is placing her self-worth in external hands.

Of course, if Sandra is concerned about her partner seeking retribution, her hesitation to speak up makes sense. Confronting Trey about his casualness about time and lack of apologies may not be a good idea, particularly if she is concerned about physical retribution or emotional or verbal abuse. In that case, it would be wiser for Sandra to evaluate whether she's in a healthy relationship. Healthy relationships do not involve violence or the threat of abuse or violence. Seeking counseling or other outside help would be important.

If Sandra has no basis for expecting that Trey would respond in a threatening way, she might turn her attention to her motives. For example, she might ask herself why she worries about feeling out of control or saying hurtful things. Does she have a track record of hurting others or is this only a fear? Have positive results ever come from expressing her anger even when doing so was uncomfortable? It might be helpful for Sandra to remind herself that it can hardly be wrong to express anger when anger is a normal, healthy emotion that surfaces occasionally in virtually every close, long-term relationship. Feeling anger is one thing; expressing it is entirely different. In questioning her assumptions about anger, Sandra could replace dysfunctional beliefs with healthier approaches. She could remind herself that responsibly expressed anger does not destroy people.

Sandra could also ask herself whether she has become too attached to the relationship. Being afraid to broach a topic that is important to her may indicate that she has come to value peace at any price and is sweeping disagreements under the rug. In the long term, this approach is unlikely to allow either Sandra or the relationship to flourish. Though speaking up may stir things up emotionally or risk temporary hurt feelings, raising the issue of Trey's lateness could help her achieve a more honest relationship and feel more free to be herself.

Eric, a fifty-year-old middle-school principal, divorced his wife of thirty years shortly after the last of their three children left for college. "For the final ten years of our marriage, there was little romance. We had become roommates," Eric recalls. The couple parted relatively amicably, remaining friends. Nine months after the divorce, Eric began dating and soon fell in love. "I felt like a teenager again," he says. After a month of "pure bliss," as he puts it, his new lover left him. Heartbroken, Eric gained thirty pounds within weeks. Six months later, he had yet to shed a pound.

As Eric struggled to hold the line against additional weight gain, he tried to understand what was making it so difficult for him to lose weight. Before his thirty-pound gain, he was already twenty pounds overweight. His doctor ruled out any medical cause. Eric was simply eating too much and not exercising enough.

He tried several diets and exercise programs. With each new diet, he'd start out inspired and hopeful. Then, somewhere, he'd lose his way. His initial resolve and inspiration seemed irretrievable, and his diet and exercise regimens each died with a whimper. After a few defeats, even when Eric recovered his will to try again, an inner voice nagged, "You've felt confident before and didn't follow through. What makes you think this time will be any different?" Over time, he lost credibility with himself. He felt powerless, alone, and defeated.

When you repeatedly fail to overcome a challenge that has a relatively straightforward solution—in this case, eating less and exercising more—it can be helpful to look for motives outside your conscious awareness. In Eric's case, his weight gain may serve a protective function. For example, it may provide him with a ready-made explanation the next time he encounters a rejection in romance. Eric could interpret rejections as being based on his overweight appearance. Such a viewpoint could offer psychic armor that softens blows received on the front lines of dating. After all, it would be his appearance, not who he is as a person, that would be rejected.

Or perhaps Eric's weight gain allows him to justify not putting himself out to women at all, in the belief that he is too heavy to be attractive. By so doing, he avoids the stress of dating and the risk of another rejection. Even though his weight gain may not decrease his attractiveness in the eyes of many potential partners, Eric's feelings of being unattractive are reflected in his demeanor around women. As a result, he is more likely to miss cues of potential interest from women. He passes up social opportunities for fear he will be shunned. His gloomy self-appraisal has become self-fulfilling.

Perhaps his weight gain is a way for Eric to appear less threatening to competitors on the dating scene. Another possibility, by contrast, is that Eric's greater girth may afford him a comforting feeling of bigness at a time when he psychologically feels small in stature and efficacy.

Perhaps his weight gain is an unconscious way of giving himself a challenge to overcome. In the logic of self-sabotage, gaining thirty pounds could be a win-win proposition. If he finds a new lover despite his weight gain, he will feel triumphant at overcoming overwhelming odds, as well as feeling more secure that he is loved for who he really is. On the other hand, if he fails to find a new lover, he will have failed in a situation nobody could have won.

Eric's difficulty losing weight may be a call for help, reflecting a hope that he might somehow be rescued. Sometimes we unwittingly test the universe with risky behavior to see whether it is a forgiving or benevolent universe.

In the simplest sense, Eric's overeating can be viewed as a way of soothing himself following a devastating emotional blow. After ten years of a virtually sexless marriage, he encountered passion again, only to have it vanish barely after it had begun. Eric is not only grieving the sudden loss of his recent love but the immense loss of a thirty-year marriage and family life. His physical pounds may be a proxy for the unexpressed grief he totes.

As is characteristic of self-sabotage, Eric's weight problem began as an effort to cope with difficult emotions. He did not consciously set out to gain weight, nor did he anticipate the associated health risks, expenses, loneliness, and emotional pain he is now encountering. Even so, Eric continues on his costly path for two reasons:

1. He does not yet view the costs of his psychic armor as greater than the benefits.

2. He fails to see enough benefits to justify the hard work of weight-loss.

Eric's current situation might have been avoided—and can still be remedied—by a full and honest exploration of the costs and benefits of his current behavior as well as of other possible approaches. He needs to find better ways to soothe his broken heart. For example, he might face his grief head-on, letting himself experience his painful feelings rather than stuffing them by overeating. He could express his feelings rather than bottling them up, perhaps by writing in a journal, talking with a trusted friend, joining a support group, or seeking counseling. Feeling and expressing grief burns calories, it doesn't add them. Eric also might exercise more, giving himself the natural feel-good endorphins of vigorous workouts.

Sometimes when we cannot see any way around loss, we substitute more palatable losses for those we dread. If we're going to lose, we at least want to choose how or what. For example, we may swim in guilt, waste time, loathe our bodies, or feel miserable rather than give up our illusions, emotional attachments, or parts of our "ego" or identity. As in Eric's case, amid the heat and light of feeling badly, we miss the point: Sometimes our illusions, attachments, and identities need to change. They are part of you, not the whole of you. They may be getting in your way.

As we'll see in the next chapter, there's a part of you that works tirelessly, using its special brand of logic and math, to maintain your illusions even when it's not in your best interests.

4

YOUR "SUBTERRANEAN ACCOUNTANT"

We lie loudest when we lie to ourselves.

—Eric Hoffer

Carlita, a forty-two-year-old physician, loved to draw and paint as a girl. "I could spend three hours drawing, and it was as if only ten minutes had passed. Even after hours of artwork, I rarely felt tired," she recalls.

By the time Carlita turned eleven, she experienced less-than-enthusiastic parental responses to her art. Her mother, though generally supportive, told Carlita that art was fine as a hobby, but that it was impossible to make a living as an artist. She suggested Carlita concentrate on "real-world" skills. In addition, Carlita's stepfather was an emotionally abusive man who told Carlita, "You better plan on becoming a doctor or lawyer and make good money, because no man is going to want to marry you."

Today Carlita has a successful medical practice but is not happy. She's had a series of difficult relationships with self-absorbed men. She yearns to take up painting again, even as a hobby, but has yet to find the time to do so.

As a girl, Carlita experienced significant no-win dilemmas. Her mother said that Carlita could be creative or successful but not both. Her stepfather devalued her attractiveness and worth. And if that weren't enough of a blow, he also warned her that she had little career choice and must seek a high-paying profession or she would not survive economically.

Young Carlita concluded that life was a series of either-or choices, and she could never have her first choice. She is a successful doctor, but her entry into the medical profession felt obligatory. She's come to expect unsatisfying romantic relationships. She feels as though she has little right to make time for the art she loves.

It doesn't make sense that someone as dedicated and talented as Carlita would suffer such a lack of fulfillment. It's too simplistic to say that Carlita unquestioningly accepted negative parental messages and consequently toed the line. Carlita doesn't blame her mother or step-father for her own choices.

But Carlita, like all of us, has a part of herself that can facilitate self-defeat. I call this part the *Subterranean Accountant*. This term is a way of conceiving of the part of you that works automatically, often without your awareness, weighing your choices in every situation.

Fuzzy Math

The problem is that your Accountant's calculations must fit into a predetermined goal: loss-avoidance. As a result, your Accountant uses fuzzy math. For example, though it makes no logical sense that you could gain by depriving or hurting yourself, your Accountant can make it add up. Your Accountant may glorify the payoffs of one course of action while ignoring or downplaying the costs. It may measure results using the wrong yardstick or stop short of finishing its calculations. Recognizing exactly how your Accountant's fuzzy math works can shed light on some of your most mystifying and painful patterns.

For example, Carlita's dissatisfying life path does make sense using the Accountant's math. Carlita was five when her father died. For three years after that, Carlita and her mother were nearly inseparable. When the stepfather arrived on the scene, Carlita was terrified of losing her connection with her mother but, sensing that a remarriage would make her mother happy, she hid her fear and grief. So by age eight, Carlita already had learned twice that she could not keep what she most wanted. First she lost her father, then her mother was no longer there just for her.

When her mother began discouraging Carlita's art, eleven-year-old Carlita saw her options as either rejecting her mother, her only constant and lifeline, or second-guessing herself. She began doubting herself, a pattern that has continued through much of her life. As extraordinary a girl as Carlita was, few eleven-year-olds have the psychological sophistication to know that if you don't get what you most cherish, it doesn't mean that it is your destiny.

Only Carlita can know for sure exactly how her Accountant tallies the benefits of withholding self-worth. We can, however, generate several hypotheses that are characteristic of Subterranean-Accountant logic. For example:

- If Carlita felt worthy, she would feel worthy of being happy. Being happy would bring the inherent possibility of losing that happiness. By feeling unworthy, Carlita may avoid kindling hope and reexperiencing the pain of dashed hopes she felt in childhood. To her Accountant that may be worth any price.

- By not pursuing her art or other activities that make her happy, perhaps Carlita differentiates herself from her mother. Her mother, after all, made herself happy by remarrying, but that hurt Carlita. Perhaps her Accountant has concluded that if Carlita is happy someone else will suffer. In contrast to her mother, Carlita foregoes her own happiness.

- In feeling unworthy, Carlita is less likely to bring attention to herself. This may help her avoid negative attention like the abuse she received from her stepfather. Or perhaps her Accountant fears that even if she gets positive attention it will eventually be withdrawn, and that would hurt terribly.

- Perhaps Carlita experiences power and control by deciding that she has little worth. She may preempt unexpected challenges to her worth from within or without by deciding from the outset that she has none.

Marcus is a thirty-five-year-old mid-level manager for a department store chain. He's had several jobs in the retail industry and done excellent work for short periods. Each time he has turned in an especially successful performance or neared a promotion, he has quit his job and moved to a lesser position at another company or taken extended time off.

Marcus grew up in the shadow of his famous and successful uncle, Raymond, who made millions through his canny acquisitions in the retail field. Raymond's acumen is well known in business circles, though what is less well known is his emotional remoteness toward family members. When Marcus's father left shortly after Marcus was born, his uncle stepped in and became a father figure. Marcus grew up feeling as though he was a minor priority in his uncle's life, albeit a minor priority to which Raymond attached major expectations.

At fourteen, Marcus joined Junior Achievement, an after-school activ-

ity in which young people create a business plan and then manufacture and sell some small product. "My uncle just glowed when my mom told him I had joined JA. I never remember seeing him so delighted in anything else I did," Marcus recalls.

Marcus's team won first-place awards for their performance. But when Junior Achievement ended for the school year, Marcus said his uncle turned his attention and affection off "like a light switch."

Marcus was a smart, capable boy who desperately wanted his uncle's love and approval. The problem was that Raymond's love and approval came only when Marcus excelled in ways his uncle valued. This dilemma plays out years later in Marcus's career self-handicapping. On the one hand, Marcus is talented and ambitious. He is genuinely interested in business and would likely have chosen it as a career even if he'd come from a different family. His uncle's prominence only added to Marcus's dreams of success in business. On the other hand, a basic need—that of love and approval from a father figure—went unmet.

Though neither consciously nor deliberately, Marcus has waged war between honoring his dreams and reacting to his uncle's neglect. The biggest casualty has been Marcus's self-esteem.

Looking at Marcus's dilemma dispassionately, we might conclude that although it is tragic that he felt little love from his uncle, that's no reason for him to undermine his life. After all, living well is the best revenge. But logical analysis plays little role in the machinations of the Subterranean Accountant. Marcus's Accountant is focused on righting wrongs from long ago. By the Accountant's logic, were Marcus to become an unabashed success in his own right, uncle Raymond would "win."

Marcus was deeply wounded in boyhood by his uncle's remoteness but could do little about it. As an adult, however, Marcus has recourse. His Accountant knows that nothing would make Raymond happier than for Marcus to become a star in his field. Being a success would validate Raymond's own choice of career. In addition, having a success-ful nephew following in his footsteps would serve as evidence to observers that Raymond was both a great businessman and great family man. Most egregiously, from his Accountant's point of view, Marcus's success would mean that his uncle *got away* with loving him condi-tionally.

To Marcus's Accountant, making his uncle happy, excusing his neg-lect, and failing to receive redress for his boyhood years of longing are too high a price even if Marcus achieved personal success and happiness in the process. Evening the score for losses from long ago is weighed more heavily than current or future happiness.

Marcus clearly demonstrates that he has the potential to be successful yet has not manifested it. This pays dividends from the Accountant's viewpoint. Marcus's wandering career track may lead observers to question, "If the old man was so great, why couldn't he impart it to his nephew?" By failing to move on, Marcus refuses to condone Raymond's remoteness. He won't let his uncle get away scot-free with hurting him. Perhaps most importantly, Marcus can singlehandedly orchestrate his own success or failure, one area in which his powerful uncle has no control.

Of course, nowhere in Marcus's thought processes are these strategies consciously delineated. They exist because of a lack of awareness. When no one is minding the store, your Accountant has free reign. In the ledger of your Accountant, acting in your own best interests is not the coin of the realm.

Black-market Economics

When you reduce the Accountant's calculations to their essence, the results are striking. In Carlita's case her Accountant is telling her:

- Never being happy is better than being happy and then losing happiness.

- Weakening yourself shows how powerful you are.

- By refusing to accept the past, you can somehow rewrite it.

Marcus's Accountant has similar reasoning:

- Being happy isn't worth it if it brings happiness to someone who hurt you.

- Not letting go of an injustice is worth continued pain, because it prevents the wrongdoer from getting away with it.

You may shake your head at the twisted logic in these statements, but logic plays little role in your Accountant's black market. Some things are deemed so important to have or to avoid that you pursue or shun them no matter what the cost. In fact, your Accountant rarely bothers to tally the costs of its actions.

In the light of day, the Accountant's shady deals and Arthur Andersen–style accounting practices don't add up. Unequal situations are given equal weight. Some qualities and experiences are overvalued while others are devalued. In general, the Accountant's calculations:

1. Rarely take into account the whole picture

2. Are based on either-or rules

3. Are based on unquestioned-but-false assumptions about life, others, and yourself

I'm not suggesting that everyone who fails to achieve his potential does so to get back at someone, or that people are unhappy simply because they are holding on to the past. But it can be revealing to sift through counterproductive patterns in your life and look for handiwork of your Accountant's equations. Although Marcus's and Carlita's stories have their roots in childhood, you don't have to trace your patterns back to that era. It's useful to generate hypotheses about how your Accountant sizes up situations so that you can uncover ill-founded and self-defeating assumptions. You'll know when one fits.

Here are some typical bargains to your Accountant's way of thinking. As you read these, notice whether any seem familiar:

- If a lover leaves you but still cares about your well-being, being unhappy is a good way of getting back at her or him.

- By devaluing your worth, you have a ready explanation any time you make a mistake or miss an opportunity. After all, what can anyone expect from an unworthy person?

- If a job or relationship ends against your will, remaining excessively angry, resentful, or wounded is a way to stay connected. It's not over until *you* say it's over.

- If you felt out of control early in life, the best response is to control everything and everyone around you.

The Accountant holds one-sided views about life, and barrels down the tracks seeking evidence to justify those views. Recognizing these assumptions offers you a chance to step back and do your own math, overriding your Accountant's version. The Accountant makes its calculations based on unspoken rules such as:

- I must never quit.

- I must be successful.

- I can't let anybody beat me.

- I can't be alone.

- I am not competent.

- I must be different from others.

- I must be like others.

- I can't survive arguments or disagreements.

- I can't be happy when others close to me are not.

- I can't break the rules.

- I can't tell a lie.

- I can't get caught in a lie.

- I can't be bored.

- I can't openly ask for what I want.

Infinite variations are possible. Each rule can lead to a slightly different form of self-sabotage. For example, believing that you must never make a mistake may lead to paralysis. Believing that you must never be caught making a mistake may lead to secretiveness. Believing that people will try to take advantage of you if you are successful, you may dumb down or hide. Believing that people will love you if you are successful (or attractive, smart, or rich), you may present a false front.

Although the Accountant's calculations are designed to avoid losses, they backfire. For example, avoiding getting close to someone for fear you might get rejected brings exactly what you fear: by avoiding getting close, you stay lonely.

In sum, many factors contribute to self-deception and self-sabotage: a need to please others; insufficient social support; feelings of inadequacy; hopelessness; low self-esteem; a lack of purpose; the need to feel in control; mistaken beliefs; and fears of failure, success, or change. At times self-sabotage springs from real or imagined flaws you feel within. When you view yourself as insufficient to meet life's challenges, you may seek shortcuts like immediate gratification, or hedge your bets by taking "acceptable" losses. Other times you may reaffirm your unworthy status by unconsciously and habitually seeking to fail, a kind of psychological homeostasis designed to avoid the internal ruckus that would ensue if you either felt unworthy yet succeeded or felt worthy yet blew it.

Keeping secrets is a powerful weapon. Few of us want to surrender the option to use it. If you could no longer distract, procrastinate, distance, rebel, or walk away with a dismissive "whatever," where would you be? Upon what could you rely? Even when you know that what you're doing is costly or self-defeating, would you swear it off forever?

Recalculating Your Subterranean Accountant's Math

You can loosen your Subterranean Accountant's grip by replacing bad math with simple, honest addition and subtraction. The way to do this is:

1. Recognize counterproductive behaviors.

2. Uncover the Accountant's logic and rules that foster those behaviors.

3. Identify the benefits.

4. Identify the costs.

5. Make a choice based on your overall best interests, rewriting or jettisoning the old rules as needed.

For example, Marcus might:

1. Squarely face his peripatetic career pattern.

2. Articulate the "logic" driving it:

   My uncle hurt me as a child.
   It wasn't fair.
   I couldn't do anything then but I can now.
   I can get even by taking him down a notch.
   One way to do this is to fail at achieving what he most values:
   consistent success.

3. Take stock of the payoffs: a sense of power; getting even; avoiding reexperiencing his childhood pain; and potentially avoiding the pain inherent in failing to achieve a cherished goal.

4. Tally the costs: low self-esteem; loss of freedom and self-determination; lack of happiness and fulfillment; lack of productivity; and conforming to an old pattern rather than moving forward.

5. Make a choice: Marcus could then decide whether the sense of power and loss-avoidance are worth more to him than freedom, self-esteem, happiness, and fulfilling his genuine interests.

Summary of Part One: The Secrets We Keep

So far I've suggested that:

1. Self-deception is innate, universal, and ranges from helpful to harmful.

2. Self-deception happens when you lose awareness, similar to the moment of falling asleep.

3. Counterproductive self-deception is characterized by misleading, distracting, overpowering, or abandoning yourself.

4. Self-sabotage results from attempts to solve internal conflicts with no emotional loss.

5. Self-sabotage is characterized by "fuzzy math" and misguided loss-brokering.

PART TWO

◆

How to Recognize the Early-warning Signs of Self-sabotage

To know that one has a secret is to know half the secret itself.

—HENRY WARD BEECHER

The process of personal change is simple. You recognize a mistake, choose not to repeat it, and then behave differently. What makes this simple process difficult is that each of us has counterproductive patterns of thinking, feeling, and acting, which, like air to the bird, we take for granted.

Since self-sabotage can take so many forms, it helps to have more than one tool for recognizing it. Part Two will show you several early-warning signs of counterproductive behavior. These include:

- Instinctive reactions that can override your ability to reflect, reason, and choose (chapter 5)

- A retreat to behavior learned in childhood, particularly when you feel blamed or guilty (chapter 6)

- Overreliance on your "usual suspects," the responses that arise by default when you feel surprised, disappointed, or challenged (chapter 7)

- The arrival of your inner "cast of characters" (chapter 8)

5

TAMING THE BEASTS WITHIN

Who hath deceived thee so often as thyself?

—BENJAMIN FRANKLIN

Harriet spotted someone breaking into her car at the shopping mall. Without thinking, she walked up to the thief and said, "What the hell are you doing to my car?" Harriet recalled: "It was this kid, maybe sixteen, and I must have surprised him. First he jumped, then he straightened up and pulled out a knife." Luckily for Harriet, the boy ran, and she was unharmed. Afterward, she wondered what had possessed her to act as she did.

We are human animals. Noticing when your behavior seems more animal than human is one way to recognize counterproductive behavior that you might not otherwise see until too late.

When an animal is threatened or startled, it generally exhibits one or more of four responses:

- Immobility: freezing in place

- Withdrawal: fleeing or hiding

- Submission: appeasing or appearing nonthreatening

- Defensive aggression: attacking, fighting back, or appearing dangerous

These responses make sense. For example, the freeze response, as scientist Joseph LeDoux has found, offers three advantages: 1. Freezing heightens the senses and allows an animal to assess the threat; 2. Since predators are drawn to movement, the prey stops moving; 3. Freezing increases adrenaline and prepares for an escape or fight.

Of course, humans are different from most animals in important ways, but some of our external behaviors and internal experiences in response to threats bear striking resemblance to instinctive animal-style responses. For example:

- Just as a rabbit or lizard becomes motionless at the first sign of a predator, we may become *immobile* when facing a threat. We physically delay by stalling or slowing down. We psychologically delay by becoming paralyzed with indecision or fear.

- Just as the deer runs and the mouse retreats to the hole, we may *withdraw* from threats. We seek physical distance by leaving or trying to appear inconspicuous. We seek psychological distance by spacing out, not caring, or turning our attention elsewhere.

- Just as a younger wolf or ape shows its belly or avoids eye contact with the alpha wolf or group leader, we may *submit* when threatened. We physically submit by appeasing or agreeing with someone who is angry. We psychologically roll over by pretending a threat doesn't exist or convincing ourselves that it's not important.

- Just as a dog may raise its hackles to appear larger or a bear may charge someone who comes too close, we *defend* ourselves. We seek physical defense by acting tough, escalating, or fighting back. We seek psychological defense through fantasies of revenge. Curiously, we also sometimes defend by attacking ourselves. Facing a threat, we'd rather do something—anything—than feel helpless. Even when our actions are detrimental to us we feel a measure of control by preempting it. At least we determine when the ax will fall, even if it falls on us. As Ernest Becker wrote, "If we don't have the omnipotence of gods, we at least can destroy like gods."

My point is not to inflict Darwinian ego-deflation on your psyche. Rather, my point is that observing animallike instinctual responses can provide a helpful perspective. We sometimes react to everyday circumstances with responses that are automatic, not chosen. They are not in proportion to the situation at hand. The following table illustrates.

Similarities in Animal and Human Responses

Animal behavior	Analogous human behavior	Analogous internal human experience
Immobility	Stalling or procrastinating	Feeling paralyzed or stuck
Withdrawal	Leaving or hiding	Spacing out or self-distracting
Submission	Giving in or appeasing	Minimizing or pretending
Defensive aggression	Attacking or fighting back	Fantasizing about revenge

The terms *freeze, withdraw, submit,* and *defend* can be equated to the four litmus test behaviors from chapter 2. The following table illustrates.

Animallike Responses to the Threat of Loss

Litmus test behavior/Goal of behavior	Equivalent animal behavior	Animal analogy	Human equivalents
Misleading: Circumvent reality	Immobility, submission	Ostrich with head in the sand	You see what you want and ignore the rest by: • Rationalizing • Distorted thinking • Pretending or acting as-if • Ignoring or denying
Distracting: Feel better	Withdrawal, submission	Cat chasing tail	You substitute pleasure for painful or complicated dilemmas by: • Fantasizing • Indulging in escapist activities

Litmus test behavior/Goal of behavior	Equivalent animal behavior	Animal analogy	Human equivalents
Overreacting: Defend yourself	Defensive aggression	Toy poodle barking menacingly at rottweiler	You take control by: • Preempting the threat by doing it to yourself • Getting carried away by your feelings • Lashing out at others
Abandoning: Escape	Immobility, withdrawal	Deer caught in the headlights	You move away from painful or complicated situations by: • Quitting or fleeing • Spacing out • Stalling or procrastinating • Hiding or trying to be inconspicuous • Hedging your bets or acting half-heartedly

The key to coping as a human animal lies in using your skills of awareness and self-reflection to do what animals presumably cannot: weigh implications and consequences. Without these, you're stuck with the liabilities of animal nature: lack of perspective and lack of awareness.

Self-awareness Tool #3: Observe Your Animal Nature

Take a moment and recall a time when you stopped short of what you wanted, got in your own way, overreacted to a threat, or disappointed yourself. Do you notice any of the animallike patterns (immobility, withdrawal, submission, or defensive aggression) in your initial behavior? If so, you have identified possible early-warning signs of self-inflicted losses. Keep these signs in mind and watch for them from time to time, particularly when you're stressed. Stop, look, and listen. By doing so, you interrupt automatic habits that trip you up. You can then think of more productive responses.

6

CAUGHT WITH YOUR HAND
IN THE COOKIE JAR

The secret of life is honesty and fair dealing. If you can fake that, you've got it made.

—GROUCHO MARX

Forty-year-old Bailey told her friend Margot that she'd missed Margot's birthday party Saturday because she was sick. In truth, Bailey was exhausted after a tough week and had spent a low-key weekend with her husband, only venturing out to see a movie. A few minutes later the conversation turned to recent films and Bailey mentioned she'd seen a good film Saturday that Margot should see. A moment later Bailey realized what she'd said. Margot responded, "But I thought you were sick Saturday." Stumbling, Bailey said, "Oh, no, I never said that. Well, I mean, the Saturday before that I was sick. I think."

Bailey says: "I felt so stupid. Our friendship is good enough that I could have told Margot the truth. But once I told that first white lie, I felt like I had to tell another and another. I was like a kid caught with her hand in the cookie jar."

Another way to recognize pending self-sabotage is to notice when you're behaving more like a child than an adult. As with Bailey, our childlike impulses sometimes get the better of us. If you spend time around children you can observe characteristic ways children try to escape blame or other negative consequences. For example, when children are caught doing something wrong, they often respond by:

- Denying that they did it
- Saying that someone else did it

- Pretending they don't know what you're talking about
- Saying that they had no choice
- Throwing a tantrum, crying, or refusing to talk
- Hiding, running, or getting mad at the adult for catching them
- Reciting some good things they've done
- Changing the subject

As a former child, you know what these experiences feel like. In children's responses we can recognize forerunners of many adult defensive reactions.

Take a moment and think of a recent time in your adult life when you felt cornered. Did you respond in one or more ways that are similar to children's responses? For example, let's say that a project you are in charge of runs into serious trouble. Perhaps you initially reacted in ways similar to those in the following table:

Common Defensive Responses			
What you say	Your goal	The reality you deny	Alternative nondefensive response
It's not my fault. Somebody else messed it up.	Shift blame	I was in charge of the project.	Fault and blame not important. I'll take responsibility for fixing it.
Something will change for the better.	Reduce anxiety	Most problems don't magically go away.	How can I brainstorm possible solutions?
I deserve an exception.	Feel special	Life isn't always fair.	We're all special but this is still my responsibility.

What you say	Your goal	The reality you deny	Alternative nondefensive response
There were extenuating circumstances.	Mitigate the costs	Every situation has extenuating circumstances.	What can I do to change or adapt to the circumstances?
I couldn't have done anything differently.	Reduce guilt	I chose my actions.	I can act differently from now on.
It's not that important a project anyway.	Hedge bets by devaluing the project	I deemed this important enough to invest my time in it.	The quality of my work is important to me.
Maybe I'm just not competent.	Preempt external criticism	I'm also capable.	What can I learn from this?
I don't need help in fixing it.	Avoid embarrassment in asking for help	We all need help at times.	Who might I consult and what resources might I tap?
This project has been ill-fated from the start.	Focus on the project's flaws instead of your own	Problems don't necessarily disqualify an entire project.	What is my goal and how can I achieve it?
I must not be that committed.	Seek a way out	Commitment is a choice, not a trait.	I agreed to do it so I'll finish.
This can't be happening.	Postpone recognition of the problem	It's happening.	It's time to face the problem and find solutions.

When it comes to finding wiggle room when something goes wrong, we possess more flavors than Baskin-Robbins. We seek to avoid responsibility by denying some part of reality.

The point about recognizing the "beasts" within is not that being descended from animals or having been a child causes self-sabotage. Sometimes animallike and childlike behaviors make sense even for adult human animals. Fleeing or hiding can be important self-preservation mechanisms. In addition, many of our animallike and childlike responses can be innocent, guileless, and refreshing. None of these behaviors is inherently bad. When you're surprised or threatened, it is natural to narrow your focus.

The point is that your automatic responses can prevent you from weighing all your options. Spotting animallike or childlike behavior can help you identify when you're not acting in your best interests. From there, you can reclaim your adult perspective and stature and choose a healthier course.

7

YOUR "USUAL SUSPECTS"

It's hard to fight an enemy who has outposts in your head.

—SALLY KEMPTON

In the movie *Casablanca,* police Captain Louis Renault ordered his men to "Round up the usual suspects" after a murder, even though he knew that his friend Rick, played by Humphrey Bogart, committed the crime. This is disingenuous detective work for a police officer, but identifying your internal "usual suspects" offers another way to recognize potentially self-undermining situations.

We each have internal usual suspects; the emotions and responses that automatically arise when we are surprised, challenged, or criticized. Perhaps you are quick to anger, tears, or despair. It's not that the emotions aren't real; they are. But they travel a well-worn pathway. These responses are where you go by *default.*

For example, Brenda, twenty-six, has noticed that when she is disappointed she initially feels sad or hurt but then generally defaults to anger. "It seems easier for me to feel angry than hurt or sad. Anger helps me feel big while hurt feels small and sadness feels vulnerable," she says. In such situations Brenda's anger may be real, but it's not honest. By recognizing anger as one of her usual suspects, she can step back and explore the full picture.

What are your emotional defaults? Hopelessness? Helplessness? Resentment? Self-doubt? Though these are authentic feelings, they may primarily serve to help you avoid discomfort but do nothing to help you face your problems. For example:

- Hopelessness can dissuade you from taking risks, which might lead to loss. The cost is that feeling hopeless can drain your energy and lead to depression.

- Helplessness may elicit sympathy and reduce pressure to act. However, long-term feelings of helplessness can sap your sense of self and increase the risk of depression, stress, and illness.

- Resentment can paper over hurt and move your focus from yourself. But when you hold on to resentment for too long, you risk cementing your connection to past wrongs instead of freeing yourself from them.

- Self-doubt in situations in which you feel uncertain or have little control can feel as though you are at least doing something rather than nothing. Yet self-doubts can spread into vital areas of your life.

You have physical and mental usual suspects as well as emotional ones. For example, you may overeat when you're angry or overspend when you're sad. You may be quick to rationalize certain behaviors or tune out certain thoughts.

If You'd Like to Go Deeper:
Rounding Up Your Usual Suspects

This exercise lists common reactions to being surprised, disappointed, or criticized. For each of the following five questions, go down the list and check any reactions that are characteristic for you. Check as many responses for each question as apply.

This list of reactions is by no means all-inclusive. You might want to write in additional responses you commonly have when you feel surprised, disappointed, or criticized.

Characteristic response	1. When you are startled, or in an unpleasant new situation, how do you usually react?	2. When you feel disappointed, how do you generally react?	3. When you feel criticized, how do you generally react?	4. When you were growing up, how were you most likely to react when criticized?	5. When you were growing up, how were you most likely to react when disappointed?
Leave	☐	☐	☐	☐	☐
Use your charm	☐	☐	☐	☐	☐
Zone out	☐	☐	☐	☐	☐
Tough it out	☐	☐	☐	☐	☐
Pretend it's not happening	☐	☐	☐	☐	☐
Second-guess yourself	☐	☐	☐	☐	☐
Blame someone else	☐	☐	☐	☐	☐
Procrastinate	☐	☐	☐	☐	☐
Distract yourself	☐	☐	☐	☐	☐
Become manipulative	☐	☐	☐	☐	☐
Get mad at yourself	☐	☐	☐	☐	☐
Fight back	☐	☐	☐	☐	☐
Feel down or depressed	☐	☐	☐	☐	☐

Become passive	☐	☐	☐	☐
Criticize someone else	☐	☐	☐	☐
Show no reaction	☐	☐	☐	☐
Lie	☐	☐	☐	☐
Deflect it with humor	☐	☐	☐	☐
Escalate the situation	☐	☐	☐	☐
Feel paralyzed	☐	☐	☐	☐
Try harder	☐	☐	☐	☐
Use drugs or similar items	☐	☐	☐	☐
	☐	☐	☐	☐

Interpreting Your Answers

Notice any usual suspects with three or more boxes checked. These may be your "default" responses. Though any of these responses may be appropriate at times, overusing them may not be your best coping mechanism.

For example, forty-year-old Rachel checked the following responses most frequently:

- Tough it out (5)

- Pretend it's not happening (5)

- Second-guess yourself (4)

- Get mad at yourself (4)

- Feel down or depressed (3)

- Become passive (3)

- Feel paralyzed (3)

Taken together, Rachel's responses indicate that when she is criticized, disappointed, or startled, she tends to deny what is happening, turn her feelings back on herself, and freeze up. Although these reactions may feel self-protective, they tend to make it harder for her to assert herself or respond with strength when she needs to. In addition, she is likely to pay an emotional price by doubting or getting mad at herself.

You might also look over your answers and notice which of the first three columns has the most checkmarks. This can indicate which of the three experiences—being startled, disappointed, or criticized—is most difficult for you to handle. Such situations may pose a higher risk of self-inflicted losses. In knowing which experiences tend to be most difficult, you can pay special attention to them when they arise. For example, you might seek support, use greater resources, and bring more awareness to such situations.

You might also notice whether any of your usual suspects has a significant difference in the number of marks between the last two columns, which focus on your experiences growing up, and the first three columns. Responses that were more common in your past than in your present life show progress. These are reactions that you've left behind as you've matured.

When you notice a usual suspect:

1. Take a moment and look more deeply at what you might be avoiding or denying.

2. Remember that you have other, more adaptive ways of responding.

8

YOUR INNER "CAST OF CHARACTERS"

Pay no attention to that man behind the curtain.

—THE WIZARD OF OZ

If it ever feels crowded inside your head, don't be surprised. You are witness to an ongoing internal conversation, only part of which you direct. One way to conceive of the complex interplay among human personality, traits, values, and personal history is that each of us symbolically ferries an internal cast of characters through our lives. Recognizing when one or more of these inner characters is negatively influencing you is another tool for spotting self-undermining patterns in time to alter course.

For example, have you ever gotten so lost in your daydreams that you found it hard to bring yourself back to reality? That journey was courtesy of what I call the Moviemaker, one of nine inner characters you'll meet in this chapter. Similarly, have you ever obsessed on a tiny detail and been unable to let it go despite the potential cost to an overall project? Thank Capt. Superior, another character you'll learn about, for that fixation.

I use "inner character" to describe strategies we consciously or unconsciously adopt when facing uncertainty, fear, or loss. When these inner characters stage psychic coups, you feel as though events are happening *to* you. Of course, these are not real characters in a clinical sense. I use "character" just as I used Subterranean Accountant, as a construct to group behaviors and tendencies and hold them at arm's length for inspection.

The inner character metaphor can help you distill a succinct recognition of your negative patterns, because it externalizes your behavior. To externalize is to step back and observe certain feelings, attitudes, and patterns. Externalizing has proven to be a particularly helpful tool in family therapy, as advanced by Australian family therapist Michael White and New Zealand family therapist David Epston. Externalizing offers psychological "binoculars," allowing you to gain perspective on unhealthy habits and patterns rather than experiencing them as inevitable parts of you.

Inner characters and the viewpoints and feelings they represent are common and completely understandable. They are a product of your diversity and complexity. They can be entertaining, harmless, and even productive. At times, however, your characters affect you powerfully and negatively. When an inner character "takes over," you lose your normal awareness.

Inner characters have characteristic signs. Recognize the signs, and you can step out of character and take back control of your life.

The nine characters, and what you do under their influence:

- Moviemaker: Entertain yourself with Hollywood-style fantasies

- Indulger: Distract yourself with escapist activities

- Persuader: Explain away uncertainty or rationalize aims and behavior

- Dr. No: Automatically oppose or become passive-aggressive

- Mini-Me: Seek safety by becoming inconspicuous

- Capt. Superior: Seek validation through perfectionism or putting others down

- Escape Artist: Avoid demands by procrastinating, spacing out, or giving up

- King Kong: Sidestep your conscience and capitulate to impulses

- Dramateer: Seek excitement by coveting super-sized emotions

One or more of these characters may be present at any time. For example, Jan is a good artist who hopes to build her art career but has great anxiety that she's not talented enough. She recounted a recent smorgasbord of characters. On a free Tuesday night, she thought about starting a painting but immediately dismissed the idea (Dr. No). She told herself she should clean the kitchen first. While cleaning, she noticed she'd been rinsing the coffee pot for nearly two minutes, absently staring out the window (Escape Artist). She put the dishes away and sat for a moment, fantasizing about what her first art show would be like (Moviemaker). Her mental movie was soon cut short with such doubts as, "What if nobody showed up?" (Mini-Me). She castigated herself for her wishful thinking (King Kong). She moved to the living room and turned on the television telling herself, "Maybe there's a show about art or a profile of a great artist," (Persuader). Despite the absence of an art-related show, the TV lineup seemed better than usual, and she settled in for the evening (Indulger). From time to time, she thought about going upstairs to paint, but the prospect of setting up her palette seemed overwhelming (Mini-Me).

As you read through this chapter's descriptions of inner characters, you may think of other characters that are uniquely yours in addition to those profiled here. Don't worry about remembering the particulars of an individual character or trying to remember all nine. Just let these descriptions rest in your consciousness and see if you notice character-driven behavior as you go through your day. It's not so important that you see which character has taken over but that you notice *when* you're in character. Once you recognize that a character has moved in, ask yourself if there are any emotional losses you're seeking to avoid or obscure. Assess whether your character-induced aims and methods are in your best interests.

Many of us could find evidence of each of these characters in our behavior at one time or another. You may find that you have a few characters that you use—or, more appropriately, that use you—most frequently.

Characters operate along a continuum. For example, the Escape Artist can range from sensible postponing to pathological procrastination. Dr. No can range from understandable ambivalence to intractable passive-aggressiveness. Capt. Superior is sometimes just a petty officer. King Kong is sometimes Prince Chimp. Sometimes you're totally under the influence; other times only partially. At times your characters take little effort to sidestep. Other times it may take all your psychic and physical strength to avoid character-inspired behavior.

Each character has a distinct way of influencing your behavior. For example, suppose that someone asks you to do something you don't want to. Typical responses when in each character:

- Moviemaker: Fantasize about different ways you could say no
- Indulger: Take the rest of the day off
- Persuader: Agree even though you can't possibly do it
- Dr. No: Say you'll get back to him then avoid him for weeks
- Mini-Me: Say that you're feeling too tired to do anything
- Capt. Superior: Tell her how it should be done
- Escape Artist: Agree, then forget about it
- King Kong: Bite his head off
- Dramateer: Get teary-eyed

Another example: Suppose that you want someone to do something for you, but you're afraid to ask. Typical approaches:

- Moviemaker: Mentally rehearse asking to the tune of imaginary background music
- Indulger: Go for ice cream
- Persuader: Assure yourself that he'll realize what you want without your having to ask
- Dr. No: Not ask, telling yourself that you don't need her anyway
- Mini-Me: Avoid him
- Capt. Superior: Begin by telling her that she owes you a favor
- Escape Artist: Tell yourself that he'd probably say no, so why bother asking
- King Kong: Contemplate the threats you'll use if she says no
- Dramateer: Flirt

The characters manifest the four litmus-test behaviors of self-defeating secret-keeping. Each character tends to rely primarily on one element, as the following table illustrates.

Primary Method for Each Character	
Distracting	• Moviemaker • Indulger • Dramateer
Overreacting	• Dr. No • Capt. Superior • King Kong
Abandoning	• Mini-Me • Escape Artist
Misleading	• Persuader

Further complicating matters is that stepping into role as any of these characters can bring either positive or negative consequences. Some of your characters' techniques, when used consciously, can help you overcome challenges and reach inspiring heights. For example, the Moviemaker's imagination can be a muse on a creative project. The Indulger can help you rest and relax. The Persuader can spark insights or spur you to triumph despite overwhelming odds. Dr. No can help you set healthy boundaries. Mini-Me can keep you humble. Capt. Superior can inspire you to excellence. The Escape Artist can help you slow down and smell the flowers. King Kong can help you find your passion. The Dramateer can add spice when you're mired in a routine. The key is to discern whether a character is playing a helpful or undermining role.

Here are sketches of the nine inner characters to help you recognize when you're under their influence.

Moviemaker

Entertains you with Hollywood-style fantasies

Examples of everyday moviemaking:

- Fantasizing about how you'd spend your lottery winnings

- Envisioning your acceptance speech for the Oscar, Grammy, or Nobel prize

- Visualizing being swept off your feet by Prince or Princess Charming

Under the influence of the Moviemaker, you script, direct, act in, and watch private colorized memories, silver-screen daydreams, and technicolor fantasies. On the way to work, for example, an adventure, romance, or horror film may restlessly spin in your mind's eye. Or perhaps you catch a sneak preview of the upcoming weekend's big event. Or you hunker down for a gritty drama recapping the previous day's unpleasant confrontation, followed by a documentary-style analysis of "What I should have said." Sometimes it may feel as if you're creating the movie, nudging it along to a desired outcome. Other times you sit, riveted, awaiting each scene as though the movie has a life of its own.

The Moviemaker provides entertainment. Your "home movies" can be uplifting or frightening but they are always engaging. That's the problem. Like theatergoers who willingly suspend disbelief, we sometimes forget that our daydreams and fantasies are mental movies. We develop expectations, assumptions, and feelings as though our scenarios are real. Even when your mind knows the movies are not real, your body and heart don't necessarily distinguish between fantasy and reality. That's why reading the words *rattlesnake bite* can evoke a bounce in your physiology even if you are reading this in a sixteenth-floor Manhattan apartment.

As I said, the key is to recognize when a character's role is costly rather than beneficial. The following table shows how.

How to Tell Bad Movies from Good Ones

Costly moviemaking
When your mental movies become the primary way to compensate for hurt, boredom, or worry, you risk living based on illusion instead of reality. The Moviemaker can wed you to unrealistic fantasies so strongly that you ignore or discount important relationships, jobs, and experiences. In retrospect you may wonder, "How could I have been so unrealistic?"

Beneficial moviemaking
The ability to envision a better future is crucial to positive change. Athletes and performers use moviemaking techniques to visualize a successful performance in advance of the actual event. Letting your mind drift, seeking new directions, and pursuing nonlinear paths are key elements of the creative process.

The difference
Costly moviemaking is used to escape a mundane or unpleasant situation using fantasies that have no realistic chance of becoming a reality. Beneficial moviemaking is directed toward giving you insights and experiences that can help you change reality for the better.

How to walk out of a bad movie
Remember the Moviemaker's big secret:

IT'S NOT REAL, IT'S JUST A MOVIE.

Indulger

Distracts, soothes, or seduces you with escapist or feel-good activities

Examples of everyday indulging:

- Taking an extra helping of chocolate decadence cake
- Maxing out your charge card to buy your fifty-third pair of shoes
- Spending hours improving your score at computer solitaire

Under the Indulger's influence, you seek instant gratification. Inexorably drawn to shopping, eating, drinking, or other distractions you sidestep pressure and unpleasantries. Whereas the Moviemaker distracts with fantasy, the Indulger distracts with activity. Under the influence of the Indulger, you'll do whatever feels good enough to crowd out what feels bad.

I remember a day some years ago when I learned that I had lost out on a career opportunity I really wanted. I felt as though a compelling force handed me my car keys and drove me to the supermarket. Standing in front of the frozen-foods case, the door open, cold air swirling around me as the glass iced up, I looked over the array of Ben and Jerry's ice creams and my pulse quickened. I picked a pint of Cherry Garcia, my favorite. I lingered. I loved so many flavors. Not wanting to feel deprived, I also grabbed a pint of Chocolate Fudge Brownie and, for dessert, Mint Chocolate Chip. It was 10:30 A.M. By 11:30 A.M. I'd finished two-and-a-half of the three pints.

Like a stress circuit-breaker, the Indulger can arrive suddenly, as it did with my 2,700-calorie "brunch." When it trips, you feel compelled to drop everything. Other times the Indulger slowly draws you in. A few minutes. One taste. A quick peek. Eventually you surrender, blotting out pressing concerns with a warm soak in your chosen distraction. You may surf the Web or play games for hours, soothing yourself with numbing repetition.

Facing the prospect of telling a loved one something you feel guilty about, rather than seize the day—*carpe diem*—and get it over with, you grab your credit cards—*carpe plasticum*—and head to the mall for retail therapy. As Tammy Faye Baker said, "Shopping is cheaper than a psychiatrist."

How to Tell Bad Indulging from Good Indulging

Costly indulging
Indulging can be costly when it is consistently and primarily used to mask or rout feelings or situations you fear. At the extreme, the Indulger can lead to addictions, binging, financial troubles, and other excesses. If you seek only to feel better fast, you risk losing sight of the long-term consequences. Afterward you may wonder, "How could I have been so irresponsible?"

Beneficial indulging
We all need escapist activities to reduce the stress of living. Such pleasures as shopping, chocolate, alcohol, sex, and traveling can be deliciously life-enhancing. If you've been depriving yourself, then giving to yourself can restore balance.

The difference
Negative indulging tries to avoid challenges or compensate for bad feelings. Beneficial indulging seeks to restore a healthy balance.

How to stop overindulging
Remind yourself of the Indulger's secret:

THIS IS ONLY A TEMPORARY FIX.

Persuader

Explains away doubts and uncertainties or justifies your aims and actions with make-it-fit reasoning, rationalization, and selective focus

Examples of everyday persuading:

- Driving with the gas gauge on empty and telling yourself, "They always build in extra reserve"

- Offering directions to out-of-towners even though you're not entirely sure how to get there

- Setting your watch five minutes ahead

Under the influence of the Persuader, you're convinced of the rightness of your thoughts, feelings, and behavior. When you face complicated experiences, puzzling behavior, or confusing feelings, any explanation, accurate or not, may feel more comforting than no explanation. The Persuader can reduce your anxiety but often does so with loony logic and simplistic thinking. For example, despite the facts you may conclude:

- "He must be angry because of something I said." (Fact: He often gets angry for no apparent reason, as you know from previous occasions.)

- "I feel incredibly attracted to her, so it must mean that I love her and she loves me." (Fact: You barely know her.)

- "Once I get a raise, I'll finally be happy." (Fact: Past raises have made little lasting difference in your happiness.)

- "I'm too shy to do that." (Fact: You've done it several times before.)

The Persuader can beckon you to a universe in which physical laws are negotiable and hours have more than sixty minutes when you want them to. For example, Mike recalls a recent morning in which he had fifteen minutes to get to work at a stuffy accounting firm where lateness is not well tolerated. His workplace is a ten-minute drive away. Nevertheless, Mike stopped to pick up dry cleaning. His record time for parking, paying, and picking up dry cleaning is eight minutes, and that included finding the dream parking space and nobody in line at the cleaners. Sure enough, Mike showed up late. "Up until one minute before I was due at work, I still somehow believed I would make it," Mike says.

The Persuader gives you permission to join treasure hunts and seek shortcuts, suspending critical judgment and embracing reasoning that you'd never accept in rational moments. The Persuader also excels at "creative" math: exaggerating or minimizing risks, rewards, and the odds of failure or success. Believing that you can predict the future may reduce your anxiety. Yet the Persuader's crystal ball is as transparent as a bowling ball.

How to Tell Bad Persuasions from Good Persuasions

Costly persuading
In search of certainty, the Persuader relies on two-dimensional analysis: either-or, all-or-nothing, and black-white thinking. As a result, you sacrifice flexibility, accuracy, and the opportunity to meet life's complexities. The Persuader is a con artist offering to make you feel better about yourself, at least in the short term. At its worst, the Persuader leads you to ignore vital information or pursue goals so indirectly that you forfeit any chance of success. In retrospect you may wonder, "How could I have been so gullible?"

Beneficial persuading
Rationalizing and explaining can be helpful coping skills at times. We all need encouragement. The inner voice that says *You can do it* can lend perspective by reminding you that nothing ventured, nothing gained.

The difference
Negative persuading narrows your perspective, shutting out information that is threatening. Beneficial persuading broadens your view by highlighting information that can empower you.

How to send the Persuader packing
Remember the Persuader's secret:

GARBAGE IN, GARBAGE OUT.

Dr. No

Seeks power by automatically opposing, invalidating, or acting passive-aggressively

Examples of everyday Nos:

- Voting *no* on every ballot proposition without bothering to read any

- Automatically declining an invitation even though you would enjoy going

- Rushing to beat another customer to the bank teller even when you're not in a hurry

Under the influence of Dr. No, you feel compelled to resist. Dr. No is akin to a two-year-old who, upon learning the word *no,* uses it for every occasion.

When Dr. No descends, you say "no" even when you want to say "yes," "maybe," or "I don't know." Dr. No's opposition may be passionate or passionless, but it generally feels utterly automatic. It's as though you derive power from squelching and a sense of identity from fighting. Only in opposition to others do you know who you are. Only by saying "no" do you feel safe from harm.

Dr. No can infuriate others with passive-aggressive behavior. You may have observed drivers in Dr. No's character. Sometimes deliberately, other times unconsciously, they linger in the fast lane, then speed up as others try to pass on the right. In a cat-and-mouse game, motorists who appear most impatient to pass are blocked the longest. Drivers who seem not in a hurry are allowed to pass in short order.

How to Tell Bad Nos from Good Nos

Costly Nos
At the extreme, Dr. No can manifest as maddeningly passive-aggressive, obstinate, or just plain disagreeable behavior. If Dr. No is a regular visitor in your life you may find it difficult to join

the party even when you want to. Afterward you may wonder, "How could I have been so negative?"

Beneficial Nos
Saying "no" is an important life skill. Standing firm on principal or honor may necessitate saying "no" even in the face of extreme pressure. Saying "no" in the service of love, health, and self-care is a crucial skill.

The difference
Negative Dr. No is defensive, warding off fears or compensating for perceived deficits. Beneficial Dr. No arises from your values. It clarifies who you are, both to others and to yourself.

How to say "no" to the doctor
Remind yourself of Dr. No's secret:

**THE COSTS OF SAYING "NO"
CAN FAR OUTWEIGH THE BENEFITS.**

Mini-Me

Seeks safety by leading you to be inconspicuous, play small, or elicit excessive caretaking

Examples of everyday Mini-Me:

- Apologizing when the other person arrives late
- Not volunteering even when you know the answer in a class or meeting
- Going to a party and spending much of the evening in the bathroom or kitchen

Under Mini-Me's influence, you seek protection by playing small. You can probably remember a time in school slouching in your chair as a teacher asked questions or on the job, trying to appear busy when your boss walked by. Shrinking in stature is Mini-Me's trademark. Mini's philosophy: If they can't see me, they can't hurt me.

For example, when Laura and her husband bought their first house, she agonized over what color to repaint the living room. "My husband and I had been in rental places for years and, you know, they're always some form of off-white. Eggshell, cream, whatever," she says.

"With our new house I asked everyone's opinion," she recalls. "For seventeen months I asked people how to paint, what's the best primer, what's the best brand of paint. I worried that if I painted it wrong or messed up the moldings I'd be judged wrongly. I was endlessly getting new paint samples. Even knowing that this was only a living room and that I could always paint over anything I did, I kept going in a big circle, afraid to settle on a color."

As in Laura's case, Mini-Me often steps in when you feel inadequate or shy. You may apologize for your presence, demeanor, or appearance. You play it safe, act indirectly, and make no waves.

How to Tell Bad Shrinking from Good Shrinking

Costly Mini-Me
Mini-Me can leave you meek with no chance of inheriting the Earth. Feeling like a junior person, you may adopt a people-pleaser personality or become desperate to be taken under another's wing. You may excessively seek reassurance, psychologically merge with others, or rarely assert your wishes and needs. You may grow overanxious and hypervigilant. In retrospect you may wonder, "How could I have acted so pitifully?"

Beneficial Mini-Me
Humility can be healthy, particularly to compulsive overachievers. When used consciously, Mini-Me allows you to move the focus from yourself to other people and tasks. This can reduce performance anxiety and self-absorption as well as let others participate more. In addition, you may be more open to learning and receiving.

The difference
Negative Mini-Me is characterized by a contraction of your sense of self. Beneficial Mini-Me fosters a slowing or shrinking in one

or more situations or areas of your life so that you can gain perspective, but it leaves your overall sense of self intact.

How to leave Mini-Me behind
Remember Mini-Me's little secret:

HIDING WON'T NECESSARILY PROTECT YOU.

Capt. Superior

Seeks validation and attention through
perfectionism or being one-up on others

Examples of everyday superiority:

- Puffing yourself up and crowing after winning a minor game of cards

- Being overly sarcastic

- Refusing to act on a good suggestion just because it wasn't yours

Under the influence of Capt. Superior, you seek to be the best and the rightest. Capt. Superior must win, for any victory is a validation of personal worth. There's no such thing as "just a game." Capt. Superior establishes his superiority as if on a noble quest. The Captain can become positional over even trivial matters. You may end up on "slight patrol," construing other people's innocent actions as personal affronts.

When Capt. Superior takes over, you feel impatient and tolerate fools badly. You surreptitiously inspect and judge others' performance, posture, and diction. In conversations you may fidget, sigh, or drum your fingers as you wait for another person to finish. You feel that you have a much better story to tell. Besides, you know that you'll make the point the other person should have but didn't.

Capt. Superior hates to be caught off-guard. Disorder or imperfec-tions in possessions, surroundings, or family members are taken as flaws in one's internal character. The Captain's house, car, children, and wardrobe are flawlessly neat and compulsively organized.

How to Tell Bad Superiority from Good Superiority

Costly superiority
For Capt. Superior, everything is a fight. You prepare for battle by seeking out others' flaws and weaknesses, stonewalling with stoicism, or looking down upon those who would dare to challenge their betters. Afterward, you may wonder, "How could I have been so self-centered?"

Beneficial superiority
Healthy self-respect is a good asset. At its best, Capt. Superior can restore balance to your life by helping you see the best in you and others. When you acknowledge your gifts, you can use them more readily.

The difference
Negative superiority is a win-lose, zero-sum game. Beneficial superiority is a win-win game in which your actions are not dependent on others' actions nor done at their expense.

How to demote the Captain
Remind yourself of the Captain's secret:

IT'S LONELY AT THE TOP.

Escape Artist

Avoids pressure and demands by hedging, quitting, spacing out, or procrastinating

Examples of everyday escape artistry:

- Daydreaming while somebody else is talking

- Remembering that you were cooking once you smell burning food

- Faxing the blank side of a document

- Beginning your tax return on April 14

Under the influence of the Escape Artist, you keep one foot out. Indecision and difficulty committing are trademarks of the Escape Artist.

For example, Jesse recalls driving to a recent party and thinking, "I'm bored now, but I'll have fun when I get there." Upon arriving Jesse found the party to be flat. He thought, "I can't wait to get out of here." He left, but his mental shell game continued. Arriving home, he wondered wistfully, "Maybe I should have stayed a bit longer. Maybe the party was just about to get good." Under the Escape Artist's influence, the grass is always greener in your mind's eye.

When pressured to perform, you may try half-heartedly or not at all. Sometimes apathy descends, anesthetizing you from demands. After all, if you don't hope, you can't be disappointed. Whereas the Indulger distracts through activity, the Escape Artist soothes through lack of activity. Even when you're aware that you're drifting, you often want it to continue. It's the path of least resistance. In a way, drifting along can be kind of relaxing.

The Escape Artist makes your feet highly susceptible to dragging. You may feel leaden or stuck as if in molasses. You may refuse to acknowledge losses or the passage of time and cling to regrets or resentments for years in the fashion of Miss Havisham of *Great Expectations*, the patron saint for Escape Artists.

The logic behind the Escape Artist's self-paralysis: Better to be paralyzed by feelings you authored than to be at the mercy of external situations. You put off decisions or actions even though they'll turn out no differently in the future. In fact, things often turn out worse because you have less time.

All forms of escape are designed to avoid loss by hedging your bets. As Scarlett O'Hara said, "I'll think about that tomorrow."

How to Tell Bad Escapes from Good Escapes

Costly escape artistry

Virtually all of us space out, withdraw, or procrastinate at times, but when this becomes a lifestyle, we forfeit momentum, efficacy, and self-confidence. At the extreme, the Escape Artist's half-hearted living can isolate you from your job, loved ones, and heart. The Escape Artist leads you to disengage—in psychological terms, to dissociate. This can become so habitual that it is hard to straighten up and fly right even when you need to. You may come to expect little from yourself. Afterward, you may wonder, "How could I have been so out to lunch?"

Beneficial escape artistry
When used by choice, the Escape Artist can foster rest and relaxation. It can encourage you not to sweat the small stuff. It can remind you that sometimes it is best to cut your losses and move on.

The difference
Negative escaping avoids living in the present. Beneficial escaping moves toward health by readying you for a time and situation when you can be more present.

How to cage the escape artist
Remember the Escape Artist's secret:

LIFE IS PASSING YOU BY.

King Kong

Sidesteps your conscience
and better judgment by capitulating
to overwhelming thoughts or impulses

Examples of everyday King Kong:

- Partying late into the night before an important test or work project

- Seething when someone brings eight items through the seven-item quick-checkout line

- Impulsively destroying something you've created because you think it is no good

Under the influence of King Kong, you give over to the monster within. Feelings, thoughts, and desires become overpowering. For example, you may fixate on distressing thoughts like, "Who is my ex with tonight, and what are they doing?" If your child doesn't come when you call, you may jump to the conclusion that it is deliberate defiance rather than consider reasonable alternatives, like the possibility your child didn't even hear you.

When you feel angry King Kong encourages you to marinate in it. For example, every time Jeremy sees his neighbor's unkempt vines crowding into Jeremy's flowerbed, he does a slow burn. "Doesn't he have eyes?" he tells himself. "I should say something. I could write him a note. Should I call or just go over? I could cut his vines myself."

Once King Kong gets going, reining in the big ape's reactions takes a mighty effort. If you feel blue you may forfeit your entire day to self-pity. If you feel ashamed you may launch into a fit of self-criticism out of proportion to the circumstances.

Under King Kong's influence you may seek an edgy aliveness by tempting fate. For example, when you feel frustrated, tired, hungry, or lonely, for some curious reason that's the time you decide to broach a sensitive subject with your boss or mate. In part this is because King Kong's devil-may-care attitude feels energizing. Imminent danger can distract you from pain or inner conflicts. If you feel empty, then figuratively or literally, toying with your life supplies quite a jolt.

When your King-sized critical eye turns back on you, you muster little empathy and compassion for yourself. You call yourself names like "stupid," "lazy," "worthless," and "loser." King Kong can lead you to deprive or punish yourself more often or more severely than anyone else would deprive or punish you.

How to Tell Bad Kings from Good Kings

Costly King Kong
Though passionate feelings are to be treasured, King Kong can lead to risky or abusive behavior. Your emotions of the moment dominate your existence. Instead of facing difficult feelings, containing them, seeking to understand them, or talking about them with others, you simply give over to them. Your justification: Might makes right. In retrospect you may wonder, "How could I have been so out of control?"

Beneficial King Kong

At his best, King Kong can help you let go and seek your passions. It can help you experience rather than ignore feelings. It can energize you to make changes.

The difference

Negative King Kong is a cop-out that denies your responsibility and acts out unwanted thoughts and feelings. Helpful King Kong seeks to give healthy expression even to those aspects of yourself that you may not like or accept.

How to dethrone the King

Remind yourself of the King's big secret:

YOU'RE BIGGER THAN KING KONG AND HE WORKS FOR YOU.

Dramateer

Seeks excitement by coveting superlatives, novelty, and super-sized emotions

Examples of everyday dramatics:

- A friend's relationship breakup becomes your own emotional trauma

- You're certain that a two-day cold is pneumonia

- Every party you give must be the social event of the year

Under the influence of the Dramateer you are tempted to exaggerate and overdo. You may banish boredom or emptiness with theatrics that, at times, even you find hard to believe. The Dramateer loves superlatives. *The most delicious cheesecake in the world. The absolute best day of my life. The most beautiful sunset ever.* Like a moth to flame, you seek more, bigger, and faster even if it gets too hot to handle.

For example, Cherie recently met a former lover at a party. Within moments, she began fantasizing about getting back together with him, though he is now married. Since then, Cherie has found it hard to concentrate on daily tasks. "Probably at least a hundred times a day I find myself fantasizing about what it will be like when we get back together," she says.

Whether or not a rekindling of Cherie's romance is possible or wise, her *Harlequin*-esque fantasies make other aspects of her life pale in comparison. And that's the point: her fantasies replace her loneliness.

The Dramateer can also drive the pace of your life as if you were a car. Sometimes it hits the brakes, lingering in indecisiveness or distraction, hoping problems will go away or that slowing down may alter the outcome. Other times it hits the gas, doing multiple tasks at once, hoping to accelerate past unpleasantries. Peripatetic activity is a Dramateer trademark. You go out to dinner and constantly look around for conversations or people you imagine to be more interesting. At parties you scan endlessly for the "in crowd."

The Dramateer leads you to temptation without taking responsibility for it. As in the classic torch song "Falling in Love Again" or Britney Spears's "Oops I Did it Again," you didn't mean to flirt, but you just couldn't help it. You didn't expect others to respond, after all.

How to Tell Bad Drama from Good Drama

Costly dramatics
At the extreme, the Dramateer's histrionics rob emotional balance and perspective. For the Dramateer, all the world's a stage. You celebrate superficiality and embrace phoniness. Looking back, you may wonder, "How could I have been so flighty?"

Beneficial dramatics
Cultivating adventures and feelings can add humor, energy, and emotion to your life. It can broaden your emotional range and stimulate you to try new experiences.

The difference
Negative drama is a facade that hides your emptiness and fears. Beneficial drama seeks to express your most authentic parts.

How to bring the curtain down on the Dramateer
Remind yourself of the Dramateer's secret:

IT'S ALL AN ACT.

Managing Your Inner Characters

Inner characters, like all forms of counterfactualizing, transport you to alternate realities. They arise in part because we don't like reckoning with an impersonal universe in which anything could happen. We construct futures, revise pasts, and assign meaning. Our characters let us play at omnipotence and immortality. Doing so isn't bad; in fact, it's very human.

The point isn't to banish your characters—that's not possible—but to manage them. The problem is that it can be difficult to know in the midst of things whether a character is self-defeating or self-enhancing. How can you tell when your steely resolve carries the courage of a Martin Luther King Jr., or simply mimics the stubbornness of a two-year-old? How do you know if your creative drive is on a par with Leonardo da Vinci's or is a distraction as elaborate as Walter Mitty's? Even da Vinci, on his deathbed, is reported to have said, "I have offended God and mankind because my work did not reach the quality it should have."

Disempowering characters are driven by unseen fears and motivations, which are then run through the errant calculator of your Subterranean Accountant. The character drives your life, and you take a back seat. When you consciously use your characters for positive ends, you're back in the driver's seat.

Negative characters offer many potential payoffs: excitement, stress-reduction, instant gratification, control, power, self-importance, self-soothing, energy, novelty, and certainty. You feel special and clever, as if you're getting away with something. Who would want to give these up? Because we like the payoffs, it is seductively easy to forfeit will, nerve, and motivation to the characters.

Characters also carry potential costs: disappointment, wasted time, dumb behavior, phoniness, victimization, and disconnections from people and life. You forfeit opportunities, self-confidence, self-respect, peace, discipline, perspective, and intimacy. You suffer rigidity, powerlessness, inner turmoil, humiliation, and physical risk.

Of course your Persuader could look at this cost-benefit ratio and declare, "What a great deal!" At the same time, in the clear light of day you might rightly question whether it's worth the price. Seeing the costs of your character-induced behavior can help you distinguish between what's harmless and what's too much.

In addition, ask yourself why a character is there in the first place.

What fear or avoided experience might the character cover? A fear of entrapment? Emptiness? Pressure? At what cost? What deep desires are not being met? Love? Peace? Fulfillment?

Characters are altered states. Our mistake is in applying normal standards to abnormal states. Characters are not bad. They just aren't reality. As with falling asleep, eventually you wake up from a character. These characters have great power, but their power comes from you. Knowing this can help you reclaim and constructively exert your power.

If You'd Like to Go Deeper: Detecting Your Inner Characters

This exercise can help you identify negative characters more clearly. Take a moment and recall a situation in which you got in your own way or felt as if you'd lost touch with your best self. Recall what you said, felt, and did. Then consult the character detector on the next page.

You can also refer to this detector the moment you have an inkling that something isn't quite right. Once you see a character clearly, it loses the power to overtake you. Remember, you may experience more than one character in any given situation.

To use this detector, start with the left-hand column and go vertically, one column at a time. After you've finished the first three columns, notice which characters have the predominance of marks. This can reveal any characters present. Or, to determine if a particular character is present, pick that character in the right-hand column and go horizontally, marking any behaviors and feelings characteristic of that character which you observe in the current situation.

Inner Character Detector			
If you're overdoing one or more of the following behaviors . . .	And trying to avoid feeling . . .	While seeking to feel . . .	Your character may be . . .
☐ Fantasizing ☐ Daydreaming ☐ Wishful or magical thinking ☐ Getting lost in memories ☐ Having an "active" imagination	☐ Bored	☐ Entertained or ☐ Distracted	Moviemaker
☐ Shopping ☐ Eating ☐ Drinking ☐ TV viewing ☐ Computer gaming or Web surfing ☐ Other escapist activities	☐ Stressed or ☐ Deprived	☐ Gratified or ☐ Satiated	Indulger
☐ Rationalizing ☐ Exaggerating ☐ Underestimating odds or risks ☐ Oversimplifying ☐ Overanalyzing ☐ Focusing selectively ☐ Viewing life in all-or-nothing terms ☐ Smooth-talking yourself	☐ Uncertain or ☐ Invalidated	☐ Justified or ☐ Validated or ☐ In-the-know	Persuader

If you're overdoing one or more of the following behaviors . . .	And trying to avoid feeling . . .	While seeking to feel . . .	Your character may be . . .
☐ Being stubborn or withholding ☐ Being distrustful or suspicious ☐ Having a negative attitude ☐ Reacting with knee-jerk objections ☐ Automatically resisting ☐ Behaving passive-aggressively	☐ Dominated or ☐ One-down	☐ In control	Dr. No
☐ Eliciting excessive caretaking ☐ Hiding behind a facade ☐ Avoiding attention ☐ Being a people-pleaser ☐ Failing to assert yourself ☐ Becoming dependent on others	☐ Exposed or ☐ Scrutinized	☐ Safe or ☐ Inconspic-uous	Mini-Me
☐ Interrupting others ☐ Being arrogant ☐ Being perfectionistic	☐ Flawed or ☐ Inferior	☐ Special or ☐ The "best"	Capt. Superior

If you're overdoing one or more of the following behaviors . . .	And trying to avoid feeling . . .	While seeking to feel . . .	Your character may be . . .
☐ Having a know-it-all attitude ☐ Winning at all costs ☐ Putting others down ☐ Being compulsively organized	☐ Flawed or ☐ Inferior	☐ Special or ☐ The "best"	Capt. Superior
☐ Numbing or zoning out ☐ Living half-heartedly ☐ Feeling apathetic ☐ Avoiding commitments ☐ Being forgetful or easily sidetracked ☐ Procrastinating or stalling ☐ Being indecisive or unable to initiate	☐ Pressured or ☐ Trapped	☐ Stress-free or ☐ No demands	Escape Artist
☐ Obsessing or becoming fixated ☐ Acting impulsively ☐ Emotionally regressing or "losing it" ☐ Self-depriving or self-criticizing	☐ Small or ☐ Irrelevant	☐ Big or ☐ Powerful	King Kong

If you're overdoing one or more of the following behaviors . . .	And trying to avoid feeling . . .	While seeking to feel . . .	Your character may be . . .
☐ Ignoring long-term consequences ☐ Taking unwise risks ☐ Avoiding responsibility	☐ Small or ☐ Irrelevant	☐ Big or ☐ Powerful	King Kong
☐ Being overly emotional or theatrical ☐ Rushing through things ☐ Taking on too many activities ☐ Holding unrealistic expectations ☐ Excessively seeking novelty ☐ Worrying or catastrophizing	☐ Empty or ☐ Hopeless or ☐ Bored	☐ Excited or ☐ Alive	Dramateer

A Word about Destructive Patterns

The signs of potentially counterproductive behaviors we've been talking about in Part Two—reacting like an animal or a child, deferring to usual suspects, and being overtaken by characters—can be amusing, adaptive, benign, or costly. Virtually all of us notice such reactions at times. Their occasional presence is normal.

However, if your overreactions or bad habits have become regular patterns with destructive consequences, it may signal deeper issues needing attention. This is particularly true in the case of addictions, eating disorders, or ongoing anxiety, depression, or relationship difficulties. The way to break these self-destructive, painful patterns and take care of yourself is to seek professional help as soon as possible.

Summary of Part Two: How to Recognize the Early-warning Signs of Self-sabotage

Telltale clues of self-sabotage can include:

- Animallike behavior that overrides your awareness and perspective

- Childlike responses that seek to deny responsibility and evade accountability

- Default feelings and behaviors that may help you feel better but don't solve problems

- An inner cast of characters that may compensate for or ward off discomfort but does so at the expense of self-awareness, efficacy, and growth

PART THREE

◆

How to Minimize Your Unnecessary Losses

When one finds oneself in a hole of one's own making, it is a good time to examine the quality of the workmanship.

—John Renmerde

Sometimes simply recognizing the signs of counterproductive behavior is enough to motivate you to change. At other times, even when you recognize that you're doing something that's not good for you, you feel as though you cannot stop. In such cases, it is likely that such deeper forces as existential issues, denial, and fear are at work. Part Three will explore:

- The existential dilemmas that can lead you to react to situations as though your survival is at stake when it isn't—and how you can regain perspective (chapter 9)

- How denial and other "covert ops" of your psyche leave you feeling defensive, mystified, or blindsided—and how you can blow their cover (chapter 10)

- The emotion at the heart of your unnecessary losses—fear. You'll see the true nature of fear, discover its Achilles' heel, and learn how to move past fear (chapters 11 through 14)

9

THE FACTS OF LIFE

The meaning of life is that it stops.

—Franz Kafka

When Jeb came home from work, his wife Cheryl, preoccupied with paying bills, did not look up, let alone smile. Jeb's mood plummeted. He recalls, "As crazy as it sounds, I felt this sinking in the pit of my stomach. I went into the kitchen wondering, 'What did I do wrong? Am I not earning enough or pulling my share? Is she angry with me?'" His worry turned to defensiveness and he began mentally preparing for an argument, recalling times he'd felt disappointed by Cheryl.

When Carol watched her eight-year-old son Andrew muff a key soccer kick, she felt embarrassed, then inexplicably upset. On the drive home, she found it difficult to be encouraging to the boy. She later apologized, but the incident troubled her for days. Normally Carol dotes on her son and is a caring and compassionate mother.

Following a mediocre job review, Lucy had visions of ending up as a bag lady. She found herself on her lunch break wondering on which corner she'd end up panhandling. She began thinking that she distrusted her boss and hated her job. By the time she returned to work, she was fuming and feeling desperate.

Maria and Ray, both thirty-six and married eight years, are at wit's end. Every time they discuss spending and budget issues they invariably end up in an argument. "It's like both of us lose all control over where the conversation goes," says Maria.

You can probably recall times when you have reacted well out of proportion to a situation and were not entirely sure why. Sometimes this happens when you confuse your relationships, possessions, ideas, or feelings as being "you." You may then react to everyday challenges as if your actual survival is at stake.

For example, Jeb's sense of self became fused with his marriage. He saw his wife's lack of acknowledgment as a sign of her displeasure. From there, he anticipated rejection. That became a threat to his entire well-being.

Carol's self-image merged with her son's athletic performance. She saw Andrew's soccer-field mistake as her personal failure.

Lucy became one with her job and reacted as if her life would be over if she lost her job.

Maria and Ray's net worth became a proxy for their self-worth when the topic of finances arose. Each felt backed into a corner instead of being on the same team.

Jeb, Carol, Lucy, Maria, and Ray were not aware that they had temporarily merged their self-images with external elements. Though each of them eventually reclaimed their equilibrium, the strength of their initial reactions shows what can happen when our self-image or identity feels threatened.

In having the ability to define who we are, we sometimes get confused about what is and is not "us." This confusion of identity can manifest in many ways:

1. Self-handicapping fight-or-flight reactions

2. Increased stress and health problems

3. Difficulty coping with limitations

4. An emotional roller coaster of expectation and disappointment

5. Trouble balancing others' needs and your own

6. Denial of your mortality

All of these can lead to unnecessary losses. Such losses can be modulated once you understand what drives them.

Existential Dilemmas

Our relationship with our existence is awash in discomforting paradox. We seek to avoid pain and loss, yet life necessarily brings pain and loss. We hope to survive, but know that ultimately we will not, at least not in our present physical form. We seek knowledge, but find that knowing can bring pain. We seek emotional connections, but learn that losing those we love can be devastating.

Underlying these paradoxes are three facts of life.

- Fact of Life #1: You carry a powerful, physiologically based, fight-or-flight instinct

- Fact of Life #2: You once were an infant

- Fact of Life #3: Your body is mortal and you know it

These facts of life can form psychological Bermuda Triangles in your daily path. Being aware of how you respond to these facts of life can help you make self-enhancing rather than self-defeating choices.

Self-handicapping Fight-or-flight Reactions

The fight-or-flight instinct, also known as the survival mechanism, lives in your lower "animal" brain, yet it must coexist with your higher "human" brain. A fight-or-flight response is present in creatures with the most rudimentary brain. You come into life with fight-or-flight software preprogrammed. The classic example of a fight-or-flight response: When a bear comes charging from the thicket to attack you, what happens in your body is similar to what happened to your earliest ancestors. Your body automatically mobilizes to help you defend yourself or escape. For example, your heart beats faster and your digestive and excretory systems temporarily shut down. This allows more blood to go to your legs and arms so you can run or fight. The fight-or-flight process bypasses your thinking brain, and for good reason: thoughtfully pondering your options in the face of a charging bear means you'll probably be dinner.

This survival mechanism is partly located in your brain's amygdala, an almond-shaped structure deep within your brain that functions as a Grand Central Station for fear and survival messages. The amygdala and associated brain structures aren't concerned about being *in* the moment, they're designed only to get you *through* each moment.

In recent years we've learned a great deal about this human hard-wired fear response and its implications for both everyday living and our responses to traumatic events. Research by neuroscientists Joseph

LeDoux and Antonio Damasio suggests that humans have an "emotional brain," which encodes memories of threatening or traumatic experiences in ways that not only last a lifetime but that can bypass our normal thinking brain. In *Emotional Intelligence*, Daniel Goleman writes that the survival instinct is designed to yield "fast and sloppy" responses rather than considered, sophisticated ones. Though your higher human brain or cortex gives you tools to seek balance and perspective, finding balance and perspective take too long when you're facing an imminent threat to your survival. Surviving life-threatening attacks often depends more on a speedy response than a precise one.

One problem with this is that the challenges we commonly face in modern civilization are markedly different from those faced by our ancestors. Rather than the life-threatening physical threats that were common hundreds of years ago, our biggest challenges tend to be slower to develop, longer lasting, and threaten our goals, values, or self-image rather than our lives. Though fast, survival-based responses are great for facing imminent physical threats, they tend to be dysfunctional for slower-moving, longer-term threats. Longer-term threats demand insight, reflection, and the ability to project into the future.

When you confuse your self-image with your actual survival as Jeb, Carol, Lucy, Maria, and Ray did, your abilities for reflection and insight are preempted by "fast and sloppy" fight-or-flight responses. "Our brain plays by yesterday's rules," as Terry Burnham and Jay Phelan wrote in *Mean Genes*.

When you think you're fighting for your survival, you will do whatever it takes to survive. You lose normal perspective. This is one reason why harmless comments or actions can escalate to relationship-threatening arguments. Road rage is another example of "yesterday's rules" in today's world.

In extreme cases, confusing your identity with your actual survival can have tragic consequences. A thirty-eight-year-old man in my community recently started off to work after hugging his eight-year-old daughter and three-year-old son. Driving on the freeway and talking on his cell phone, he accidentally dropped the phone. While he reached down, searching the floorboard for his phone, his car drifted into the base of a concrete overpass and he was killed. In the final seconds of his life, the man *became* his conversation. In focusing on the survival of his conversation, he lost his actual, physical survival.

How can such things happen? You and I are the product of eons of evolutionary fine-tuning designed to increase our ability to survive. We know logically that an interrupted conversation can be resumed, but an interrupted life cannot. Prior to his accident, the man had every reason to expect that he would return home that evening to his children and wife.

Increased Stress and Health Problems

Given how dramatically society has changed in the last few centuries and how slowly our bodies evolve, our fight-or-flight instinct may be working overtime. Lacking the real charging bears our ancestors faced, our survival mechanism is now left to defend against threats to our self-image, ideas, and possessions as it once did against physical threats. The consequences are rarely as deadly as with the driver and his cell phone, but some fight-or-flight overreactions can become a nettlesome part of daily life.

Excessive fight-or-flight reactions take their toll on health. Research indicates that people who are quick to anger or who often overreact to stressful situations evoke the fight-or-flight response to their detriment, facing greater risk of death from heart disease and other ailments. As the *New York Times*'s Jane Brody wrote, "Trouble results in those people who repeatedly call this survival mechanism into play for reasons that are hardly life-threatening: being stuck in traffic or behind a slow driver, confronting the breakdown of an appliance, or having to wait for someone who is late, for instance."

What You Can Do about Fact of Life #1:
The Fight-or-flight Instinct

Although you cannot hurry evolution, you can take a cue from the direction human evolution seems headed. You cannot quash your fight-or-flight reactions, but you can use your well-evolved higher functions—your abilities to reason, reflect, and direct your awareness—to temper, balance, and provide perspective when fight-or-flight kicks in. Even more importantly, you can be aware of who and what you identify as "you" so that you fight for your life only when your life is actually at stake.

Difficulty Coping with Limitations

Everybody wants to rule the world.

—ROLAND ORZABAL OF TEARS FOR FEARS

Gary, a forty-eight-year-old journalist, is normally even tempered. But when he wants or feels entitled to something and is told no, he becomes an emotional basket case. "When someone stands in the way of my getting what I want, I go ballistic," he says.

Though your ancient fight-or-flight mechanism is notable for its speed, remnants of your not-so-ancient days as an infant are remarkable for their intensity. The point of the second fact of life—that we all once were infants—is that infants react dramatically to losses and limitations. The roots of these early reactions remain with you for life and can lead you to hold on too tightly, deny your feelings, avoid attachments, or pretend that you feel differently than you do.

We begin our lives not knowing who or what we are. We notice that we have caregivers. At first we're not quite sure who they are, how they got here, or whether they are part of us or separate from us. Magically, they seem able to comfort, feed, and soothe us. As we grow, we discover to our dismay that our magical caregivers have limits. The people with the capacity to cater to our every need don't always do so. "As the infant ages, parents begin to seem like servants who are falling down on the job," writes psychoanalyst Robert Karen. We also discover that we ourselves have limits. We can't always get everything we want when we want it. We don't always feel good, and we don't always know how to make ourselves feel good.

Infants react dramatically to this lack of gratification and power. "Children do not yet know that time heals. When children feel something, they believe it is forever," wrote Rabbi David Wolpe. They may retreat within, pretend things are otherwise, or throw a tantrum. In these responses, we can almost see the budding forerunners of adult self-distracting, misleading, overreacting and abandoning.

However, life follows a "tough love" policy. A necessary part of our development is to find adaptive ways to come to grips with despair, frustration, and rage. Yet no matter how well we adapt, the roots of our early reactions remain with us for life.

In a sense, we're all born narcissists. We are each the center of the world. Nobody seems as real to us as we seem to ourselves. We want what we want when we want it. Though few adults suffer clinical narcissistic personality disorder, most of us carry traces of infancy's narcissism like remnants of a prehensile tail.

If you fail to outgrow early narcissism, you may never move past your early disappointment that others can either soothe you or not. Persons with strong narcissistic tendencies are "holding out for heaven," writes Robert Karen. They find it difficult to live fully in the present moment, because they don't want to accept life's inherent limitations. They want to believe there is somewhere over the rainbow where limitations don't apply.

Unhealthy narcissism covers profound fears of flaws and emptiness. Persons with narcissistic personality disorder tend to bridge this abyss by acting larger than life, disguising their own vulnerabilities by dominating others, or seeking from others the adulation they don't know how to supply from within. They may be arrogant, self-centered, or controlling. They view other people as things rather than as equals because, from a narcissistic view, being equal means not being special.

Such responses are dysfunctional and extreme reactions to the hurts, losses, and inequities we all face in life. Any of us may occasionally have milder versions of these tendencies, as in Dr. No's and Capt. Superior's preemptive put-downs of others, and Mini-Me's and the Escape Artist's hedging of bets by fading into the background.

Such behavior may be a sign that you are experiencing a loss of control, limitation, or lack of gratification that is more disturbing than you are consciously aware. Recognizing this can help you step back and reevaluate your reactions.

An Emotional Roller Coaster of Expectation and Disappointment

Imagination is very rapid; it jumps from admiration to love, from love to matrimony, in a moment.

—JANE AUSTEN

Randy, an architect, is an avid tennis player. For two years running he won the singles championship in a tournament. The first year he triumphed in a dramatic, come-from-behind fashion. The second year he powered through his opponents, playing unbeatable tennis. As the third year approached, Randy was still basking in the glory of his prior championships and antici- pating a three-peat. He began wondering how this year's victory would unfold. He visualized a third trophy on his cabinet. His expectations became so real that he began harvesting the good feelings from his antici- pated victory and exporting those feelings to other areas of his life. He was having a tough time in his job, but instead of facing his job problems, he turned to daydreaming about his expected victory. He told himself that his job problems didn't matter because he would feel better soon. As his attach- ment to his expected victory deepened, his positive feelings increased.

Then he lost the tournament.

It would have been disappointing for anyone to lose as the odds-on favorite. But that's how games are, and we generally get over such losses. Randy's problem was that he had borrowed on the expected emotional rewards and extended them to make up for a lack of positive feelings in his job. Expectations can excite and motivate, but over-attaching to expectations is taking a loan with a horrendous balloon payment. When Randy lost the tournament, he had to grieve not just his tournament loss but the heightened, deferred pain about his job as well. In becom- ing overinvested in victory preceding the tournament, Randy over- looked an important reality: He hadn't yet won.

Unrealistic expectations that compensate for a dull or lonely present can place you in the hands of a loan shark. The letdown from failed expectations often costs far more than any temporary relief you found in your expectations. What would have been a 4.0 on the emotional-loss Richter scale jumped to a 7.0. When Randy lost the tournament, the losses rippled through his life.

Of course, getting attached to your expectations can be helpful when you do so in ways that give you energy and focus to achieve your expectations. For example, if Randy had used his time and energy to visualize winning ground strokes, a positive mindset, and other things that he knew from experience would help his game performance, his mental and emotional investments in preparation for a third trophy could have helped him play better tennis. Instead, he used his expecta- tions to feel more worthy as a person and ignore problems at work. Had he confined his expectations to feeling hopeful of winning without get- ting attached to the outcome, perhaps by reminding himself of his worth regardless of the tournament results, he could have avoided such emotional losses.

Trouble Balancing Others' Needs with Your Own

It seems impossible to love people who hurt and disappoint us. Yet there are no other kinds of people.

—FRANK ANDREWS

Pat, a thirty-three-year-old accountant, lives with her boyfriend, Paul. As in several earlier intimate relationships, there's something tentative in Pat's commitment. "Paul is a good man but I don't see myself spending my life with him," she says. She worries that he's not as smart as she. She isn't convinced of his commitment to her. It would be nice if he were taller.

Pat relegates her relationship to romance's waiting room. She waits for Paul to prove that he is "The One" or, alternatively, to disappoint her. She waits to feel something stronger or more definitive.

By keeping one foot out, Pat hedges her bets. When she is disappointed by people or events, this insulated stance cushions her disappointment. She can tell herself that she didn't really try that hard or that it didn't matter. At the same time, she can keep alive her belief that she will easily immerse herself in an intimate relationship when Mr. Right comes along. Pat downplays today's hurts with hopes for tomorrow's love. Unfortunately, this approach siphons vibrancy from her relationship.

We are social animals who seek to connect emotionally with others. Emotional connection is different from emotional over-attachment. When you over-attach, want becomes need. For example, if you view avoiding a relationship break-up as your most important goal, you may preserve the relationship even at the expense of loving and cherishing yourself or the other person.

Our history as infants can affect our coping styles in intimate relationships. Infancy deals us such painful experiences as feeling helpless; lacking inner resources; and fearing annihilation, abandonment, or engulfment. Just as Randy felt entitled to win the tennis tournament, an unhealthy sense of entitlement, either too much or too little, can torpedo close relationships. Persons with an extreme sense of entitlement may automatically approach interactions expecting to be admired. By contrast, people who feel a lack of entitlement may resign themselves to mediocre relationships in which they live in fear of being left or betrayed. In either case, unhealthy entitlement makes it hard to get to know others, be open to new experiences, or cultivate give-and-take. Intimacy, love, or growth simply aren't on the screen.

Over- or under-entitlement can manifest in various ways: denying your feelings, pretending you feel differently than you do, avoiding connections with others, finding it difficult to trust or get close even when you want to, rejecting others before they can reject you, or clinging too tightly.

What You Can Do about Fact of Life #2:
Vestiges of Infantile Reactions

The uncomplicated, passionate responses of infants are something we may envy or strive to emulate as adults. As with animallike and childlike reactions, it is important to distinguish between helpful and counterproductive responses. The average two-year-old has a fifty-word vocabulary while the average adult has a lexicon of more than fifty thousand. By the same token, as an adult you have many more choices in how to respond to emotionally charged, potentially self-sabotaging situations than you had as a child.

Self-awareness Tool #4:
Take Stock of Your Roots in Infancy

When you feel confused, in turmoil, or threatened, ask yourself which of your feelings are based in the actual situation at hand and which may arise from a primal reaction to loss, limitations, or not getting what you want. When you recognize feelings driven by emotional charges of decades earlier, you can respond more appropriately to the current situation.

Denial of Your Mortality

Time sneaks up on you like a windshield on a bug.

—JOHN LITHGOW

Acknowledging our mortality can be discomforting. Sometimes denial of mortality goes too far, and we ignore or avoid anything that reminds us of mortality, including situations involving any kind of loss or ending.

Darryl awoke on his forty-seventh birthday with an unsettling thought: "I've lived more than half my life. Based on the law of averages, men live to their mid-seventies, which means I have more time behind me than ahead of me."

Thoughts about your mortality can strike at any age, but they often take on greater immediacy at midlife. Why? Even when you turn forty or fifty, little has changed from a year earlier. You can expect, on average, many more years ahead. Perhaps a more intriguing question is why some of us suddenly view our mortality in a new light when we've known it for years.

We each approach awareness of our mortality differently. Some find it empowering to confront or embrace their mortality because it puts the issue on the table. Others function optimally by giving little attention to the issue. Some reach peace with the fact of mortality long before facing it. Others struggle from time to time.

Our concerns about mortality aren't particularly logical. If you are age thirty-five or older, you've already had a longer life than the vast majority of the estimated one hundred billion humans who have walked this planet. If you live in a developed country, you can expect to live longer on average than your neighbors in developing countries. In this sense, time is tyrannical.

On the other hand, time is democratic. You choose how to spend whatever time you have. Had you been born in 1800, when turning thirty-five was statistically unlikely, how might you have experienced your life and time? Do you use your time more preciously than your ancestors did? If we live more years than ever, why do so many of us often feel so rushed?

The following table shows the average life expectancy for American men and women. As averages, these figures are neither a death sentence nor a guarantee. Your genes and lifestyle significantly affect the quality and length of your life.

Average Life Expectancy in the United States				
	WOMEN		MEN	
Current age	Average life expectancy	Average years of life remaining	Average life expectancy	Average years of life remaining
10	80.1	70.1	74.9	64.9
15	80.2	65.2	74.9	59.9
20	80.3	60.3	75.2	55.2
25	80.4	55.4	75.6	50.6
30	80.6	50.6	75.9	45.9
35	80.8	45.8	76.3	41.3
40	81.0	41.0	76.7	36.7
45	81.3	36.3	77.2	32.2
50	81.8	31.8	77.9	27.9
55	82.4	27.4	78.8	23.8
60	83.1	23.1	79.9	19.9
65	84.2	19.2	81.3	16.3
70	85.5	15.5	83.0	13.0
75	87.1	12.1	86.1	10.1
80	89.1	9.1	87.6	7.6
85	91.7	6.7	90.6	5.6
90	94.8	4.8	94.1	4.1

Source: National Center for Health Statistics, 2000

Did you notice any reactions as you looked over this table? If you're a forty-five-year-old woman, are you comforted or disconcerted to know that, on average, you are likely to live another thirty-six years? Does that feel like too much, too little, or the right amount of time? By contrast, women of your great-grandmother's generation in 1900 lived to an average age of forty-nine.

More importantly, what do you want to do with your remaining years? Reckoning with your morality can be imprisoning or freeing. When it manifests as existential dread or death anxiety, it can imprison.

The good news is that you can use the knowledge of your mortality for your benefit. Just as exploring your inner characters or childlike responses may have given you access to parts of yourself that influence your behavior without your knowing it, being aware of how you view your mortality can shed light on how you cope with losses.

Try this experiment. Read the following statement, then pause and notice how you feel.

"I will eventually lose everything I have, everyone I know, and all that I cherish."

Take a moment and notice any emotions, thoughts, or reactions. Do you feel sad? Irritated? Anxious? Do you minimize or dismiss the statement? Do you look for a way out of its finality and totality?

A central dilemma in life is how to connect emotionally in a world in which you will lose all that you care about. How can you appreciate what you have and live for today while knowing that loss is a when, not an if, proposition?

Reckoning with who you are in the existential sense can be disturbing. *I am here, now, alive. But I am finite. I won't exist someday, at least not in this form.* It's not logical. It doesn't add up. It begs for resolution. The resolution may come through denial, pessimism, or overreactions to loss.

How would you finish the following sentence:
My general approach to knowing I will die someday is to:

- Worry about it

- Ignore or deny it

- Feel peace in the knowledge

- Put off thinking about it until I'm older

- Find a way to put this insight to use

- Turn it over to God

- All of the above

- None of the above

What You Can Do about Fact of Life #3:
Knowledge of Your Mortality

A paradox about death and loss is that accepting the inevitability of loss can bring freedom. We live in uneasy coexistence with the truisms that we will die and that we can't control everything. After a lifetime of resisting the fact of your mortality, it can be liberating to embrace it. Terminally ill people who accept their impending death—who *choose* it as their reality—often find lightness, forgiveness, and peace. Having nothing left to lose doesn't make you desperate—it frees you. Attachment makes you desperate.

The Facts of Life, Revisited

Our lives begin with upsetting limitations and end with the biggest limitation of all: physical death. This creates uniquely human dilemmas. Evolutionarily speaking, we are descended from animals who react without thinking. Developmentally speaking, we began our lives as infants who desire without limits. We possess the remnants of animal, fight-or-flight instincts, and infancy's unbridled grandiose urges. However, unlike animals and infants, we know that our reactions have consequences, that we can't have everything we want, and that we will eventually die, at least physically. The result is an uneasy truce that is tested by limitations, losses, or endings.

The fight-or-flight mechanism, infantile urges, and mortality concepts in this chapter may seem so obvious or so far removed from your daily life as to be irrelevant. The point is that it is helpful to recognize when the dilemmas inherent in these issues become activated in daily life. Dilemmas such as *What do I consider to be me? What do I want?* and *How can I control my destiny?* touch us deeply whether they are activated by a dire threat to your survival or coffee spilled on your brand-new outfit. By raising your awareness of what's at stake, you reduce the likelihood that you'll respond in ways more appropriate to long ago and far away.

In addition, it may be comforting to recognize that everybody faces these existential dilemmas. Feeling excessive guilt or self-judgment over tendencies that are innate in all of us is just another form of self-sabotage.

10

YOUR PERSONAL "DEFENSE DEPARTMENT"

Denial is not only infuriating to others, it leaves one with the sense of harboring a horrible person within.

—ROBERT KAREN

Mecha notices that when others give her constructive criticism or feedback at work, she brings the conversation to a quick halt by saying something like, "I'm a Virgo and we don't change." Though her comments succeed in deflecting criticism, she often feels out-of-sorts for hours afterward and notices coworkers seem to be tiptoeing around her.

Underlying Mecha's astrological conversation-stoppers is her anxiety about not doing things perfectly. Her standards are so high that she constantly feels she is letting herself down. When anyone points out how she might improve, even when the advice is correct and delivered in a supportive way, Mecha becomes defensive. If Mecha could see that her defensiveness is in response to her internal pressure-cooker, not others' constructive comments, she could stop fleeing potentially helpful advice and maybe even temper her unrealistic standards.

Like Mecha, we all have a personal Defense Department designed to keep internal emotional and psychological peace. Psychological defense mechanisms, the shell games of your psyche, are all variations on the theme of denial.

A certain amount of denial can be adaptive. Ignoring, forgetting, or pretending can help you through rough times. However, like a faulty circuit breaker, denial sometimes trips prematurely or stays off too long. We don't always notice when we're in denial about loss. We don't always recognize when our fight-or-flight instinct is working overtime.

We are not always aware when we avoid our feelings or overreact to events.

Denial is the glue that binds the parts of ourselves that disturb us. The good news is that if denial is the glue that allows for self-deception, awareness is the solvent that dissolves denial.

Challenging Your Denial

Denial carries a warning label: "Break at your own risk." Breaking denial can feel disorienting, embarrassing, and painful. Think of a time you discovered a shocking or disappointing truth about someone. For example: a friendly neighbor discovered as a fugitive from justice; a trusted doctor too distracted to diagnose you correctly and too busy to answer your questions in your time of greatest need; a school-teacher you always thought had it together, now convicted of drug dealing. Without denial, you're robbed of illusions that muffle fear and pain.

Though we all experience occasional denial-breaking epiphanies, in my experience denial generally erodes in steps over time. Even dramatic epiphanies are usually preceded by subtle preparatory work and growth, which you may not recognize. This is particularly true regarding owning up to ways you've deprived or hurt yourself. When another person deceives, abandons, or sabotages you, you may feel violated or angry. When you do these negative things to yourself, your reactions are more complicated. Coming to grips with self-defeating behavior brings three recognitions:

1. You are the source of what hurt you.

2. You had the ability to act in a healthier way.

3. You didn't do so.

Though recognizing any form of denial can be difficult, recognizing denial about what you have done to yourself can be especially difficult. Seeing losses and missed opportunities may bring difficult feelings, including shame, guilt, regret, sorrow, angst, rage, and grief. The ache from hurting yourself is like no other. You undermine the one who watches over you. Some losses you inflict on yourself are irrevocable.

Self-sabotage is an autoimmune disease of the self. As with any autoimmune disease, if you ignore it, you risk being weakened further.

At the same time, when you acknowledge your capacity for self-inflicted wounds, you may feel as if you are caged with an enemy.

The incomprehension, grief, and loss we may feel when we fully recognize the harm we've done to ourselves is difficult to tolerate for more than a few moments. Your Defense Department reserves some of its most potent weapons to avoid the full impact of such moments.

Try this experiment. Think of a time when you recognized an unsettling truth about yourself. For example, perhaps you:

- Failed because you wanted to fail

- Thought you loved another, but were fooling yourself

- Hid despair behind a pleasing demeanor

- Were too busy to do warm-up stretching, and injured yourself

- Had to buy the expensive item, then couldn't pay your taxes

I'm asking you to look consciously at some of your smallest, greediest, most callous, or most short-sighted moments. As you gaze, notice if your Defense Department is at work. Notice thoughts such as:

"I know all this already."

"What's he talking about?"

"This doesn't apply to me."

"This is irrelevant." (Or overemphasized, overblown, or just plain stupid.)

Notice any feelings. Irritation? Impatience? Ennui? Notice any physical sensation, perhaps restlessness, cramping, or tiredness. Notice if perhaps your focus wanders to a suddenly important phone call or the kitchen that needs cleaning.

These may be your defenses at work. Of course, much of what your Defense Department offers up as roadblocks has a grain of truth. Your kitchen may need cleaning, and you might feel tired. But why are these so pressing right now?

Defensive facades are habits held in place by a lack of awareness. Yet nobody can know you as well as yourself. Only you can decide when your denial is counterproductive. The answer to denial isn't to try to get rid of it; denial itself is an attempt to get rid of something. Instead, let's accept denial as a fact of life and see how you can work with it.

Dissolving Your Denial

Denial tends to obscure awareness of self-sabotage. However, from Part Two you know several early-warning signs of potential self-sabotage. When you see these warning signs, ask yourself two questions:

1. What potential benefits are my actions offering me?

2. What is being avoided or obscured by my actions?

For example:

Linda, a forty-four-year-old financial planner, recalls her previous weekend's cycle of procrastination. She had promised herself she would clean her apartment Saturday morning, then have the rest of the day to do as she wanted. Saturday morning she picked up a magazine article she had been meaning to read. A half-hour later she logged on to check her E-mail and spent two hours on the Web. She made lunch and ate in front of the television, watching a movie she'd seen previously. By 2:30 P.M. she had done no cleaning.

"I stared at the vacuum and tried to force myself to clean for even five minutes, but I just sat there. When I was reading or watching TV, I couldn't let myself enjoy it because I was supposed to be cleaning," Linda says.

One benefit of her procrastination was obvious: Linda avoided the dirty work of cleaning. As Linda thought about it, she saw other payoffs. She got to do whatever she wanted instead of what she felt she should have. She got to rebel, be entertained, and escape demands, even though her leisure time was tainted by her "I am supposed to be cleaning" voice.

The second question—what is being avoided or obscured by her behavior—sheds additional light on her procrastination. Linda has trouble giving to herself. She feels as though she must earn pleasant experiences and has to justify taking time off. Underneath that is a deeply rooted feeling that she doesn't deserve to relax and must keep her guard up.

On a superficial level, Linda's day consisted of avoiding cleaning and feeling guilty about it. That familiar drama obscured deeper, unsettling questions such as *Am I deserving? Can I relax? Is it safe?* No amount of television watching or household chores can put such issues to rest. By recognizing when you deny or avoid questions of self-worth, control, and safety, you can step back in the ring with your doubts and fears to face and eventually master them.

To dissolve denial is to get sober. When you focus your attention on times you've sabotaged yourself, you may initially see less-attractive aspects of yourself. Stay with it. Recognizing denial and the self-sabotage it masks may take humility, humor, courage, and perseverance. The payoffs: freedom, peace, fulfillment, and a future with potentially fewer self-defeats.

Take a moment and recall a time you finally understood the truth after struggling with denial. You may have felt lightness after dropping a pretense, or a surge of energy after owning up to a misstep. To achieve these payoffs, you had to willingly face the prospect of emotional discomfort. You had to let go of the illusion that no loss is possible. You had to be willing to deepen and focus rather than simplify and distract. When you face painful emotions instead of trying to leap-frog them, you create psychological wake-up calls. You recognize that you had been sleepwalking while thinking that your eyes were open.

There is no easy salve to the time and effort lost in denial. However, just as you can do things when you're awake that are impossible when you're sleeping, you can accomplish and experience things once you're out of denial that are impossible when you're in denial.

If You'd Like to Go Deeper: Unmasking Denial

Think of a current or past situation that troubles or puzzles you. Ask yourself one or more of the following questions. Your answers can illuminate denial and some of the reasons it is operating. In so doing, you loosen denial's grip.

1. Are any of my thoughts, feelings, or actions serving to . . .

   - Sidestep or camouflage more painful feelings?

   - Procrastinate or avoid something?

   - Assuage my guilt?

   - Preempt loss?

   - Take the focus off me?

2. Do I feel distracted or fixated?

3. How grounded and authentic do I feel right now? Is this how I want to feel?

4. If someone I deeply admire asked me what I'm in denial about, what would I say?

5. How would the best part of me handle this situation?

11

THE TRUTH ABOUT FEAR

All men should strive to learn before they die what they are running from, and to, and why.

—JAMES THURBER

At the start of the book, I wrote that we keep secrets from ourselves because we fear emotional and other losses. When we're afraid, we are more susceptible to fuzzy math, distortions, impulsive actions, and a restricted view of our options. Beneath the Subterranean Accountant, animallike and childlike reactions, usual suspects, inner characters, existential overreactions, and denial is fear. Bottom line, fear is why we get in our own way. To consistently do what's best for you, you ultimately have to face your fears.

Take a moment and recall a time when your fears got the better of you and you were unable to move forward. What happened? How did you feel about yourself afterward?

Then recall a time when you stood your ground in the face of fear. What made you do it? How did you feel during and afterward?

Fear can be a motivator for good or ill. It's neither wise nor possible to rid yourself of all fears. When you understand how fear works, you can more readily move ahead in the face of counterproductive fear. Fear can be remarkably powerful, but it is also quite fragile. Two characteristics give fear both its power and its fragility:

1. Fear is a mental movie that gets stuck at the worst part.

2. Fear highlights worst-case scenarios without regard to their likelihood.

Fear Is a Mental Movie That Gets Stuck at the Worst Part

Lorraine, thirty-three, works at a community nonprofit helping single mothers of children with severe birth defects. The director of her agency has asked Lorraine to give a presentation at a fund-raiser next month.

"I'm literally petrified," Lorraine says. Although Lorraine is articulate and passionate about her work when talking one-on-one, the thought of standing before more than a hundred potential contributors makes her blanch. "In my mind's eye, I see myself walking on stage shaking so badly that I bump into the podium, knock over the water glass, and spill my note cards. I open my mouth to begin and nothing comes out. I stand there unable to speak or leave the stage and everyone's staring at me. Needless to say, nobody contributes a dime," she says.

Fear's job is to warn you about unwise risks. It does this by carrying your mind to the doorstep of your most-dreaded consequences and dropping you there. Once it does that, fear considers its job completed.

Fear functions like an internal horror movie that pauses at the worst part. Imagine going to see *Psycho* and having the projector freeze just as Norman Bates, knife in hand, peers through the curtain at his unaware, showering, soon-to-be-victim. To dissuade you from taking risks, fear leaves you face-to-face with the worst-case scenario.

For example, most people surveyed express a fear of heights at least in certain situations. Imagine yourself standing on a cliff overlooking a several-hundred-foot sheer drop-off. Most of us, if we stop to think about it, don't fear falling off a cliff primarily because we fear falling through the air. After all, parachutists pay good money for the privilege of falling. Rather, you probably fear falling from a cliff because your mind flashes a freeze-frame of whatever would be the most terrifying part of the fall for you. Perhaps it's the accelerating velocity of your plunge, the moment before you hit bottom, or the end result: You, crashed on the rocks.

Fears and anxieties are born of what-ifs. "What if it gets worse?" "What if I lose control?" "What if this feeling never goes away?" Your what-ifs follow a cycle:

1. This is uncomfortable.

2. I want it to stop.

3. What if it doesn't stop?

What if it doesn't stop? The core of fear is that what hurts or frightens you may never end. Fear is a doorman who lets you into the House of Horrors but won't show you the way out.

In real life, however, events and time don't freeze. The moments you fear may indeed come, but they also pass. You probably have had the experience of feeling anxious about a problem or concern, then stopping to ask yourself, "What's the worst that could happen?" Such a question can reduce your anxiety and help you cope, because it defines your fears rather than letting them run wild. You remind yourself that there is life after fear.

Fear Highlights Worst-case Scenarios Without Regard to Their Likelihood

Fear's worst-case scenarios tend to get your attention, but they aren't necessarily accurate or realistic. Remember, a fear is only one possible future. A big step in moving past counterproductive fears is to ask yourself whether a given fear is based on likely and realistic assumptions or on extreme, faulty assumptions.

Fear spawns two hybrids: *fear-thoughts* and *survival rules*. These are like overly watchful twin dogs that bark at both friend and foe. I use the term *fear-thoughts* because these are neither purely emotion nor thought but a combination of both. The emotion fear is a collection of sensations and physiological reactions that warn you of danger. The thought "I might get hurt" is an example of a mental warning to be careful. Fear-thoughts are a combination of emotions and mental warnings. Fear-thoughts are expressed in terms such as "If this doesn't work, I'll be in deep trouble" or "If that happens again, it will be a disaster."

Survival rules, so named by family therapist Virginia Satir, are often-unfounded but rarely questioned assumptions—about life, yourself, and others—that you feel you must follow. Survival rules dictate the thoughts, actions, emotions, and situations you must or must not experience. For example: "I must never give in" or "I should be polite no matter what."

Identifying your fear-thoughts and survival rules lays bare any faulty assumptions that give rise to and maintain counterproductive fears. Seeing these assumptions allows you to refute excessive or unfounded fears. It is like pulling a string of rock candy from the sugary liquid in which it formed. From a distance, it looks like a foreboding, solid, encrusted column, but if you break any of the rocks, you expose a fragile, pliable string. Similarly, by identifying and reality-testing your potentially self-defeating fear-thoughts and survival rules, you break away the defenses born and nourished by denial.

Fear-thoughts and survival rules work in tandem. For example, the fear-thought "What if I make a mistake?" is fed by the survival rule "I must be perfect." Fear-thoughts and survival rules differ in the form in which they appear.

Fear-thoughts are "what-if" scenarios. They are thoughts that ask *What if x happens (or doesn't happen)?* The fear-thought then provides the answer to that what-if, an answer that is generally the worst outcome you can imagine. The problem is that a fear-thought can frighten you so much that you forget that it is just one of many possible scenarios, and you come to see it as a probability or a certainty.

Survival rules are "or-else" scenarios. They are thoughts that dictate *I must (or must not) do x, or else.* The or-else may not be clearly articulated, but what is implicit is that breaking a survival rule will bring the worst turn of events you can imagine. As with fear-thoughts, survival rules can frighten you so much that you forget that they are assumptions and treat them as inevitabilities.

The following table illustrates.

Fear-thoughts and Survival Rules		
	Definition	Examples
Fear-thoughts	Mental "what-if" scenarios that highlight the most anxiety-producing possibility	• If they disagree with me, I'll completely lose confidence. • If I lose, I'll never be able to recover.
Survival rules	Tacit "or-else" assumptions and rules about life you believe you must follow to survive	• I must never show my fears. • I should always be in control of my feelings. • My happiness depends on winning.

Like fairy tales from hell, survival rules and fear-thoughts don't just lack a "they lived happily ever after" ending, they lack *any* ending. Survival rules and fear-thoughts remove you from the equation. They omit or obscure recognition of the various ways you can cope.

Survival rules, like fear-thoughts, fixate your attention so that you tend to ignore evidence to the contrary. Survival rules like "I cannot show my emotions" and "I must be in control" hold you hostage to a host of untested and unrealistic assumptions about what *could* happen.

Fear-thoughts and survival rules can shape your attitudes and moods, particularly when you are unaware of them. For example, "I'm too old to make new friends," "I have little to look forward to," or "I better hold on to what I have, because it's the best I can get." Each of these assumptions is arguable. By accepting them, you're dealt an incomplete hand.

Mind FITs

There is a simple way to recognize and overcome fear-thoughts and survival rules. Fear-thoughts and survival rules share the same architecture. They happen when the mind throws a "FIT." You believe that an unpleasant situation will last *forever*, means something *innate* about you, and will affect your *total* life.

This Forever-Innate-Total combination is seen in panic attacks as well as other anxiety disorders. The fear of future fear can become stronger than the original fear. As FDR said, "The only thing we have to fear is fear itself."

Recall Lorraine, from earlier in this chapter, who was petrified about a speech she had been asked to give. Even though the speech was a month away, she was becoming increasingly anxious, mentally picturing herself freezing up during the speech. She worried that:

1. Her agonizing moment of embarrassment would never end (duration: forever)

2. She lacked any ability to give a speech (cause: innate)

3. Everything in her life would be affected by her failure at the podium (impact: total)

Mind FITs stop time, at least in your mind, and that sets off a powerful, anxiety-producing chain of assumptions. You fear being stuck forever at the point of greatest discomfort. With no forward movement in time you feel helpless, as if your innate strengths and qualities are gone. You become fixated on what frightens you the most. In so doing, you lose perspective of the whole of your life, including your strengths, relationships, and resources. The result can be blanket paralysis.

Mind FITs are common and generally happen outside of our awareness. Yet they carry tremendous impact because they weave together three crucial elements of existence: time, cause, and scope. These three elements reinforce each other to make you feel trapped and helpless, as follows:

- *Time—Forever:* In assessing what the feared situation will feel like, your mind fixates on a picture of yourself at your most-feared moment. As a result, you feel trapped.

- *Cause—Innate:* In assessing the cause of the feared situation, you find the cause within you. You view the troublesome situation as a consequence not of your behavior but of your very character. Rather than thinking that you may have done something bad, you assume that you *are* bad. You feel trapped because, if the problem lies within you, how can you get away from it?

- *Scope—Total:* In assessing the result of your feared situation, you focus only on the costs, failing to recognize the aspects of your life that won't be affected by an unpleasant outcome. Once again, you feel trapped, because if the problem affects your entire life, what will you have left to comfort you?

You might take a moment and recall a recent incident in which you felt greater-than-normal distress. Recall any thoughts and concerns you had during the distressing incident. Do you recognize any of the forever, innate, or total elements of a Mind FIT? Thoughts with even one of the elements can diminish your confidence.

The following table illustrates how mind FITs can distort everyday situations.

Mind FITs		
Common situation	Typical thoughts and feelings	Nature of distortion
You're suffering from a cold that drags on	This cold is never going to go away.	*Forever*: It won't end.
	I must be in bad health.	*Innate*: The cold is evidence of something innately wrong with me.
	I can't work, exercise, sleep, or do anything when I am sick.	*Total*: It will affect everything.
Your relationship is in question	If we split up I'll never be happy again.	*Forever*: I'll always be in pain.
	I'm unattractive.	*Innate*: This breakup is evidence of something wrong or lacking with me.
	I'll be so devastated that I will lose my job, friends, health, and self-confidence.	*Total*: A breakup will affect every part of my life.

Though fear-thoughts and survival rules seem forever, innate, and total, their components—emotions and thoughts—are anything but. By nature, emotions and thoughts are *temporary* not permanent, *external states* not innate traits, and *limited* aspects of your life not the totality of who you are.

Emotions are:

- *Temporary*. Have you ever had a feeling that did not eventually pass?

- *External*. Since anything can trigger emotions and since you can't control them, how can your feelings say anything innate about you?

- *Limited*. You cannot actually be consumed by feelings, though it may feel like it at the time. You are more than your feelings. You *have* feelings.

Like feelings, thoughts are also temporary and limited states, not permanent, all-inclusive traits. Though you can direct much of your thinking, a good deal of your thinking happens randomly. To see this for yourself, take a moment and try to stop all your thoughts. You'll probably observe that your thinking is not entirely within your control. Furthermore, thoughts may bear no resemblance to reality. Thinking something is so doesn't make it so. As with feelings, you *have* thoughts, but you are much more than your thoughts.

Recall the two examples from the preceding table: a cold that drags on and a relationship in question. It takes only a few moments to generate a much different set of interpretations from the same set of facts. The following table illustrates.

Counteracting Mind FITs		
Situation	**Alternative interpretation**	**Reality-based correction**
You're suffering from a cold that drags on	This cold feels miserable but it will pass; colds always do.	*Temporary*: By definition, a cold passes.
	It must be the cold and flu season.	*External*: Colds are going around, so even healthy people are more likely to catch one now.
	I may not be able to run a marathon right now, but maybe this is my opportunity to read that book I've been putting off.	*Limited*: Being sick affects some things but not others.

Situation	Alternative interpretation	Reality-based correction
Your relationship is in question	If we split up, I may feel a lot of emotional pain for a time, but I will eventually recover.	*Temporary*: I have overcome grief before, and I will do it again.
	We both tried to make it work, but the chemistry just wasn't there. We'll both be better off in relationships that allow our best qualities to be expressed.	*External*: The relationship doesn't say anything innate or unchangeable about me. Changing the situation may add to the quality of my life.
	If this relationship ends, it will give me more time and energy to focus on creative ventures.	*Limited*: Without denying my loss or pain, I recognize that positive opportunities can come with a breakup.

When you forget the forever-innate-total nature of fear-thoughts, they gobble psychic space. When you remember that a fear-thought is a stuck horror movie masquerading as your one-and-only, never-ending entire life, you regain perspective.

You may find it useful to keep this FIT tool handy. The next time you feel distressed, pause and determine whether you are viewing the situation as:

- Forever or temporary
- Innately caused or the result of external factors
- Totally pervasive or a limited situation that is only one aspect of many in your life

Exploiting Fear's Weak Spots

The way to overcome fear is to exploit its vulnerabilities. When troubling fear-thoughts appear, flag them for closer inspection. Take what-if thoughts and ask yourself, "Okay, if what I dread did occur, what would happen next?" or, "If I don't get what I think I must have, then what?"

One convenient way to do this in a troubling situation is to take a sheet of paper and, on the left side, list each of your worries about the situation. Then, for each worry, ask yourself the question "If my worry came to pass, then what?" or "If what I'm worried about happened, what would it mean?" Repeat either or both questions several times for each worry, each time writing your answers on the right side until you carry that worry to its most extreme conclusion.

For example, if you are afraid of feeling out of control in a given situation, ask yourself, "If I lose control, then what?" Does that mean you will never get control back? Will you end up in a straitjacket or jail cell? Keep asking "Then what?" In doing so:

1. You'll gain the perspective to separate real threats from overblown fear-thoughts. You'll then be able to plan thoughtfully for and address any real threats.

2. You'll lay bare the exaggerations and irrationalities your worst-case scenarios use to frighten you.

Similarly, when troubling survival rules appear, ask yourself, "or else what?" For example, with the survival rule "I must not show anger" ask, "I must not show anger or else what?" If you show anger, will you die? Get stuck there forever? Explode? Lose control and hurt yourself or others? The or-elses underneath survival rules need to be subjected to critical, honest analysis. Keep asking "or else what?" and pursue your survival rules to their conclusion.

Of course some survival rules make sense. *Don't walk across a busy street without checking for traffic* has a pretty solid or-else: You may end up crunched by a car. But many survival rules have no legitimate consequences in the or-else department. *Don't let others see your true emotions,* for example, is a survival rule that may be prudent in a few instances but is unwise or nearly impossible in many situations.

With a little work, you can become facile at recognizing your fear-thoughts and survival rules. Fear-thoughts and survival rules rest atop exaggerated, irrational, and unlikely what-ifs and or-elses. When a fear-thought or survival rule zips by on your mental highways, pull it over and ask to see its "then-what?" or "or-else-what" license. If you hear such thoughts as, "I couldn't survive the embarrassment," "I might do it wrong," or "That's the way I've always done it," you've likely captured a fear-thought or survival rule. Feel free to revoke its "license" to travel your inner highways.

When fear spins out worst-case or unrealistic fear-thoughts and survival rules, it is simply doing its job. Your job is to pick up where fear stops. Restart the horror movie. Realize that there are other possible outcomes than the worst-case one. Determine whether the assumptions underlying your fears are realistic.

You have the last word.

12

GOING TO THE HEART OF YOUR FEARS

We either make ourselves miserable or we make ourselves strong. The amount of work is the same.

—CARLOS CASTENADA

Fear is an alarmist. To silence fear's false alarms, you need to cut overblown fears down to actual size. One way to do this is to recognize that despite the infinite variety of potentially frightening situations, whatever is distressing you in any given situation can be distilled to one or both of the following:

1. Concerns about your basic worth, nature, or abilities

2. Experiences you most dread and would do virtually anything to avoid

Knowing that virtually every fear imaginable comes down to one or both of these can make the universe of fear more manageable. Within each of these two categories are slight variations on the overall theme.

For example, when it comes to our basic worth, nature, or abilities, our deepest fears are that we are one or more of the following:

- Flawed
- Unworthy
- Empty
- Fragmented
- Weak
- Bad

In addition, we tend to dread experiences in which we feel:

- Out of control
- Trapped
- Alone
- Deprived

- Dominated
- Rejected
- Hurt

- Unsafe
- Hurtful

These fifteen fears could be termed core fears. Everybody has core fears. Sigmund Freud, for example, acknowledged that one of his worst fears was feeling helpless.

When you're frightened, mystified, confused, or overwhelmed, it is helpful to identify which core fears are at play. All core fears represent some kind of loss. By identifying the specific feared loss, you make fear more manageable. You define the problem succinctly rather than feeling as though you're facing capital-F Fear, that is, fear itself, or all fears rolled into one.

When you name what is troubling you, you can more readily tame it. As you read the following descriptions, you might notice if any seem particularly familiar or carry an emotional charge for you.

Core Fears	
CONCERNS ABOUT YOUR BASIC WORTH, NATURE, OR ABILITIES	
You feel . . .	**Words you might use to describe how you're feeling . . .**
Flawed	Defective, inferior, broken, clueless, fraudulent, inarticulate, gullible, or in doubt about your quality or equality
Unworthy	Undeserving, wrong, unlovable, worthless, a loser, invalid, lacking in self-acceptance, ashamed, or having nothing to offer
Empty	Insignificant, understimulated, bored, numb, listless, overly needy, emotionally flat, hopeless, superficial, or in terror of an internal void
Fragmented	Fragile, not well put together, not whole, lacking integrity, lost, unmoored, or as if you are coming apart emotionally, mentally, or physically
Weak	Small, unable, incompetent, lazy, a failure, ineffectual, inhibited, unimaginative, incapable, undependable, timid, indecisive, disorganized, or lacking in courage, strength, resilience or efficacy

You feel . . .	Words you might use to describe how you're feeling . . .
Bad	Dishonorable, blameworthy, at fault, indecent, cursed, dishonest, illegitimate, disloyal, or lacking in basic goodness

EXPERIENCES YOU MOST DREAD

You feel . . .	Words you might use to describe how you're feeling . . .
Out of control	Overwhelmed, unstable, panicky, overstimulated, volatile, on the brink, unable to bring yourself back, or unable to feel grounded or soothe yourself
Trapped	Pressured, on the spot, engulfed, under a microscope, the focus of negative or unwanted attention, or lacking a viable path of escape
Alone	Disconnected, isolated, unloved, lonely, invisible, abandoned, lacking human connections, without spirituality, or cut off from other living beings
Deprived	Disappointed, thwarted, defeated, bankrupt, beaten, or unfulfilled
Dominated	Controlled, one-down, dependent, used, betrayed, unjustly treated, subservient, lacking in autonomy, or under the thumb of another person
Rejected	Cast off, disliked, unwanted, unpopular, disapproved of, not valued, not attended to, or like the first-round loser in the *Survivor* TV show
Hurt	Unhappy, suffering, depressed, sick, sad, or in emotional or physical pain
Unsafe	In danger, attacked, threatened, criticized, vulnerable, or lacking protection
Hurtful	Rejecting, arrogant, quarrelsome, grandiose, judgmental, ruthless, inconsiderate, destructive, untrustworthy, selfish, self-centered, unloving, antagonistic, or as if you've used or damaged another

In troubling situations you usually experience more than one core fear. Over a lifetime, certain core fears may solidify and become what you most avoid. Your core fears are the fundamental operating principles of your loss-avoidance. They comprise your unique mental "background noise." Carl Jung called these aspects of ourselves part of our "shadow," metaphorically, the part of us hidden from view and blocked from the light. Like an actual shadow, your psychic shadow follows you wherever you go whether you like it or not. We tend to deny or disown our shadow, displacing it through activity or projecting it onto others.

To view a part of your shadow, take a moment to imagine an experience that you fear you could not psychologically or emotionally survive. For example: becoming paralyzed or blind, losing a spouse, or becoming bankrupt. Then ask yourself what would be the most difficult part of that experience.

Marcy, a healthy and athletic twenty-eight-year-old, dreads the thought of a back or neck injury that would leave her paralyzed. "I wouldn't be able to walk, run, swim, or ski. I'd be totally dependent on others," she says.

I ask Marcy what would be the worst part of being paralyzed. She barely hesitates, then says in staccato fashion, "I'd feel incredibly deprived and desolate, and I'd have no way to make it better. I'd feel needy, embarrassed, vulnerable, and a burden. I'd lie there regretting all the times I hadn't enjoyed what I had. I'd mentally go over the events that led to my paralysis. I'd feel guilty, horribly depressed, and angry with myself. I'd blame myself, the event, and anyone contributing to the event for ruining a perfectly good life. I wouldn't be able to feed myself. I wouldn't be able to have sex. I'd be facing the prospect of many years accompanied only by my thoughts and dependencies and robbed of the experiences I cherish."

Becoming paralyzed is a tragic event that few of us will face, but virtually all of us fear. Thinking about such worst-case scenarios can be distressing but doing so obviously won't make them more likely to happen. The value of asking yourself questions about what you most fear is that it can illuminate the kinds of losses you try hardest to avoid even in everyday situations. Marcy's core fears include feeling trapped, deprived, dominated, and hurt.

Core fears are common and understandable. The problem comes when these fears are triggered out of proportion to events at hand. You probably can recall a time when a loved one's fears overpowered his ability to see clearly. Looking from outside, you perhaps could see the source of his fears and more accurately assess their likelihood than could your loved one. In such cases, we tend to have greater empathy and compassion for our loved ones. For example, knowing *why* your mate won't talk about his feelings or *why* your teen has become monosyllabic can help you create empathy. As Mary Pipher wrote, "People are most alike in their feelings and least alike in their thinking." Identifying the fear at the core of a troubling situation can help you extend to yourself the same compassion and empathy you offer to others when they are afraid.

Why Identifying Core Fears Is Helpful

When you view every situation that you face as an unfamiliar one against which you have little successful experience, you're likely to feel daunted. An alternative is to recognize that though the particular situation may be new and unique, at the heart of any challenging situation is one or more of a finite number of core fears that you've faced before. It's the difference between facing fifteen fears thousands of times until you master them, as opposed to facing fifteen thousand fears only once and never getting a second chance.

You have on numerous occasions already successfully faced the core fears that underlie any challenge that may await you. You can use the experience you already possess as a guide. You don't have to reinvent the wheel. For example, let's say you're feeling flummoxed in a new job. You don't know all the rules, everything seems to be happening much faster than you're used to, and you're not sure who your allies are. Recognize the core fears underlying these concerns: feeling flawed, incompetent, and out of control. Then recall one or more times when you felt flawed and overcame that fear. How did you did you do it? What was the key? Do the same for each of your core fears.

Tracking Your Fears

Fear can affect us deeply, but it is hardly omnipotent. Fear's vulnerability is that it leaves tracks. Even when an ostrich has its head in the sand its upturned fanny gives an unmistakable clue of its presence. When you recognize the presence of fear, you have two choices:

1. You can be *reactive*, turning to denial, inner characters, animallike or childlike responses, and the usual suspects.

2. You can be *proactive* by moving closer, looking deeper, and openly facing your fears.

Trudy, a computer consultant, moved cross-country three months ago. She works out of her home, and most of her contact with others is on-line. As a result, she has made few friends in her new location. The one friend she has made, Marlene, has become a cornerstone of her social life. Trudy has a love-hate relationship with Marlene. Marlene can be extremely generous and caring, but when Marlene drinks, which she does several times a week, she becomes mean and self-centered. Under the influence, she becomes loud, critical, and inappropriate, which embarrasses and hurts Trudy when the two are out together.

Trudy masks her feelings during Marlene's incidents and has yet to confront Marlene when Marlene is sober. She has come to expect little of Marlene, a turn of events for which she feels sad and resentful, though she tries not to dwell on these feelings. Trudy compensates by reminding herself that Marlene has footed the bill for several lavish dinners and outings and has already booked a two-week vacation to Italy for the two of them next summer.

"I hate feeling like I can be bought, but Marlene really can be fun at times and I do enjoy our travels, which I could not afford on my own," Trudy says.

Trudy's quandary stems from core fears of feeling alone, deprived, and unsafe. She fears that if she were to lose her friendship with Marlene, loneliness would descend upon her with a vengeance. She doesn't confront Marlene about her alcoholism for fear of being hurtful to her friend but also for fear that Marlene might verbally attack her. This shows a core fear of feeling unsafe.

Part of Trudy's tolerating the situation comes from a lack of sense of self-worth. It's as if she feels that a friendship fraught with alcoholic drama is the best she can get, because once people get to know her they wouldn't like her.

For Trudy to get proactive and move past her counterproductive behavior, she will need to confront herself as well as Marlene. She'll have to face her loneliness and poor self-image. She will have to recognize that she has a lot to offer and can have quality relationships. She'll have to decide what behavior she will tolerate from Marlene and communicate this to her friend.

Naming Your Fears

You can use a simple method to identify your core fears in any given situation. Take a moment and think of a situation that troubles you, then ask yourself these questions:

1. *What* specifically am I avoiding?

2. *How* am I avoiding it?

3. *Why* am avoiding it?

Put together a 1-2-3 statement like this: I'm **avoiding** (specific action or situation) **by** (method of avoidance) **because** I don't want to feel (core fear).

For example: *I'm* **avoiding** *returning a friend's phone call* **by** *playing computer games,* **because** *I know he's mad at me and I'm afraid he will criticize me.* This clarifies what you are avoiding, the specific avoidant behavior you are using, and the reasons you give to avoid the feared loss. Pay special attention to the *because* clause. In this example, if your worst fear is that someone will be mad at you, and you don't want to be criticized, what worries you most? Is it that:

- You will lose control and attack back, saying things you'll regret? (Core fears: feeling out of control and being hurtful.)

- Your friend will leave and you fear losing the connection? (Core fears: feeling rejected, empty, and alone.)

- Your friend is a hothead and might become verbally abusive? (Core fears: feeling unsafe, dominated, and trapped.)

- You'll feel bad about yourself? (Core fears: feeling hurt and that you're a bad person.)

- You won't be able to stand the tension or stress during a heated conversation? (Core fears: feeling weak, fragmented, and out of control.)

How Core Fears Translate into Action

Our core fears are recognizable in our counterproductive behaviors. The following table illustrates some of the common but potentially counterproductive ways we compensate for core fears. Of course many of the behaviors listed in this table can be appropriate or adaptive at times. The question to ask yourself is whether your behaviors are automatic reactions to fear or are consciously chosen and adaptive responses. As you read through these, you might notice any coping behaviors that tend to be most problematic for you.

Potentially Counterproductive Ways of Coping with Core Fears	
A core fear of feeling . . .	May lead to counterproductive coping behaviors such as . . .
Flawed or Unworthy	• Excessively seeking reassurance or compliments • Putting yourself down before anyone else can • Overly clinging to possessions or memories of past achievements • Seeking to be famous, rich, special, or more attractive than others • Isolating yourself so others won't see your flaws • Quitting before getting what you want • Avoiding thinking about happiness, fulfillment, or inner peace • Settling for poor jobs or bad relationships • Always putting others' needs first • Obsessing about your minor flaws to avoid facing feared deeper flaws • Treating others as unworthy by humiliating or rejecting them • Excessively needing to explain or justify your actions, desires, or reasons • Not hoping for or expecting good things • Being overly defensive • Assuming that your thoughts and contributions are inadequate
Empty or Fragmented	• Overintellectualizing • Filling your emptiness through addictions or compulsive activity • Desperately clinging to a set of beliefs, group, or identity • Fantasizing that someday you'll be famous, rich, beautiful, or powerful • Avoiding introspection • Relegating yourself to the edge of society • Avoiding being alone or having nothing to do

A core fear of feeling . . .	May lead to counterproductive coping behaviors such as . . .
Empty or Fragmented (continued)	• Numbing or zoning out • Avoiding challenging or confronting situations • Provoking crises or exaggerating emotions to distract from emptiness • Distracting through meaningless or inappropriate activity • Seeking caretaking from others • Holding tight rein on your thoughts and feelings
Weak or Bad	• Always trying to be one step ahead • Constantly working on yourself to become OK • Seeking excessive validation from others • Seeking endless purification through religion, rituals, or activity • Not standing up for your rights • Giving up easily • Isolating yourself so you don't "poison" or "corrupt" anyone • Preempting criticism by criticizing yourself or apologizing for yourself • Punishing yourself • Thinking Pollyanna-positive • Being antisocial or having a "bad girl" or "outlaw" persona • Expecting the worst so you will feel more prepared when it comes
Out of control	• Being compulsively busy • Obsessively organizing your environment • Being perfectionistic or having impossibly high standards • Avoiding new experiences • Resisting pleasure • Cutting yourself off from your feelings
Trapped or Dominated	• Trying to control others • Working endlessly to anticipate future dangers

A core fear of feeling . . .	May lead to counterproductive coping behaviors such as . . .
Trapped or Dominated (continued)	• Avoiding giving definitive answers or opinions • Always leaving yourself an out • Avoiding group activities • Being wary, suspicious, or aloof • Testing the loyalty of loved ones • Provoking arguments to keep distance from others • Automatically rejecting others' requests, feelings, or opinions
Alone or Rejected or Deprived	• Emotionally over-attaching to relationships • Seeking instant intimacy • Overfocusing on taking care of others • Settling for superficial relationships so that it will hurt less if they end • Adopting a people-pleasing demeanor • Telling yourself that you don't need others • Avoiding situations in which you might be judged or evaluated • Holding low expectations • Not asking for help • Denying or minimizing your desires • Ignoring or shelving your dreams • Rejecting others before they reject you • Searching others' vulnerabilities to find ammunition if they reject you • Scanning others' expressions and tones of voice for signs of rejection • Becoming envious and fixated on what others have • Getting upset when you are not immediately heard, seen, or understood
Hurt or Unsafe	• Seeking symbols of safety such as guns or aggressive dogs • Anesthetizing with substance abuse • Denying your pain • Avoiding letting yourself grieve losses • Distracting yourself

A core fear of feeling . . .	May lead to counterproductive coping behaviors such as . . .
Hurt or Unsafe *(continued)*	• Building protective emotional fortifications • Acting rude or intimidating
Hurtful	• Blaming others for causing your actions • Seeking reassurance from others that your actions were OK • Isolating yourself • Denying that you've hurt anyone • Provoking confrontations so you'll have justification to hurt others • Pretending that your actions were a mistake or "just part of the game" • Punishing yourself

13

TAKING CONTROL OF YOUR FEARS

I've developed a new philosophy. I only dread one day at a time.

—CHARLIE BROWN

The more you know about what drives your fears, the more you can take the air out of fear's sails. Core fears carry so much energy and history that we often assume that giving in to our fears is less costly than facing them. We fall for the stacked calculations of our Subterranean Accountant.

Identifying your fear-thoughts, survival rules, mind FITs, counterproductive coping behaviors and, ultimately, your core fears in a given situation allows you to honestly assess whether your behavior is more beneficial than costly. The following examples illustrate:

Bonita, a thirty-eight-year-old pediatric nurse, has felt lonely and overwhelmed for several weeks. She's tried to ignore it. She won't let herself cry or express frustration. She won't ask friends for a sympathetic ear or friendly shoulder.

Why does an intelligent, caring woman who deals heroically with illness and pain in the tiniest and most helpless of beings not allow herself the same caring? In part, Bonita fears the strength of her dammed-up loneliness and depression. She worries that her pain would debilitate her. She fears that if she were to ask for help and a friend was too busy or didn't empathize, she'd feel foolish. She also worries that she'll burden her friends or that they would be overwhelmed by her feelings. Though Bonita recognizes the signs of depression in her behavior, she feels that as a health professional she should be able to handle it by herself. In addition, she tells herself that there is no reason she should be depressed when she compares her life to those of the sick children she sees daily. Bonita readily accepts that helpless, young human beings deserve unlimited help but believes that for adults like herself, help is scarce and undeserved.

Bonita's fear-thoughts and underlying core fears:

1. If I opened up to my feelings, they would be too powerful to handle and I'd feel even more overwhelmed and depressed. (Weak, out of control, hurt.)

2. If I voiced my feelings, I might realize they are exaggerated and then I'd feel like an unstable, clueless alarmist. (Flawed, fragmented, bad, unsafe.)

3. If I told my friends how I feel, I'd burden them. (Alone, rejected, hurtful.)

Her survival rules and underlying core fears:

1. I cannot lose control. (Out of control, unsafe.)

2. I should be able to handle my problems on my own. (Unworthy, bad.)

Bonita is mentally boxed in. Her fear-thoughts tell her that her feelings are too big to handle yet are also not worth worrying about. Her survival rules dictate that she must handle her problems but cannot seek help or resources to do so. Her fear-thoughts and survival rules frighten her with visions of losing control, then leave her to face her fears without assistance.

When we fail to question our fear-thoughts and survival rules, we question ourselves. Bonita concludes that since her problems seem less serious than those of others, her feelings must be exaggerated. Therefore she feels undeserving of the compassion she freely gives others.

Bonita's implicit sense of worth is based on being competent, strong, and self-sufficient. She dreads thinking of herself as unable to maintain self-control. As a result, she unwittingly narrows her choices to either:

1. Seek help at the risk of losing control, feeling incompetent, and inconveniencing others; or,

2. Suffer in solitary silence.

Based on such a skewed equation, Bonita continues to suffer.

This kind of step-by-step analysis may initially seem awkward and time-consuming. As you become more familiar with your core fears, this process becomes easier, quicker, and more natural. It can help you counterbalance the catastrophic distortions of fear-thoughts and survival rules.

Julianne, a twenty-nine-year-old writer, finds it hard to hope for positive things. She has applied for a new job, is well-qualified, and received positive feedback from the interviewer. As she waits for her prospective employer to check her references, she weakly reassures herself that it will work out. But she feels on edge, worried that some undefined "bad" thing will surface in her background and she won't get the job. Though the interviewer told Julianne that she was impressed, Julianne wonders if the interviewer said that only to be nice.

Julianne's fear-thoughts and the core fears driving them:

1. If I let myself hope for something and it doesn't happen, the disappointment will be overwhelmingly painful. (Weak, out of control, hurt.).

2. If I believe that I'm going to get the job but don't get it, I'll no longer be able to trust my instincts. (Flawed, trapped.)

3. If I don't get the job, it means there's something wrong with me. (Flawed, unworthy, bad.)

Her survival rules and underlying core fears:

1. I cannot survive disappointment. (Weak, rejected, deprived.)

2. I must have infallible instincts. (Flawed, fragmented.)

Believing herself unable to survive disappointment, Julianne seeks to ensure that she doesn't trigger it. She reduces her expectations and second-guesses herself, which in turn makes it harder to believe that good things will happen. The unfortunate result is that by playing to her fear of disappointment Julianne solidifies her unhappiness. She narrows her choices to either:

1. Have confidence at the risk of rejection and crushing disappointment; or,

2. Doubt herself and feel in turmoil.

Her desire to be hopeful about a single job prospect can hardly hold its own against fears of being rejected, flawed, and undeserving.

Julianne's fear-thoughts and survival rules show the power of forever-innate-total (FIT) thinking. Is she lets herself hope that she'll get the job, she fears that she will *never* be able to trust her intuition again if the job falls through. In addition, she worries that the prospective employer will discover something *innately wrong* with her. Julianne fears that the disappointment she'd face if this happened would be so *total* that it would overwhelm her.

Were Julianne to pause and deconstruct her mind FIT she'd realize that even if she did believe she would be hired but wasn't, the consequences would be temporary, external, and limited.

Temporary: Though she might be disappointed, the feelings won't last the rest of her life.

External: Having a mistaken instinct or intuition isn't anything innate. Her intuition is still intact even if it misses on occasion. In fact, when her intuition is wrong, it is likely the result of factors specific to the situation—for example, the great hope and great stress she feels about this job prospect. Emotions and stress, like thunderstorms, come and go. Stress can obscure your intuition, but it doesn't take it away. The sun remains when a thunderstorm passes.

Limited: Though it may be painful to lose the job she wants, it doesn't have to affect every aspect of her life. She already has a job. Other jobs are likely to come along. And her job is only one aspect of her life, not the entirety of who she is.

Bob, forty-eight, was recently promoted to the executive ranks and became engaged to his lover of four years. He tells himself he should feel proud, confident, and ecstatic but instead feels numb and empty. He wonders if his numbness reflects something wrong with his job or engagement.

Bob's fear-thoughts and underlying core fears:

1. If I don't feel happy, perhaps I have the wrong job or fiancée, which means somebody is going to be hurt. (Deprived, hurt.)

2. If I do have the right job and fiancée but I don't feel happy, I must be broken. (Flawed.)

3. If I am broken, I will always be broken. (Weak, deprived, hurt.)

4. If I'm not broken, that means I have passed up countless opportunities for happiness, a tragedy for which there is no remedy

and from which I shall never recover. (Empty, bad, trapped, deprived, hurt.)

His survival rules and core fears:

1. I must feel what I'm supposed to feel. (Flawed, bad.)
2. I should be innately emotionally facile regardless of my history. (Flawed, unworthy.)

In truth, Bob has plenty of emotions, but he misses their cues. He has unwittingly trained himself out of looking within. As a result, he hasn't learned to interpret the language of the heart. If Bob were to recognize that he is emotionally out of practice rather than emotionally incapable, he might feel freed. But he cannot accept such an interpretation for fear he'd wonder what was wrong with him for missing "Emotions 101." In addition, if Bob were to accept that he is capable of feeling but simply out of practice, he worries that he'd feel guilty for spending so many years cut off from his feelings when he had the ability to do otherwise.

Bob's dead-end, worst-case scenarios trap him. Either Bob has the wrong job and fiancée or he's broken and can never recover. His survival rules are absolute, allowing no room for individual differences and discounting the reality that emotional awareness and flexibility are learned, not inborn.

Fear-thoughts and survival rules have payoffs just as denial and inner characters. Instead of being willing to see himself as a beginner at emotions, Bob casts himself as a broken person. Using the math typical of self-defeat, Bob prefers to view his numbness as a result of his being flawed rather than his lacking practice. This is a curious but not uncommon reaction. Feeling flawed or broken hardly feels good, but it does contain Bob emotionally. After all, he tells himself, this is the way he is. He cannot fix what's broken.

If Bob were to accept that he is not broken but had merely missed an emotional education—something he could still learn—he might feel threatened. He would face his heart's unfamiliar terrain without his stonewall defense of *I'm broken and that's that*. Exploring his emotional life might feel terrifying, out of control, or disappointing. If he discovered that he could more readily feel joy, ecstasy, gratitude, and light-heartedness, Bob fears that this would invalidate forty-eight years of living. To Bob, the prospect of feeling good makes him fear feeling awful. He is happiness-phobic.

Bob's Subterranean Accountant gives him the narrowed options to:

1. Challenge his assumptions and explore his heart but risk guilt and emotional turmoil; or,

2. Continue to feel numb and confused but at least avoid feeling out of control.

His choice is to feel confused and numb rather than out of control.

Arlene, a thirty-three-year-old office worker, is her harshest critic. She dwells on her mistakes and replays slights and criticisms from long ago. She seeks frequent reassurance and approval from others. When socializing she'll ask her friends a half-dozen times if her appearance is OK. Arlene seems hungry for reassurance that she isn't a bad person. Her biannual job performance review triggers both dread and great anticipation. Fearing bad feedback, she wishes she could avoid the review entirely. But a part of Arlene secretly would like a performance review every day if she could get it.

Arlene's life is driven by trying to do the right thing, get approval, and avoid disapproval. She tries to find out whether she is OK based on what others say. Because external opinion weighs so heavily, she finds it hard to let go of even accidental slights. She is hypersensitive to both praise and criticism and on constant alert for both.

Arlene's fear-thoughts and core fears:

1. If others disapprove of me, I am no good. (Unworthy, bad, rejected.)

2. If I receive disapproval, I could not handle my disappointment. (Empty, weak, hurt.)

Arlene's survival rules and core fears:

1. My value and worth are determined by others, not by me. (Unworthy, fragmented, alone, dominated.)

2. I must do everything I can to gain approval and avoid disapproval. (Rejected, hurt.)

Arlene lives not knowing who she is. She believes that she lacks the ability to grant herself legitimacy as a human being. She feels as though she must keep earning the right to be here, a right that she fears could be revoked at any time.

Arlene's sense of worth is based on what others think about her. If she were to explore this dynamic, she could create the opportunity for newfound freedom. In going deeper, however, she'd have to risk others' rejections. More importantly, she'd have to face the immense grief she carries from years of self-rejection in seeing herself as illegitimate. Hamstrung by the freeze-frame of her internal horror movie, she cannot imagine becoming whole or forgiving herself after admitting how she has hurt herself.

Her fear-induced options are to:

1. Believe in herself at the risk of crushing disappointment, rejection, isolation, and feelings of unworthiness; or,

2. Hand her self-esteem over to others and work night and day to get it back.

She puts her self-esteem in others' hands. The payoff is that, though she doesn't have ultimate control, she feels she has interim control. If she does well and someone approves, she feels OK, at least for the moment.

Terry, a thirty-year-old stockbroker, is quick to notice others' faults and envy their strengths. Terry feels surrounded by "average" people and is on the lookout for the "best" people. His heart seems permanently clenched over those who have more than he. He works long hours and takes few vacations. In his relationships, he keeps a mental list of his partners' shortcomings. Though he voices perhaps 1 percent of what he thinks, 1 percent of his huge reservoir of disapproval is a tremendous amount of criticism. In the face of such criticism, his partners understandably feel uncherished.

Terry's fear-thoughts and underlying core fears:

1. If I have less than others, I will feel intolerable deprivation. (Weak, deprived.)

2. If I ease up, it means that I am not as good as the "best" people. (Flawed, unworthy.)

His survival rules and the core fears that drive them:

1. I have to be perfect, superior, and the best. (Flawed, unworthy.)

2. I cannot feel deprived or inferior. (Flawed, deprived, dominated.)

3. I must work hard enough and be vigilant enough to become OK. (Unworthy, rejected.)

4. If average people like me, it means nothing. (Unworthy.)

5. If the best people like me, it means I, too, am the best. (Unworthy.)

Terry's fault-finding and perfectionism cover his lack of a sense of self. His search for flaws in others is an attempt at self-reassurance. Doing so shifts the focus from his faults and sets him up as the person rejecting others, thereby preempting their doing so to him. His approach also keeps alive a fantasy that there are perfect people out there and, if he can be with them, he will be perfect, too.

This perspective reduces his options to either:

1. Become less judging and more accepting but risk feeling deprived and inferior; or,

2. Stay vigilant and feel in control even though it will bring continued isolation.

Rather than face his feared flawed self, Terry searches endlessly for perfection.

Terry's reluctance to accept imperfect reality is not uncommon. Such fantasies offer insulation and safety by allowing us to believe that perfection is just around the corner. The cost is that we rob ourselves of living in the moment. In *The Forgiving Self*, Robert Karen wrote: "We'd rather not love at all than face the truth about the past and abandon forever our unconscious dreams of a future made whole by perfection." Your fears are children of loss. Loss-avoidance, once again, is central.

Bonita, Julianne, Bob, Arlene, and Terry are suffering. They are experiencing loneliness, low expectations, numbness, self-criticism, and lack of intimacy. Their Subterranean Accountants tell them that the costs are worth it. The painful paradox is that such fear-avoidant behavior often brings us more of what we fear, not less.

Bonita, the pediatric nurse who is denying her depression and going it alone, risks worsening her depression the longer she ignores the problem and refuses to ask for help.

Julianne, the hopeful job applicant trying to avoid disappointment, risks a lifetime of deprivation by not trying for what she wants.

Bob, the executive afraid to explore his emotional numbness following his promotion and engagement, risks facing even stronger emotions the longer he represses his feelings.

Arlene, the office worker seeking external reassurance of her inner worth, risks a lifetime of being held hostage to the daily whims of others and cut off from the true source of self-worth.

Terry, the stockbroker trying to hide the inner flaws he feels so acutely by pushing others away, risks losing the growth and self-acceptance that can accompany intimacy and emotional vulnerability.

Core Fears Are Perceived Deficits

Core fears and concerns are perceived deficits. Losing your job, for example, might kindle fears that you're a failure, bad, incompetent, or flawed. What's missing is confidence in your worth, ability, and adequacy. That deficit can leave you scrambling to beg, borrow, or steal worth from external sources or trying to disguise your unworthiness.

What would happen if each time you identified a core fear you asked yourself: "What am I afraid that I lack and how can I supply it?"

The very question changes your starting point. You recognize that what you fear lacking is hidden, not gone. You remind yourself that you have the ability to define your worth. You can then notice ways in which you are worthy and seek experiences and relationships that validate your innate worth and abilities. This will transform your actions from loss-avoidance to expansion-seeking.

If you try to ignore or rid yourself of your core fears, you risk isolating vital parts of yourself. For example, if you are ashamed for making a mistake, you may hide your errors. Though this may offer short-term relief, it alienates you from your self. When you squarely confront core fears, you have less need to pretend, look the other way, hide, or overreact. Your fears are a part of you, but they are not the essence of you.

If You'd Like to Go Deeper: Identifying the Heart of Your Fears

If you are having difficulty pinpointing core fears or most-avoided experiences, or if you want to go deeper and find additional perspectives, the following questions can help crystallize your core fears. For each question, you may find that listing any fear-thoughts and survival rules, as demonstrated in the examples earlier in this chapter, can help pinpoint your core fears.

1. What kinds of situations or experiences drain your energy?

2. What kinds of situations or experiences make you feel small?

3. When you were a child, what kinds of experiences most frightened you?

4. What situations or experiences do you try hardest to avoid?

5. What was the most difficult loss you ever faced?

6. What do you most regret?

14

TOOLS FOR FEAR-BUSTING

You can discover what your enemy fears most by observing the means he uses to frighten you.

—ERIC HOFFER

Once you identify the heart of your fears, you are poised to overcome them. Here are ten fear-busting techniques.

Ten Fear-busting Techniques

1. When fear plays the survival card, call its bluff

Our worst fears devolve into concerns about our survival. When your fears deal the survival card, play it out. Ask yourself: *Is my actual, physical survival at stake? What is the likelihood that a life-threatening situation will materialize? What are my options for action? What is the time frame? What have I done in similar situations in the past?*

For example, a salesperson might worry, "If I don't make more sales, I won't be able to pay my mortgage and I'll have to sell my house. I couldn't face the trauma of that." To refute this, she could ask herself, "If I don't make the sale, will I lose my home for sure? If I lose my home, what then? I might be disappointed, but would I survive?"

In truthfully answering these questions, our salesperson would likely realize that even if she did have to sell her house the consequences would probably be less severe than she fears. In fact, it's possible that selling her house might free her to pursue nonmaterial goals that she's always dreamed of. In addition, it's also possible that she will eventually earn enough to have a house she loves as much or more than her current home. Positive outcomes become visible once you take survival fears out of the equation.

2. Lay bare the contradictions inherent in fear

Our fears are riddled with contradictions. For example, Bonita, the pediatric nurse who felt unable to cope with her depression, believed, "If I can't handle my own problems, I don't deserve help from others." She need only sit with this for a few moments to see the illogic of this self-defeating assumption. In truth, when we can't handle our own problems we most need help from others. Bonita is living proof, as she helps dozens of sick children and their worried parents. Sometimes simply recognizing a contradiction loosens the muck around it enough to free yourself.

One of the biggest contradictions of fear is inherent. When you listen to your fears, you can become convinced that you are powerless. The paradox: You are so powerful that you use your own fears to convince yourself that you lack power.

3. Reality-test fear's assumptions

Fear makes the leap from possibility to probability, and it does so on the backs of unrealistic and illogical assumptions. For example: "If this relationship falls apart, I'll never find another love."

Such a fear is based on such unfounded assumptions as:

- We only get one love per lifetime.

- Whether I meet appropriate partners is completely outside of my control.

- I don't have the ability to mourn, heal, and move on.

Another example: "I could never tell my lover some of my negative thoughts about him."

The underlying assumptions:

- If you love someone, you won't have negative thoughts or feelings about him.

- People who love you will leave you, retaliate, or fall apart when they hear a negative judgment.

- There is something wrong with me if I sometimes think negatively about my lover.

Recognizing illogical assumptions that hold you back is akin to a spring cleaning. Be alert for words like "never," "always," "can't," and "must" and then clear away the mustiness with fresh perspectives.

Two of the most troublesome fears involve shame and guilt. Shame is identity-based. We are ashamed of who we are. Shame "feels like swallowing poison," wrote Howard Raphael Cushnir in *Unconditional Bliss*. Guilt, by contrast, is activity-based. We feel guilty for what we did. Shame paralyzes us with a negative self image. Guilt handcuffs us with negative emotions.

In the case of shame, honestly ask yourself, "Am I really a bad person?" Reality-test by seeing the whole picture. Include a full assessment of your strengths and gifts.

In the case of guilt, ask yourself, "Are the consequences of my actions truly as global or despicable as guilt would have me believe?" or "Are others really as fragile or helpless as my guilt suggests?" Recall a time when you've been the recipient of actions similar to those you feel guilty for inflicting on another. How did you overcome that situation?

4. Tackle fear's "emotional reasoning"

Fears live in a jungle in which feelings must be true and thoughts can't be questioned. For example, you may treat feelings as facts: "I'm furious at him, so I must be right and he must be wrong." Or when you feel sad but can find no logical reason for it, you dismiss your sadness. Or you collapse emotions into actions: "I'm frustrated, so I'll berate the clerk."

This phenomenon is dubbed "emotional reasoning" by researcher David Burns. Feeling something is so doesn't necessarily make it so. When you see your fear-thoughts for what they are, they become akin to dangerous animals in a zoo—harmless to you in their cages, though interesting to visit from time to time.

5. Look beyond fear's oversimplifications

Fear tends to omit important details and nuances. To counteract this, put back what your fear-based simplifications leave out.

You may remember Bob from the previous chapter, who viewed his emotional numbness following his promotion and marital engagement as evidence that he was "broken." Bob saw his emotional ability in stark terms: If you don't feel how you're supposed to, you must be broken. Bob's simplification leaves out the effects of his history, natural variations in emotionality among individuals, and the ability we all have to deepen our emotional repertoire. Emotions occur along a continuum. Bob looked only for obvious, blunt feelings. In truth, Bob was feeling hints and nuances of emotions all the time. He just didn't recognize them as emotions.

6. When weeding out fears, go for the roots

The remedy to dysfunctional loss-avoidance is not to avoid but to move closer. Many forms of self-defense teach that if you cannot escape an unarmed attacker you may be better off moving as close to the attacker as possible. This seems counterintuitive and risky, yet moving in close can reduce the force of an attacker's punch or kick because the attacker cannot reach full extension. You also gain greater access to an attacker's vulnerable areas.

Similarly, when you move closer to your fears, you can take away their momentum. You can often see the roots of your fears in past events. When you're unaware of the roots of a longstanding fear, you approach it as an unfamiliar situation each time you experience it. You may remember Julianne, who was on pins and needles after her job interview and seemed incapable of believing in herself. If Julianne were to go deeper, she might see the roots of her fears in a series of unfortunate disappointments in her adolescence. Julianne overlooks two things:

1. Much of her current anxiety stems from past hurts.

2. She has survived every disappointment to date, belying her fear that she can't do so.

In recognizing the deeper issues, Julianne could take positive action, for example, thinking of times in her life when she was pleasantly surprised.

7. Do the math

The calculations of fear often don't add up. When you weigh the pros and cons of how you are responding to a particular fear, you regain equilibrium.

You may remember Terry, who became sarcastic and critical to deflect his feelings of imperfection and deprivation. If he were to put his fears on the table, Terry would have a perfect opportunity to do a simple cost-benefit analysis. Is the sense of protection he gains from his emotional defensiveness worth the hurt he inflicts on others as well as the intimacy, joy, and peace he is missing? Is the distractive value of all-work-and-no-play worth the toll on his health? One of the freeing effects of dissolving denial or acknowledging your core fears is that you can be honest about the costs. If you can't admit a secret, you won't generally admit its costs. Once a self-defeating secret is out of the closet, you don't have to deny its costs.

8. Measure fear's track record

Fear can arise with full potency no matter how many times that fear has been proven unfounded in the past. Your Subterranean Accountant, however, does not tally fear's win-loss statistics. You can. From time to time, keep track of how many of your fears actually materialize. Take a moment and write down some concerns about what might happen to you in the next week. Then, at week's end, go back and see what actually happened. How much of what you fear came true? If you wonder whether you are worrying too much, this will provide an objective measure.

Another simple way to return inflated fears to their normal size is to take a few moments and list some past successes you have had in facing that specific fear. You, too, have a win-loss record. Recalling even one victory over a fear levels the playing field because it takes "I can't" out of fear's arsenal of self-defeating thoughts.

9. You have many more choices than what fear offers

Fear reduces you to either-or thinking. The "either" and "or" tend to be shortsighted. When you are in an irritating or puzzling situation, think of a range of possible interpretations.

For example, when someone is tailgating you, possible explanations include:

1. He's an angry, hostile driver who tailgates everyone.

2. He's drunk or high.

3. He never learned good driving habits.

4. He's distracted.

5. He just found out that his wife has cancer and is rushing to be with her.

In actuality, you would probably never know which explanation was closest to the truth. Looking at the situation from different views will free *you*. If you can see only one interpretation, particularly negative interpretations, you are more likely to feel hostile, defensive, or anxious. When you can entertain alternative possible explanations, especially those which give others the benefit of the doubt or touch compassion within you, you can stop taking things personally. Most of us would feel quite differently about a tailgater who had just received news of his wife's illness than we would if we knew the driver was angry or drunk, even though the tailgater's behavior would be exactly the same.

Your explanations for others' behavior often determine your attitudes and reactions even when you forget that you made up the explanation. If you're going to make things up without sufficient evidence, why not make up explanations that reduce rather than increase your stress? In so doing, you use the same techniques of denial as your Subterranean Accountant, but with a major difference: You do so with awareness and by conscious choice.

You also can use this approach in viewing your own actions. For example, when you make a mistake, come up with at least three different interpretations for why. Make sure none of them is self-critical.

10. Ask proactive questions

Your questions determine your focus. As Tony Robbins said, "The quality of your life is nothing but the quality of the questions you ask. If you ask questions like, 'Why me? Why does this always happen to me?' then you'll be totally disempowered."

The right question can move you from a reactive to a proactive stance. For example:

- If you find that you tend to criticize yourself or others to excess, keep the question "What positive thing can I say at this time?" close at hand.

- If you feel emotionally numb, ask, "What am I feeling right now?" or "What was the last emotion I recall?"

- If you're an overwhelmed overachiever, a question might be, "What would be most satisfying right now?"

- If you'd like to improve the quality of your primary relationship, the next time you are around your mate, keep in mind the question, "What would she most appreciate from me right now?"

The possibilities are unlimited. For example, Spencer Johnson, in *One Minute for Myself*, offered the question, "What is the best way to take care of myself right now?"

Creative questioning can give fresh perspectives and innovative solutions. For example, when faced with a perplexing challenge, look at it from several different angles. Ask yourself:

- How might I handle this problem in a different culture, setting, or time period?

- If this were my only problem, how would I solve it?

- If this were my smallest problem, how would I handle it?

- If I knew I could make a difference, what would I do?

- How much will this matter in a year?

- How would I assess this situation if I were ten years older or younger than I am now?

Fear Versus Courage

Overcoming fear takes courage. We sometimes hold misconceptions about courage. Courage is neither the absence of fear nor the opposite of fear. Courage is a behavior as well as a feeling. Courage means acting even when you're afraid.

None of us knows in advance whether we'll act courageously in any given situation even if we've acted with courage in similar situations in the past. Acting courageously does not depend on feeling a certain way. It rarely feels good to face fears, at least initially. Your feelings may or may not change once action is under way. If you wait until you feel courageous before tackling a challenge, you're unlikely to do anything.

When the Tin Man, Scarecrow, and Cowardly Lion in *The Wizard of Oz* went to the wicked witch's castle to rescue Dorothy, they confronted their greatest fears. Similarly, sometimes your wisest course is to provoke or seek what you most fear. Fear of rejection is one such case. When your fear of being rejected is more painful and debilitating than actually being rejected, you may be better off seeking the dreaded consequence so you can move past it rather than hiding in fear. Often the negative consequences are less than what we fear. In surviving, we expand and feel strengthened.

Much of the courage you seek may only be available *after* action. The woman who saves a child from a runaway car was probably not feeling courageous as she walked down the street moments before the incident. She was probably not even feeling courageous when she lunged for the child. She didn't have time to access her courage bank or think about the great deed she was about to do. Though many heroes may have an explanation for the behavior in retrospect, many never feel certain why they acted as they did.

Courage is a gift your actions leave you with.

Summary of Part Three:
How to Minimize Your Unnecessary Losses

1. Everyday events can tap into existential dilemmas and lead you to:

   • Confuse ideas, possessions, relationships, and feelings with your actual survival

   • Experience primal responses to feeling powerless or ungratified

   • Adopt unrealistic expectations or take counterproductive stances in relationships

   • React intensely to limitations, loss, or endings

   When you see these kinds of reactions, remind yourself that everyday events merit everyday responses, not life-or-death ones.

2. Denial is well-armed but when you ask the right questions your Defense Department will stand down.

3. Fear stops time at the worst possible moment. You can restart the clock any time you want.

4. When you feel overwhelmed, identify the core fears or concerns at work. Doing so will help you go to the heart of what bothers you instead of just focusing on the symptoms.

5. Once you reach the heart of your fears, you can use numerous ways of reality-testing to overcome those fears.

PART FOUR

◆

Unearthing the Treasures You Keep from Yourself

It is never too late to be what you might have been.

—GEORGE ELIOT

The overreactions, denial, and self-sabotaging secret-keeping fostered by fear are roadblocks to your innate drive for wholeness and balance. When you move past these roadblocks, you see what's on the other side of fear: the treasures you may be keeping from yourself.

- Chapter 15 will help you better recognize and embrace your core desires and values and use them to motivate you to act in your best interests.

- Chapter 16 will show you how to view yourself in positive, realistic ways rather than in a self-undermining fashion.

- Chapter 17 will help you clarify what matters most to you. This knowledge can help you incorporate what really matters into your decisions and actions.

- Chapter 18 will show you a simple approach you can use at any time to restore healthy balance in your life.

15

MOVING FROM FEAR TO DESIRE

Too much of a good thing is wonderful.

—MAE WEST

Identifying core fears takes you all the way down to the ghost in the machine of self-sabotage. Fear is only half the story, not the end of the road. Fears are inextricably twinned with desires. As you become more adept at setting aside counterproductive fears, you gain greater access to your deepest desires.

We tend to be motivated by a combination of:

1. Fear, which primarily leads us to avoid

2. Hope and desire, which primarily lead us to seek

Both fear and desire are present in most situations. Fears often speak more loudly than hopes and desires, because they carry the speed and power of the fight-or-flight instinct. Fear and denial function like planetary eclipses, obscuring or distorting essential parts of your psychic terrain. In addition, your Subterranean Accountant may overestimate danger and underestimate your strengths and resources. To strengthen your ability to act in your best interests, it is just as important to recognize your desires, strengths, and potential as it is to recognize how your denial and fears work.

Like fear, desire is tremendously powerful, but it can be quite fragile. Your desires can be eclipsed when:

1. Your fears and activities consume so much of your attention that you have *scant time* or *energy* to attend to your hopes and desires.

2. Denial causes you to *overlook* or *forget* your hopes and desires.

3. Your fears, inner characters, and self-defeating beliefs convince you that you *can't have* or *don't deserve* what you most desire and value.

Karla, a third-grade inner-city teacher, was named "Teacher of the Year" in her second year of teaching. Now in her fifth year, she has become overwhelmed by her teaching load, paperwork, the school's physically deteriorating conditions, and the threat of violence her third-graders face from older students. She recalls "I was driving in this morning, and I was stunned to realize that I had not complimented any of my students in days. I can't remember the last time I laughed or was moved by one of my kids. I can't believe how I've been so focused on the school's problems that I've overlooked what is precious about these kids and teaching."

Karla's extraordinary appreciation of and dedication to her students never left her. It was obscured by what it took to get through her day. Burnout and being overwhelmed do not necessarily indicate that you've lost your desires. Rather, burnout and being overwhelmed are signs that you need to look at what is taking energy and attention away from your desires.

Minnie is a twenty-seven-year-old construction worker. She is upset over the previous night's conversation with her mother, who criticized Minnie's job and urged her to go back and finish college. Minnie recalls "My mother never even went to college. College is her dream, and she's trying to live it out through me. She has no idea how hard it would be for me to get back in the swing of things at college with all those kids. If she thinks my job's pay is lousy, being a student pays nothing."

As Minnie reflects, she discovers why she is so upset. She once dreamed of being an architect. She would draw incredible sketches of homes. Both her high school art teacher and a draftswoman friend encouraged her to pursue her talent. But during her first year in college, she developed meningitis and had to withdraw from school. Although Minnie has recovered physically, the barriers to returning to school have seemed too daunting. "Every time I think about going back to school I feel emotionally overwhelmed and exhausted. When my mother brings it up I just want to leave the room," she says.

Though Minnie healed physically, she still suffers psychologically. It hurts when she thinks about her abandoned dreams of being an architect. Over time she has let herself recall her dream less and less often. When the issue does come up, as with her mother's urging, she tells herself that she neither deserves nor can achieve her dreams.

Self-awareness Tool #5: Reclaim Overlooked, Abandoned, or Forgotten Desires

When you feel a sense of emptiness or a lack of purpose or motivation, ask yourself whether any of these factors is playing a part:

1. Your fears or activities are crowding out your deep desires.

2. You have forgotten or overlooked your deepest desires.

3. You're convinced you can't have or don't deserve what you desire.

If your desires have been crowded out, ask yourself how you might make room and invite them back. Making yourself take a vacation or a class you've always dreamed of may give you breathing room to rekindle your desires.

If you notice any forgotten desires, or recognize desires that you have never articulated until now, let yourself dwell in the energy of those desires. Focus on what excites you about them. Visualize yourself doing what you most desire. Now isn't the time to worry about the practicality of the desire. At this stage, desire is akin to a spark trying to start a campfire in the wind. Protect newly remembered or articulated desires so they can fully ignite.

If you're convinced that you can't have or don't deserve what you desire, remind yourself of who convinced you of that. Use the reality-testing techniques from the last chapter to assess the accuracy of self-depriving assumptions.

Core Desires

You can probably recall times when you pursued your deepest desires, stood up for noble causes, or dared to dream impossible dreams despite the presence of fear. Most likely you transcended your fears or pursued your dreams even in the face of fear.

It's important to know three truths about desire:

1. You have unique and powerful core desires whether or not you're aware of them.

2. You can use your fears to identify your desires.

3. You have many ways of recognizing and promoting your core desires.

When it comes to our basic worth, nature, or abilities, our deepest desires are that we are:

- Valid
- Worthy
- Whole
- Complete
- Strong
- Good

The experiences we tend to most desire are of feeling:

- Stable
- Independent
- Connected
- Fulfilled
- Accepted
- Happy
- Safe
- Generous
- Creative

The following table describes each of these core desires. As you read the following descriptions, you might notice any core values and desires you have forgotten about, convinced yourself you don't deserve, or have failed to recognize.

Core Desires	
HOPES ABOUT YOUR BASIC WORTH, NATURE, AND ABILITIES	
You feel . . .	**Words you may use to describe how you're feeling . . .**
Valid	Authentic, healthy, genuine, legitimate, OK, or unique
Worthy	Deserving, equal, lovable, needed, or valuable
Complete	Grounded, centered, self-sufficient, true to your purpose, or true to your self

You feel . . .	Words you may use to describe how you're feeling . . .
Whole	Well-integrated, stimulated, expansive, open-minded, well-rounded, or your best self
Strong	Able, competent, resilient, successful, reliable, imaginative, hard-working, industrious, courageous, decisive, confident, or intelligent
Good	Honorable, blessed, positive, noble, honest, fair, special, or trustworthy
EXPERIENCES YOU MOST CHERISH	
You feel . . .	Words you may use to describe how you're feeling . . .
Stable	At peace, in control, self-soothing, calm, steady, or at ease
Independent	Self-reliant, autonomous, or free
Connected	Intimate, loving, trusting, trusted, loved, or a sense of belonging or oneness
Fulfilled	Content, engaged, satisfied, grateful, or sated
Accepted	Desired, valued, seen, needed, liked, popular, or approved of
Happy	Hopeful, optimistic, excited, eager, lighthearted, joyous, relaxed, passionate, or playful
Safe	Secure or protected
Generous	Empathic, giving, accepting, inspiring, considerate, loyal, or graceful
Creative	Growing, expansive, creative, learning, generative, innovative, or contributing

Each of these core desires matches one or more core fears. The following table illustrates.

The Fear-Desire Connection	
Core desire	**Corresponding core fear**
Valid	Flawed
Worthy	Unworthy
Complete	Empty
Whole	Fragmented
Strong	Weak
Good	Bad
Stable	Out of control
Independent	Dominated or trapped
Connected	Alone
Fulfilled	Deprived
Accepted	Rejected
Happy	Hurt
Safe	Unsafe
Generous	Hurtful
Creative	Flawed or weak

Core fears are one side of the coin. The flip side bears your hopes and desires. When you fear, you also care, wish, and desire. This is a subtle but powerful shift in perspective. Recognizing this duality means you need not be ashamed of your fears or disown your self-defeats. You can view your fears and self-defeats as guideposts to your deepest values and desires.

For example, let's say that you fear aloneness and are dealing with it by clinging to others, feeling desperate, or further isolating yourself. What are the corresponding values and desires? Your fear of aloneness may reflect a striving for connection, belonging, and love.

Similarly, if you feel bad about yourself, you may cope by withdrawing, overachieving, or having low expectations. Yet a sensitivity to your "flaws" reflects an innate desire for wholeness, worth, and feeling proud of yourself.

Peter fears rejection and tries to fit in with whomever he is around, even at the cost of sanding down the edges of his personality. He does so out of fear of disapproval.

Inherent in Peter's wanting to fit in are his desires for connection, intimacy, and contribution. If he looked only to his fears, he might feel ashamed of his efforts to fit in. In seeing his desires, Peter could remind himself of his more noble motives and seek healthier strategies to express them.

Helene fears being dominated by others and becomes overly suspicious. Her suspiciousness cheats her out of peace and happiness.

Helene's defensiveness isn't a sign that she is bad, only that she's using a bad strategy for coping with her fear of being dominated. Helene knows that when she feels controlled, she finds it harder to blossom, grow, give to others, and live to her full potential. One solution would be for Helene to experiment with gradually trusting others more. In doing so, she could assess whether her suspicions are truly warranted. She could also assess whether having greater trust brings happiness that she cannot experience when she's being suspicious.

We don't always recognize that our fears and desires are joined at the hip. We feel bad about ourselves for what we lack, or feel shame for clumsy efforts to capture what eludes us. In the process, we overlook our inherent goodness. None of us is bad for trying to avoid loneliness, even if our efforts to do so are self-defeating. When you fear aloneness, it is partly because you want connection, and that's healthy. You simply may be trying to connect in costly or inefficient ways.

One advantage of seeing the desires inherent in your core fears is that you shift your focus from a *character trait* to a *behavior*. For example, instead of seeing yourself as bad, flawed, or worthless, you can see yourself as a good, strong person who sometimes makes mistakes. When you *are* a mistake, you have no place to go. When you *make* a mistake, you can correct it, learn from it, and make future successes.

Take a moment and think of a troubling situation in your life and identify a core fear. If you like, refer to the table of core fears on page 139. Then ask yourself what core desire underlies this core fear. You may want to refer to the table of core desires on page 174. Which desires can you identify?

Promoting Your Core Desires

Just as you distilled fear-thoughts and mind FITs to their core fears, you can extrapolate your core desires from any situation. When you do, you highlight strong motivators. For example, think of a goal you have and ask yourself:

1. What am I seeking?

2. How am I seeking it?

3. Why am I seeking it?

Put your answers into a 1-2-3 statement like this: **I want** (result you're seeking) and am **trying to get it by** (your efforts or contemplated action) **because**, more than anything, I value (core desire or value).

For example, if you find yourself wanting to reach out to a stranger and aren't sure why, ask yourself, "What core desires underlie my wanting to reach out?" Perhaps you want to comfort another or to feel good, loving, or worthy. Whatever core desires you recognize are important, positive parts of you. You may achieve the results and experiences you want more easily when you are motivated by desires and hopes rather than fears. The shift from avoidance to seeking is a powerful one. When you act based on valuing connection rather than on avoiding loneliness, you tend to act in healthier ways.

A second way to recognize and promote your core desires is to use this 1-2-3 format in reverse. Think of a troubling situation and then think of a core value or desire you cherish. For example, let's say a relationship with a friend has become strained following a disagreement. You've started to avoid your friend. When you are together, the conversation seems superficial and awkward. Refer to the list of core desires on page 174 and pick one or more desires that are most important to you with regard to the friendship. Think of how you would like the friendship to feel.

Perhaps you value connection. Take this value and put it into a 1-2-3 format: I **value** (connection) so I will **seek** (specific desired result) **by** (actions to be taken).

Your desired results might include rekindling the friendship, clearing up misunderstandings, and becoming close again. Then, think of actions to pursue your desired result. For example, I will **seek** *to clear the air between us* **by** taking a few moments to compose myself, *put myself in my friend's shoes,* and then *call and express my willingness to listen.*

Another approach is simply to ask yourself, "If I were motivated by my core desires rather than by my core fears, what would I do right now?" When you recognize that you have within you tremendous desires, visions, goals, passions, and dreams, you don't have to seek them outside yourself.

Embracing the Profound Within You

Your core desires and values are more than just the opposites of your fears. Core desires spring from deep within. For example:

Marty, eleven, was recently at Little League baseball tryouts. Marty, who is small for his age, noticed three older kids bullying another boy, Philip. Marty knew Philip casually; they shared homeroom. Seeing Philip shoved and his shirt ripped, Marty walked over to the group and said, "What's going on?" One of the bullies said, "We're kicking the crap out of this cry-baby." Another bully, fifteen pounds heavier than Marty, challenged him, "Why? Are you a friend of his?" Marty looked the bully in the eye and said, "Yes. He's my best friend. Now leave him alone."

Sandy, a thirty-seven-year-old marketing executive, was inching along in Fourth of July holiday traffic when she noticed a teenage girl in the break-down lane standing by a car with the hood raised. Because of the traffic, Sandy was already late to a getaway weekend she'd been anticipating for months. But she pulled off the road and asked if the young woman needed help. The stranded motorist was in tears, partly from the heat and exhaust fumes and partly because she was bewildered about what to do. She had no phone, little cash, and no auto-club membership that would arrange a tow or repair. Sandy invited the girl into her air-conditioned car and called her own auto club. When the tow-truck driver arrived and said he couldn't tow a nonmember's car, she paid him eighty dollars to take the girl and her car to a nearby station. Sandy followed the tow truck and, once at the station, waited until the teenage girl contacted a friend who agreed to come and pick her up. Sandy's Good Samaritan actions took two hours.

Sandy recalls, "I'm not entirely sure why I did that. I was exhausted and desperately in need of some R and R. Odds are that if I hadn't stopped, the girl would have worked things out somehow. But I felt a connection with that girl the minute I saw her. I remember when I was seventeen. I was not very street-smart and felt quite vulnerable. I couldn't pass her by, knowing she was probably afraid and in potential danger from the crazies out there. I knew I could help."

Helen, a forty-four-year-old artist and breast-cancer survivor, volunteers at her local hospice. She is by no means in the clear from her illness, as her cancer was removed only eleven months earlier. Her friends and family urge her to take time off, go easy, and enjoy life. But Helen recalls the emotional support she received months earlier from Gretchen, a sixty-eight-year-old woman she met during a hospital visit. Gretchen, who had terminal cancer, brightened Helen's spirits every time she visited. Helen never fully understood how Gretchen could set aside her own illness and nurture others so fully. Helen remembers Gretchen sitting by her side for hours holding her hand as she rested following surgery and chemotherapy sessions.

Shortly after Helen's chemotherapy ended, Gretchen was moved into hospice for her final days. Helen practically moved in, staying close, cradling Gretchen as she took her final breath. Within a week, Helen was volunteering for hospice home-care visits. Despite Helen's devastating illness and surgery, the loss of her friend, and her natural uncertainty over whether her own cancer would stay in remission, she chose to spend her time offering emotional lifelines to others, just as Gretchen had done for her.

Marty, Sandy, and Helen have fears as do you or I, but in these instances they marshaled the courage to act from their deepest desires. Marty risked attack to stand up for an outnumbered classmate. Sandy extended herself to protect a vulnerable young woman. Helen gave of her heart to others in their final days.

Each of us possesses core desires as powerful as Marty's, Sandy's, and Helen's. I see core desires all around. I see it in my friends who volunteer to teach illiterate adults to read. I see it in my neighbor who is an unofficial "Welcome Wagon," greeting newcomers with brownies and flowers. I see it in my bright-eyed neighbor who has taken up studying Italian at age eighty-two.

I see core desires in underpaid teachers who believe in their students, as my eighth-grade English teacher, Mrs. Murray, and eleventh-grade history teacher, Mr. Bell, believed in and encouraged me. Such teachers not only change their students' lives for the better, they alter the lives of all those whom their students touch across a lifetime.

I see core desires in the courage of millions of parents doing their best to raise their children, necessarily foregoing some of their personal dreams.

I see core desires in psychotherapy clients who come each week, willing to push the envelope of their emotional limits. They risk discomfort, answering my questions, and asking uncomfortable ones of themselves, in an effort to enhance their lives and the lives of those around them.

All these actions are expressions of core desires. Your core desires point to and arise from the best in you. The more you recognize your deepest desires, the more readily you can embrace and promote them.

If You'd Like to Go Deeper: Clarifying Your Desires

The following questions can help you further clarify your personal values, passions, hopes, and dreams. You might want to give yourself some time in a setting where you won't be distracted as you ponder these questions.

- What experiences fill you with energy and make you feel expansive?

- When you were growing up, what experiences most empowered you?

- What triumph has meant the most to you?

- What are you most grateful for?

- What are you proudest of about yourself?

- What do you most value in yourself?

- What gives you a sense of worth?

- If you could do or have anything right now, what would it be?

- What relationship has most changed your life for the better, and how?

- What experience has most changed your life for the better, and how?

- What question has most changed your life for the better, and how?

- What promise has most changed your life for the better, and how?

- What are you most passionate about?
- What is most needed in the world?
- What would you normally never do that you'd like to try?
- If you had six months to live, how would you spend it?
- If you could do whatever you wanted for one week, how would you spend the week?
- What would your ideal day be like five years hence?
- What could you do all day and never tire of?
- What would you do even if you weren't paid to do it?
- If you could have six lives, what would you do with your other five?
- What do you most want to be remembered for?

16

EMERGING FROM THE SHADOWS:
A PORTRAIT OF YOUR HIDDEN SELF

Our deepest fear is not that we are inadequate; our deepest fear is that we are powerful beyond measure. It is our light, not our darkness, that most frightens us.

—NELSON MANDELA

We buy $677 billion of property, casualty, and life insurance annually, according to A. M. Best and Company's 1999 figures. Sometimes we forget that insurance doesn't prevent loss, it helps only in recovering from loss. Similarly, emotional-loss prevention insurance does not exist. However, emotional-loss *recovery* insurance does. You buy it with self-acceptance, flexibility, and relationships with others.

We tend to approach personal challenges in one of two ways:

1. Survival-based: Fearing yourself insufficient to meet the challenge or unable to survive a loss, you organize your actions, feelings, and thoughts around bargaining with, avoiding, or denying risks. Survival-based living is driven by fear and loss-avoidance.

2. Growth-based: Recognizing that you can't control life or avoid all risks, you build your resources, awareness, and flexibility so that you can face whatever comes up as best you can and grow from the process. Growth-based living is driven by desire.

Survival-based living increases your risk of unnecessary losses. Growth-based living reduces it. You might take a moment and recall a time when you felt "in survival." Perhaps you felt especially overwhelmed, pessimistic, or on the defensive. Survival-based living is rooted in assumptions of scarcity like *I'm not good enough, I won't get what I need,* or *There's not enough to go around.*

Growth-based living, by contrast, is rooted in acceptance. You acknowledge that scarcity may exist, but foster choices based on abundance. You're aware of the potential of loss, but choose to attach emotionally anyway. You are aware of your limitations, but exercise your ever-present option to live in the now. As *The Four Agreements* author Don Miguel Ruiz wrote, "The best way to say 'Thank you, God' is by letting go of the past and living in the present moment."

Survival-based living fosters an either-or outlook. When you notice aspects of yourself you don't like, you disown, ignore, or shun them. The problem is that selective self-acceptance tends to be self-defeating. Disowning parts of you isn't like pinpoint laser surgery. As we saw in the last chapter, when you avoid facing your fears, you tend simultaneously to obscure your desires.

Instead of a survival-based, either-or approach, you can cultivate a growth-based, "both-and" approach. One of the best ways to move from survival-based to growth-based living is to accept and even embrace all parts of yourself. It is particularly helpful to identify and accept those aspects of yourself that you may have cast off, overlooked, or underappreciated. Later in this chapter you will find two approaches to help you see yourself more accurately so that you can reclaim and integrate these cast-off and underappreciated parts of you.

Cultivating Paradox

We are beings full of paradox. The intriguing richness of paradox is that both sides are true. They coexist even though they conflict. When you cultivate internal paradoxes, you grow. You approach wholeness.

For example, we often tend to shy away from either our limitations, our potential, or both. We all have limitations, some of which are non-negotiable. As I have said, we chafe against limitations, in part because they can unconsciously remind us of infancy when we encountered our first nonnegotiable limits. We also may rail at limitations, in part because they remind us of the inevitability of our physical death. Like giant invisible hands, our unconscious memories of infancy's disappointments and knowledge of our mortality can add an emotional charge to our normal reactions to everyday limitations.

At the same time, we can be oddly ambivalent about our potential. Perhaps we fear that fully accepting our potential would feel too out of control or unfamiliar to tolerate. Perhaps we worry that seeing ourselves at our best would deprive us of our inalienable right to kick back, quit, or fail when we feel like it. Maybe we anticipate that if we were to embrace our capabilities, any future disappointments or failures would feel worse by contrast. Perhaps we hold ourselves back from our potential for fear that achieving great things would make others jealous of us or dislike us. Or maybe we're concerned that acknowledging our powers would, paradoxically, invalidate how we've lived to date. As Caroline, a forty-six-year-old teacher says, "When I really acknowledge all that I am capable of, I remember the times I've failed to use it. That makes me feel guilty."

Self-acceptance includes accepting both your limitations and potential. You have finite capabilities and reach. You can deny loss, but you can't control it. At the same time, your potential is infinite, and your worth is immeasurable. You determine your potential and worth. You do so by how you live, not how you die.

When you accept the paradoxes and limitations of life and death, time and loss, worth and potential, you gain more conscious use of your life. As Anaïs Nin wrote, "I postpone death by living, by suffering, by error, by risking, by giving, by losing."

The answer to feeling ambivalent about your potential is not to be cautious or careful. The answer is to honestly assess your strengths and potential as well your limitations, and follow a growth-based approach that denies neither.

Knowing Who You Are

We have to dare to be ourselves, however frightening or strange that self may prove to be.

—MAY SARTON

Search the world's best-known spiritual, philosophical, and social sciences texts and you'll discover a common, central message: *When you don't know who you are, or you don't live true to yourself, it hurts.*

When you're not sure who you really are in a spiritual, existential, or psychological sense, you may look for clues in all the wrong places. One of life's challenges is to drop illusory or self-defeating avoidances and protections, and to do so without excessive suffering. For example, let's say you worry about your "flaws" or feel unworthy. Such fears may arise when you lose touch with your true nature. When you view yourself as flawed or lacking, you scramble to hide or fix your flaws.

You may envy others who seem to possess qualities that you fear that you lack.

On the other hand, what if everything truly important has always been inside you? You possess the ability to feel love, validation, courage, peace, and confidence. You may wait until an external event prods you to experience these feelings, and forget that the capacity for every imaginable emotion is already within you. Just ask any actor. External events don't generate your feelings, they tap into feelings you are already capable of generating.

At times you may assume that your worth or goodness is based on how you feel, what you do, who you know, or what you have. When you believe that your well-being is primarily contingent on external factors, you seek to change or hold on to those circumstances. You put your well-being outside your control.

In truth, your sense of well-being is primarily contingent on internal factors. Value does not innately reside in external situations or objects. You bestow it. As Walt Disney once said, "I love Mickey Mouse more than any woman I've ever known."

Have you ever come up against a challenge and thought something like, "It'll be too much work," "Nobody can do this," "I don't see how this could benefit me," or "I'll think about it later"? Such thoughts use your power to deny your power. You can choose to feel invalid, undeserving, or not good enough, but you, by definition, are valid, deserving, and good enough, no matter what it may feel like. Though much of your identify may be derived from relationships and circumstances, in any given moment you are whole and complete regardless of circumstances.

It is not: "I'll be OK *when* I'm successful, loved, or safe."

It is: "I am *already* OK."

You might pause for a moment and notice any random thoughts you are having. Are you aware of any chatter, doubts, or self-distractions? If so, this may be the voice of part of you, like the Subterranean Accountant or inner characters, that leads you to get in your own way. These "rogue" aspects of you are just doing their jobs. If you were to accept that you are OK and whole at all times no matter what was happening in your life, these rogue parts of you fear that they would be out of a job. In truth, you cannot fire self-defeating or counterproductive aspects of yourself. You do, however, have final say on whether you act from these parts, or from the best parts of yourself.

Take a moment and think of a time when you felt hopeful, fulfilled, even ecstatic. I suggest that such experiences were derived from within you, though they may have been triggered by external circumstances and relationships.

When you view yourself as worthy and complete, you don't have to seek survival, protection, or sufficiency to become OK, whole, or good. You already are.

Crafting a Life

The self is not something one finds, it is something one creates.

—THOMAS SZASZ

You are crafting a life. You are the only one who is responsible for taking yourself through your life from start to finish. You've had that responsibility all along, whether you've acknowledged it or not. You are the one who decides how to spend your life. You craft your life when you convince yourself that you have little hope or power, just as you craft your life when you allow yourself to feel full of potential and goodness.

In a sense, crafting a life is like being the CEO of a large company, full of divisions and employees, each with strengths and weaknesses. A corporation needs its research and development people to research and its sales force to sell, not vice versa. Among your "employees" are your inner characters and Subterranean Accountant. Among your divisions are your Defense Department and Bureau of Fear. You can't expect fear, for example, to do anything other than its job, which is to raise alarms. But remember, all these folks work for you. You are the CEO. You can listen to fear's alarms, but you don't have to take its advice. You get the final say. Your score, not that of the Accountant, is what matters in the end.

You are a powerful being, so powerful that you diminish yourself or enhance your life using the same techniques. The difference lies in awareness. Seen in this light, your self-defeats are messengers. Their message: *You have temporarily forgotten who you are.*

Your "Hidden Self"

Have you ever felt internal prohibitions or urges that, no matter how irrational, were ruthlessly compelling? Have you ever felt antipathy or admiration for another person and not known why? Such experiences are orchestrated by your "hidden self."

Your hidden self, what Jung termed your "shadow," includes unwanted, overlooked, and wished-for aspects of your personality, identity, and values. These aspects can orchestrate much of what you do, think, and feel. What's more, they do so outside of your awareness. You may react favorably or unfavorably to people and experiences, unaware that a part of you is pulling the strings. Each time you bring more of your hidden self into the light, you give yourself an opportunity to reclaim parts of yourself that you intentionally or unwittingly may have walled off.

One way to identify aspects of your hidden self is to note qualities you tend to dislike or admire in others. As Herman Hesse wrote, "If you hate a person, you hate something in him that is part of yourself. What isn't part of ourselves doesn't disturb us." Qualities you judge and avoid in others may represent aspects of yourself that trouble you. By the same token, qualities you admire in others may represent aspects within you that you haven't fully embraced, or desire more of. Your reactions to others offer fertile ground for learning more about yourself and for fostering increased compassion for yourself and others.

Ignoring parts of yourself that you dislike, or pretending they don't exist, is akin to ignoring a wound. Until you see it, you can't heal it. By the same token, identifying aspects of yourself and others that you admire, but have been overlooking or reluctant to embrace, can show you hidden treasures within. Articulating your hidden wish list of qualities you strive to emulate and achieve brings them into the open where you can pursue them directly.

If You'd Like to Go Deeper: Painting a Portrait of Your Hidden Self

This exercise will help you more clearly identify unwanted, overlooked, and wished-for personal qualities.

Part 1: Unwanted qualities

The following questions ask about qualities and emotions you dislike or avoid in yourself and others. You may want to answer each question based on your overall perceptions about your life. Or you may find answering these questions easier if you relate each question to a particular area of your life, such as work, health, emotional life, friendships, primary relationship, or family life.

In answering each question, you may simply want to write down whatever comes to mind. Or you may want to refer to the accompanying lists of qualities and emotions on page 190 to help stimulate your thinking. The lists are by no means exhaustive. You may have other qualities and emotions you want to add.

Answer each question in any way you like. There are no right or wrong answers. You may have multiple answers. The best answers are those that reflect your values, perspective, and experience of yourself. Pay special attention to any answers that carry an emotional charge.

1. Personal qualities or traits that most bother me in other people:

2. Emotions I find hardest to tolerate in other people:

3. Personal qualities my parents most disapproved of in me when I was growing up:

4. Emotions my parents most disapproved of in me when I was growing up:

5. Emotions I least like to experience:

6. Personal qualities I'd least want others to think of me as having:

7. Personal qualities I least like in myself:

Unwanted and avoided personal qualities

aggressiveness	humorlessness	naiveté
aloofness	hypersensitivity	negativity
antagonism	impulsivity	pessimism
arrogance	incompetence	superstitiousness
closed-mindedness	impatience	uncertainty
coldness	indecisiveness	ruthlessness
cluelessness	lack of discipline	self-centeredness
cynicism	laziness	selfishness
detachment	obsessiveness	shyness
dishonesty	paranoia	stinginess
disloyalty	perfectionism	stubbornness
distractibility	rebelliousness	timidity
gullibility	rudeness	volatility
hostility	lack of imagination	

Unwanted and avoided emotions

anger	greed	jealousy
anxiety	grief	loneliness
belligerence	guilt	moodiness
boredom	hatred	regret
depression	helplessness	resentment
disappointment	hopelessness	resignation
embarrassment	humiliation	sadness
fear	insecurity	shame
frustration	irritability	stress

Part 2: Admired and wished-for qualities

The following questions ask about qualities and emotions you admire or seek in yourself and others. Just as with Part 1, you may want to answer each question based on your overall perceptions about your life. Or you may answer the questions by thinking about a particular area of your life you wish to understand better, such as work, health, emotional life, friendships, or family life.

In answering each question, you may want to refer to the accompanying lists of qualities and emotions on page 192 to stimulate your thinking. The lists are by no means exhaustive. You may have other qualities and emotions you want to add.

Answer each of the following in any way you like. There are no right or wrong answers. You may have multiple answers. The best answers are those that reflect your values, perspective, and experience of yourself. Pay special attention to any answers that carry an emotional charge.

1. Personal qualities I most admire in others:

2. Personal qualities my parents were most proud of in me when I was growing up:

3. Emotions my parents most approved of in me when I was growing up:

4. Emotions I most enjoy experiencing:

5. Emotions I would like to experience more, but find elusive:

6. Personal qualities I most hope that other people attribute to me:

7. Personal qualities I am proudest of in myself:

8. Personal qualities I aspire to enhance in myself:

Admired and wished-for personal qualities

assertiveness	friendliness	self-awareness
certainty	generosity	self-discipline
clarity	genuineness	self-reliance
competence	honesty	selflessness
confidence	humility	social adeptness
courage	imagination	sophistication
curiosity	intelligence	spirituality
decisiveness	loyalty	strength
dependability	open-mindedness	thoughtfulness
directness	optimism	tolerance
efficiency	patience	trustworthiness
empathy	promptness	unflappability
energy	reliability	warmth
fairness	resourcefulness	

Desired emotions

affection	gratitude	passion
calmness	happiness	peacefulness
compassion	hopefulness	playfulness
contentment	inspiration	pride
elation	joy	satisfaction
excitement	lightheartedness	serenity
fulfillment	love	tenderness

Interpreting Your Self-portrait

First, look over your answers from Part 1 of this exercise. Taken together, these answers give a flavor of some of the attitudes, emotions, personal qualities and traits you avoid, dislike, or struggle with in yourself and others. As with art, you may find many insights and multiple valid interpretations among your answers. You may especially want to notice:

- *Qualities you listed more than once.* These least-favored attributes may point to deep moral convictions or values that you hold and don't like to see violated. They may also point to ways of being you avoid or overreact to in yourself or others. Such ways of being can increase your risk of counterproductive behavior.

- *What bothers you in others.* Do any of your closest friends, family members, and coworkers have these qualities? If so, how does that affect your relationships? For example, if you dislike shyness and timidity do you tend to look down on loved ones who show these qualities, or do you have compassion for them? If you dislike aggressiveness or arrogance, do you tend to avoid, criticize, or feel intimidated around friends when they come across as aggressive or arrogant?

- *What your parents disapproved of in you.* Do any of these qualities point to parental injunctions and prohibitions you may still be following as an adult? If so, are those injunctions helpful to you or have they outlived their usefulness? If you had a contentious relationship with one or both parents, are you rebelling even as an adult by seeking the opposite of what your parents wanted? Does your rebellion feel constructive or destructive? Is it a consciously chosen or automatic reaction?

- *Personal qualities and emotions you dislike in yourself and hope others do not attribute to you.* How do you cope when you notice unwanted qualities or emotions in yourself? Do you judge yourself harshly? Try to eliminate them? Feel distressed upon recognizing them? Do your recognitions trigger counterproductive behavior? For example, if you dislike feeling indecisive or lazy, recall the last time you felt that. What happened next?

Once you've finished looking over your answers from Part 1, turn to your answers from Part 2. What is the flavor of these answers? What types of qualities do you desire and admire? Do you tend to favor active qualities like energy, excitement, intensity, assertiveness, and decisiveness? Or do you favor "quieter" attributes like patience, tolerance, calmness, lightheartedness, and empathy? In particular, you might notice:

- *Personal qualities and emotions you most like to experience and/or are proud of.* For example:
  1. Do you sometimes try too hard or take unwise risks to experience these wished-for qualities? If so, having greater awareness of this potential may help you find balance.
  2. Are you experiencing enough of these desired qualities? If not, you may be setting yourself up for self-sabotage the longer you deprive yourself of what you most want.

3. Do you acknowledge yourself when you recognize your actions, qualities, and experiences that you are most proud of? When you live up to your ideals, make sure you give yourself a hearty pat on the back. Doing so reinforces positive behavior.

• *Qualities and feelings your parents approved of.* We all seek parental approval, usually for life. Did you feel as a child that you received adequate approval from your parents? Did the approval come for qualities that mattered most to you, or for qualities that mattered most to your parents, assuming the qualities were different? In looking over the qualities your parents most approved of and the qualities you like best in you, are there similarities, or is the tenor of each markedly different?

If you had a contentious relationship with one or both parents, you might notice if there are qualities your parents most wanted you to emulate that you are trying *not* to achieve even as an adult. For example, if your parents highly valued self-discipline and you find discipline elusive in your adult life, is it possible this represents Subterranean Accounting? Even though the lack of discipline may cost you a great deal, does it give you a "win" by defeating parental wishes even years later?

At the other extreme, are you still trying to gain parental approval? Is this a positive motivation and influence in your adult life?

• *Aspects of others you admire.* Are the qualities you admire in others qualities that you also possess? Are there qualities that you feel you will never have? When you admire something in another person, do you generally tell them?

• *Qualities you aspire to enhance in yourself.* How are your efforts to enhance these aspects progressing? Do you feel optimistic and confident about the prospects? Do you have a plan for achieving what you aspire to?

Finally, compare your answers from Part 1 and Part 2. Notice what you least want others to see in you and least like in yourself (questions 6 and 7 in Part 1). Then notice what you hope others attribute to you and are proudest of in yourself (questions 6 and 7 in Part 2). These answers can provide a succinct portrait of your "shadow"; aspects of yourself you least want as well as those you most desire. These are the qualities that, for good or ill, stir your heart. Your answers can highlight goals you may want to work harder to promote and embrace within yourself, as well as potential pitfalls to be aware of.

Ponder the qualities you most and least want others to see you as having (question 6 on both Part 1 and Part 2). If some of the people closest to you were with you right now, would they be surprised by the qualities you listed? Do you think they attribute any of your least-wanted qualities to you? Do they see the qualities you hope they do? You might find a trusted friend and ask. This is one way to find out whether you come across to others as you think and hope you do. If you do not, why not? Is it because others don't see you clearly? Is it possible that you present yourself in ways that are incongruent with who you aspire to be?

You might also compare the qualities that bother you most in others to the qualities you admire most in others. Do you notice any correlations? For example, if you dislike coldness, did you list qualities like warmth and empathy among what you most admire? Is there any correlation between your least-liked and most-admired qualities?

Your responses to this exercise may reveal areas for introspection, growth, and self-acceptance. Identifying unwanted and wished-for aspects can help you measure how well your relationships and daily activities match your deepest values. Taking such a measure can help you identify goals, activities, and resources to reevaluate, replace, adjust, or promote.

Building an Accurate Self-image

One doesn't discover new lands without consenting to lose sight of shore for a very long time.

—ANDRE GIDE

Self-defeats can arise from having an unrealistically low view of your strengths, just as they can arise from having an overblown view of your weaknesses. As family therapist Frank Pittman wrote, "People who think too little of themselves are just as happy as people who expect too much of themselves." Embracing your individual strengths is as important as taking stock of your failings. What good are your strengths if you don't know you have them?

In leading workshops with groups ranging from unemployed job seekers to retired elderly persons, I've found that self-esteem and mood can change dramatically when people simply list the accomplishments, experiences, and insights of which they are most proud.

We know from cognitive therapy that when people who feel depressed realize that their explanations of events are inaccurate or self-defeating, and then adopt new explanations, their depression can lift. If you tend to think about your problems and defeats but overlook your successes, you are gathering evidence that may create pessimism and a lack of self-confidence. Change your focus, and your mood can change.

Try this experiment. Think back over the past week. Recall at least one thing you did, said, thought, or felt that you are proud of. Review where you went, what you did, to whom you spoke, and any notable feelings, experiences, or insights. If you notice any negative thoughts, simply let them pass by. If it takes a while to find something you are proud of, that's fine. Most of us are out of practice at acknowledging our accomplishments. Keep at it.

Once you've identified at least one experience or accomplishment you are proud of, write it down. If you identify more than one, all the better. Recall the setting, what happened, and any sensations and thoughts you had. Mentally picture it. Again, let any negative thoughts simply pass by. After you've clearly pictured your proud moment, notice whether you view yourself any differently than before you recalled the positive experience.

If You'd Like to Go Deeper: Acknowledging Your Accomplishments

The phrase "You are what you do" reflects a limiting view. Yet we can also limit ourselves by *failing* to notice all that we do. Our self-definitions often are based on distorted views or little evidence. Negative self-views can arise from a single incident followed by mind-FIT thinking that generalizes about your entire character.

In this exercise, you will gather evidence and then see what emerges from the evidence rather than from a generalization. You'll answer a series of questions about what you have accomplished and experienced during the last twelve months (or any time period you like). To do this most effectively, give yourself some private time when you won't be disturbed. You might find it helpful to gather your appointment book or schedule for the last twelve months to jog your memory.

As you're answering these questions, if thoughts arise that dismiss your accomplishments or label them as not enough, let those thoughts pass by. If you like, imagine sending any critical thoughts to your local landfill or recycling center. Or visualize sending them to me; I have a huge imaginary landfill for negative thoughts that I invite my clients and workshop participants to donate to. There is plenty of room for yours, I promise, and the landfill is ecologically sound.

If you look over this exercise and it seems overwhelming or irrelevant, you may want to pause and examine your thoughts and feelings. It may be that this exercise just doesn't speak to you, and that is important to honor. But this is an exercise in which you tell the truth about accomplishments you feel good about. You can find plenty of accomplishments, I promise you, so why would you avoid such an experience? What is the downside of reckoning with your best self? If you are tempted to pass this exercise by, you may want to do a quick check of your denial and notice if any core fears have arisen. If so, doing this exercise will help you get in touch with your core desires. Even answering five or six of the following questions can be beneficial.

List **accomplishments, positive experiences,** and **insights** of any kind or size that you've had during the last twelve months in each of the following areas:

- While helping others:

- While making something:

- While listening to another person:

- While on vacation or relaxing:

- While traveling:

- While fixing something:

- While overcoming fears or setbacks:

- In writing, art, music, dance, drama, or other creative and expressive arts:

- In standing up for yourself:

- In designing or planning something:

- In your work life:

- In your family life:

- In your friendships:

- In romance:

- In any honors you've received:

- In negotiating or persuading someone:

- In finishing something you had struggled with:

- In saying "yes" even when it was hard:

- In saying "no" even when it was hard:

- In doing something they said couldn't be done:

- In physical fitness:

- In a game or sport:

- As a parent, son, or daughter:

- As a woman or man:

- As a citizen:

- As a consumer:

- As a spouse or partner:

When you've finished, take a moment to review your answers. Are you surprised by any of the accomplishments, positive experiences, or insights that you recalled? Notice your emotional state. Is it different from when you began this exercise? Your reactions reflect an awakening of your mind, body, and heart. Each of your answers is an experience or accomplishment you added to the world. They wouldn't exist if you were not here. You've created thousands of successes, contributions, and positive experiences in your life. Don't discount, diminish, or forget that. These experiences and accomplishments reflect who you are at your best. You can be that person any time you want.

17

WHAT MATTERS AND WHAT DOESN'T

Our lives begin to end the day we become silent about things that matter.

—MARTIN LUTHER KING JR.

Thirty-four-year-old Jessica has blazed a trail of awards and rewards in a New York ad agency for four years. The agency's partners have considered her their hottest creative director for her innovative work with several large accounts. In the last three months, however, Jessica's creations for two major clients, an electronics company and an automaker, have been uninspired.

"I once lived and breathed advertising. I couldn't wait to get to work in the morning. I thought of slogans in the shower, when I was working out, and even in my sleep," Jessica says. The only time in the last few months she has felt her former creative self was when working pro bono for a non-profit organization that helps babies born to drug-dependent mothers. As she thought about it, Jessica realized that the urban wallpaper of homeless and addicted street people had gotten to her. "I can't blindly walk past what some of my friends call New York's 'human garbage' as I once could," she says.

She begun to question the importance of enticing consumers with cars and DVD players while people are starving at her feet. This change in values has surprised her. In her twenties, Jessica rarely concerned herself with issues of the urban poor.

Feeling as if your life lacks meaning or purpose can lead to wasted time and poor choices, because you feel that there is little at stake. The impetus to seek deeper meaning often follows a loss. For example, in the wake of the terrorist attacks of September 11, 2001, many people found themselves reassessing what was important.

You don't have to wait for an external loss to strike before reassessing what matters. One way to clarify a sense of purpose for your life is to shift temporarily to an "end of life" perspective. That is, to imagine yourself nearing the end of your days and picturing how you might assess what had mattered most in your life.

If you've known a loved one who became terminally ill, you may have noticed changes in his outlook. Perhaps his priorities shifted, he wasted less time, or he stopped sweating the small stuff. Near the end of life, given the time and willingness to reflect, many people tend to seek a reckoning with how they've lived. They wonder: *Did I use my life well? Did I make a difference? Did I treat myself and others well? Was my life meaningful?*

The state that gives rise to such questions is often one of letting go and nonattachment. With nothing left to protect or expect, we often return to our deepest feelings of love, gratitude, and compassion.

You may recall in your youth feeling full of hope for your life and perceiving a lack of such idealism among some older adults. Perhaps it seemed as if others settled too easily. Did you ever vow that you would never give up on your deepest dreams? Have you kept your promise? The end-of-life perspective can help you assess whether important dreams and values have fallen by the wayside.

Our everyday consciousness or "ego" tends to be preoccupied with looking ahead, solving problems, being in control, and knowing for sure. Although these are valuable functions, many of the most memorable moments in your life have likely come in situations involving love, loss, death, birth, sex, and risk—situations that are inherent opposites of your ego's daily concerns for control and predictability. A brush with death, either in fact or in thought, knocks your ego off stride. In such moments, you may have a deep recognition that the person you thought you were won't always be here. Your ego doesn't have a snappy comeback to that. Your ego assumes that it is "you" and that you will last forever. When your ego's hold loosens, even momentarily, you have an opening in which to create life-changing experiences. An end-of-life consciousness is something you can create by design, even if only for a few moments.

People who are looking back over their lives list some of the following experiences as what they have cherished most. As you read this list, you might think of what you cherish most about your life.

- Having loving and nurturing connections with other people

- Creating a family and sense of community, however you define it

- Having a special, loving relationship with another person

- Pursuing your deepest passions

- Expressing yourself through activities that are most important to you

- Contributing to others and to the world

- Accepting, loving, and making peace with yourself

Life Is an Open-book Exam

You have probably known or heard of people who have neared the end of their lives and realized that they had largely lived untrue to themselves or their values. You can avoid this fate. Despite the mystery, unpredictability, and difficulty of existence, your life is an open-book exam.

You may recall in school taking an open-book exam in which you were given the questions, then allowed to look through your textbooks to find the answers. No studying was required, and all the answers were there. It is possible for everyone in the class to get an A on an open-book exam.

You may be decades away from your death, but I suggest that you likely already know what will have mattered most to you when you near the end of your life. If you don't know or aren't sure, temporarily adopting an end-of-life perspective when thinking about the nine questions that follow in this chapter may help you crystallize what matters most to you.

Take a few moments to ponder the first three questions. If you like, write your thoughts in the space provided or on a sheet of paper. Or you may want to share these questions with a loved one and both answer together. These are simple questions but they can bring surprisingly powerful insights and feelings, particularly if you take time to give more than superficial answers.

- How satisfied are you with the way your life has unfolded?

- What, if anything, do you regret?

- What do you still want to accomplish and experience?

Your answers to these questions may reflect some of your deepest values. As you think about your level of satisfaction, regrets, and remaining priorities, do any of your answers surprise, concern, sadden, or lighten you? You may want to give yourself additional time to think about these questions, either now or later.

Here are how two people I interviewed answered these questions:

Charlene, a twenty-nine-year-old marketing director, admits, "I'm not very satisfied. Seems like I've blitzed through friendships and relationships in my twenties with little to show for it. I've got plenty of people I can call to go to a concert, show, or exhibit, but when I'm home sick with the flu I can't think of a single friend I'd call and ask if they would drop by with some chicken soup."

Charlene regrets valuing novelty and adventure over depth in her friendships. What she still hopes to accomplish and experience: "I'd like to meet someone who'll see me as I really am. I'd like to marry and have children."

Kate, a fifty-five-year-old interior designer, says, "I'm mostly satisfied, but I've been worrying lately about my father." Growing up, Kate had a contentious relationship with her alcoholic father. In the past two decades, she's had only perfunctory contact with him through holiday cards and occasional phone calls. Those contacts were often upsetting and reminded her why she had chosen to distance herself. Since her father developed emphysema, Kate is facing new feelings.

"It seems like my thirties and forties whizzed by. It's as if, while I wasn't looking, my parents turned into old people. I thought they'd be here forever. I wish I had asked my dad back when he was healthier, and when he was sober, about his days as a boy, in the war, and in the depression," Kate says. With her parents' mortality in sight, Kate has begun to think about the things she'd like to say to them, ask them, and give them.

Now take a moment and ponder three more questions. Again, take your time and write down your answers.

- What do you cherish most in your present life?

- What experiences and accomplishments have you treasured?

- When do you feel most true to yourself?

Here are how two people answered:

Lane, a forty-year-old artist and mother of two, says that she has most cherished nursing her children through the normal illnesses of childhood and helping them solve school and social dilemmas. "They were so helpless as sick kids, and they were so trusting of me for the right advice," she says.

Her most treasured accomplishments include raising her children, having a loving marriage, and selling her paintings. Lane says she feels most true to herself when she is painting or on family vacations.

Brett, a fifty-five-year-old physical education teacher, says that some of his most cherished experiences have been when former students drop by and thank him for his "drill-sergeant-with-heart" approach to teaching. "One former student, now in his late thirties, told me that most friends his age have knee injuries and can't run anymore, whereas he had just finished his third marathon. He said that the way I pounded into those kids' heads the importance of warm-ups and stretching is probably what has kept him injury-free," Brett recalls.

Brett also says that being at his father's side, holding his hand when he died following a battle with heart disease, was one of his most cherished moments. Brett says he feels most true to himself when he is working out, sitting next to his wife on the porch swing, or doing things to help his aging mother.

Now take a few moments and ponder the final three questions:

- What would give your life the greatest sense of completion before you die?

- What would you most want to say or do with your loved ones before you die?

- What do you want to leave behind of yourself?

Take a few moments and review all nine of your answers from this chapter. You may also want to review the admired and wished-for personal qualities you identified in the previous chapter. Consider how much of your time, will, and energy you spend in accord with these precious values and standards. If you see that your daily routine doesn't reflect and support your core values and standards, you've received a priceless wake-up call. Rather than feel shame or hopelessness, take heart. By discovering what you are doing that gets in the way of having what you most cherish, you can change course. The more precisely you know what you want for tomorrow, the more efficiently you can adjust your life today.

In *It's a Wonderful Life*, actor Jimmy Stewart's character, George Bailey, depressed and considering suicide, is granted a fantasy look at how his home town of Bedford Falls would have turned out for the worse had he not been a part of it. In your wonderful life, you can take a similar eye-opening journey. At any moment, no matter what your age, you can assess your life with the powerful perspective of someone looking back from life's end. You can know the questions you're likely to ponder on your deathbed, a time when you no longer need to hide or protect anything. Your answers to this chapter's questions may shed light on what matters most to you. These are the values that light up your heart.

18

DECODING THE LANGUAGES OF YOUR MIND, BODY, AND HEART

The heart has its reasons which reason knows not of.

—BLAISE PASCAL

Feeling is what you get for thinking the way you do.

—MARILYN VOS SAVANT

I don't let my mouth say nothin' my head can't stand.

—LOUIS ARMSTRONG

The last vacation that Rachel, a thirty-three-year-old writer, allowed herself was a three-day weekend in the mountains five years ago. She writes six days a week; her "day off" is used to catch up with laundry, bills, and shopping. She works out at a gym every day but derives little joy or relaxation from her routine. Two months ago, she began developing painful stomach aches but has yet to see a doctor. Recently, after watching a touching greeting-card commercial, she burst into tears and wept for ten minutes.

In the *Wizard of Oz*, the Scarecrow, lacking a brain, couldn't think. The Tin Man, without a heart, couldn't feel. The Lion, lacking courage, couldn't act. Despite their deficits, working as a team they charmed and rescued Dorothy and Toto, too.

You have within you what each individual in the trio of Oz lacked: a team consisting of a thinker, doer, and feeler. When your mental, physical, and emotional selves work as a team, your life flows. When your mind, body, and heart work at cross purposes, as when you overreact or give over to negative inner characters, you lack a healthy balance.

Your mind, body, and heart—shorthand for your mental, physical, and emotional selves—are the DNA of your daily experience. I use the terms *mind, body,* and *heart* as constructs. Distinguishing between mental, physical, and emotional functions is a self-awareness tool similar to the inner cast of characters, Subterranean Accountant, and personal Defense Department. In the heat of battle and the rush of everyday, a quick check-in with your mind, body, and heart can help you:

1. Recognize when you're living out of balance and identify how to restore healthy balance
2. Clarify confusing situations and generate effective responses
3. Achieve optimal well-being

Mind, body, and heart have disparate roles. Our minds seek to explain, create, and control. Our bodies seek to experience, accomplish, and grow. Our hearts seek to attach, give, and feel. The following chart illustrates:

Mind, Body, and Heart	
	What each includes
Mind	Thoughts, attitudes, goals, self-talk, self-image, and your relationship with yourself
Body	Physical self, sensations, physiological processes, behaviors, and your relationship to the outside world
Heart	Emotions, moods, intuitions, hopes, passions, and your relationships with others

Sometimes your mind, body, and heart work together, one for all and all for one, as with the Three Musketeers. Other times, given the different natures of the mind, body, and heart, they function more like the Three Stooges.

What Happens When Your Mind, Body, and Heart Work at Cross-purposes

Problems arise when your mind, body, or heart:

- Hijacks the others or bosses them around
- Feels left out or ignored
- Gets confused about its identity
- Forgets that it's interdependent

Have you ever tried unsuccessfully to remember where you put something only to recall its location once you stopped thinking about it and did something else? Have you ever felt negatively toward someone, then had a heart-to-heart talk and found your judgments giving way to genuine affection? These are examples of your mind, body, and heart's synergy.

Your mind, body, and heart are interconnected, as the late twentieth-century scientific revolution in psychoneuroimmunology demonstrated. A change in any one of the three affects the other two. We know, for example, that a positive change in beliefs can lead to reduced depression and healthier behavior. This is news you can use. When you feel depressed or pessimistic, reality-testing your thinking as we did in chapter 14 can replace hopelessness with hope. Feeling hopeful can spark new perspectives and push aside a depressed mind-set. As depression lifts, lethargy evaporates. You do more and feel happier. Your mind, body, and heart are working as a team.

Much of your mind, body, and heart synergy is innate. For example, if you're emotionally upset, crying emits tears, which carry away ACTH, a substance that increases the stress hormone cortisol. A drop in ACTH leads to a drop in stress hormones. That is why you often feel better after a "good cry." Similarly, when you feel anxious, you may pace, rock, or drum your fingers. Research has found that such rhythmic movements can release chemicals that soothe the mind and calm the body. Knee-bouncing, foot-tapping, knitting, or rocking can increase serotonin, the "feel good" neurochemical that antidepressants like Prozac make more available in your brain.

This mind-body-heart synergy can work for or against you. If you're a competitive, type A personality, when you win a game of racquetball, your sense of self may expand, your confidence will soar, and your mood may become pleasantly fluid. If you are male, you may even experience a temporary rise in testosterone levels, further elevating your mood. Lose the match, however, and you may doubt yourself, become cranky, and be bathed in down-regulating hormones that lead to moodiness.

Your natural synergy is disrupted, for example, when your mind tries to rule your heart. You've probably met people who seem removed from their feelings, talking about themselves in the second person or discussing emotional events in stilted tones. In such cases, the mind is working overtime to prevent experiencing emotions. There is a balance between tempering emotions and muffling them, and the mind doesn't always strike the right balance.

Adrianne feels increasingly frustrated about her meddling in-laws but has yet to talk about it with her husband. Instead, she tries to ignore her frustration and dismiss her concerns as unkind and unfair.

Deny the heart its feelings and they may surface in other forms. "When we ignore a part of ourselves, it is irritated with us, just as we are irritated when someone we know ignores us," wrote therapist Martha Baldwin. You may lash out at others, act irrationally, or get injured. You may obsess ceaselessly, further increasing your frustration. Unable to gain clarity, your mind may get personal. Your inner critic may snarl, as in Adrianne's case, "What's wrong with you?" and your self-confidence tanks. Or perhaps you blame someone else, spreading your frustration.

It's important to listen to and understand your feelings. When you misinterpret emotions, you're at odds with yourself. For example, irritability is a common feeling, but it can mask such feelings as depression, aggression, sadness, and fear. Thinking that you're irritable when the problem is deeper may prolong your pain. Such emotional confusion tends to be particularly true for men. From an early age, boys are reinforced for having two or three emotional responses—primarily competitiveness, aggression, and withdrawal—as Dan Kindlon and Michael Thomson wrote in *Raising Cain: Protecting the Emotional Life of Boys*. Girls, by contrast, are encouraged a wider range of emotional expression. It is as if girls are given the sixty-four-color box of emotional crayons while boys are handed three primary colors. By adulthood it can be difficult for some men to be as emotionally literate as women.

Recognizing When You're
Living out of Balance

We hear others use the term "out of body" or "out of his mind," but how often do you recognize it when you are "out of heart" and numb to or unaware of what you are feeling? When you don't consult your body to recognize the physical cues that come with emotions, or when you let your mind ignore or mislabel your feelings, you risk falling out of heart.

One way to return to heart is to notice feelings without trying to do anything about them. Your mind and body can provide clues to help you clarify your feelings. Check in with your body. Where do you feel tense or clenched? How is your breathing? Do you feel hot or cold? These can all be cues to emotional responses.

Your mind, body, and heart, like the three branches of U.S. government, offer checks and balances to keep you healthy. Your well-being depends on how well you listen to and nourish each. An ignored mental, physical, or emotional life will make itself known in progressively more dire terms. Your mind may ruminate obsessively. Your body may ache or fall ill. Your heart may race with panic attacks.

The following table illustrates the possible effects of ignoring an aspect of yourself:

Imbalance Among Mind, Body, and Heart	
	Signs that you're out of balance
Mind	Ruminating, distractibility, racing thoughts, persistent confusion, excessive cynicism, or harsh self-criticism
Body	Pain, fatigue, numbness, tension, or lack of body awareness
Heart	Emotional volatility, emotional flatness, depression, or anxiety

A lack of balance is costly. For example, if you are taking care of a parent, children, and a number of people at your job while also running a busy household, you may eventually feel burned out, overwhelmed, and deprived. Such feelings can alert you to identify what is out of balance.

Mentally, you've lost perspective. Remember, nobody can give endlessly or give without also sometimes being given to. Physically, you're overworked. None of us can function without taking time to recharge. Emotionally, you've become lopsided. Although you are expressing great love for others, you have dropped the ball on treating yourself lovingly.

One solution would be to take a day and gratify yourself. Arrange for someone to cover for you. Drop your *shoulds*. Do whatever you feel like in the moment. If you're tired, give over to sleep completely. If you're hungry, eat ravenously. Play. Do nothing. By gratifying your basic needs in the moment without hesitating or second-guessing, you can counteract habits and situations that sapped your energy.

Think of your mind, body, and heart as gifted children. You're the parent. Each of your children deserves all the compassion you can offer. As you would with a gifted child, offer your mind, body, and heart adventures uniquely suited to each. From time to time, tune in and let each have what it wants and needs. If your body wants to run, rest, eat, or float, let it. If your mind wants to fantasize, analyze, do crosswords, daydream, or tell jokes, let it. If your heart wants to socialize, be alone, cry, laugh, hurt, or soar, let it.

Self-awareness Tool #6:
Check In with Your "Children"

As parent to your mind, body, and heart, take a moment and ask yourself: Which of my children most needs attention right now? What do my mind, body, and heart need? Caretaking? Soothing? To be heard? What specifically could I do to fulfill each inner yearning?

Clarifying Confusing Situations
and Generating Effective Responses

Your mind, body, and heart are expert consultants available to you 24/7. For example, let's say you feel frustrated and don't know why. Your mind, body, and heart each have resources and perspectives to offer.

- *Consultant #1: Your mind.* You could turn your feelings of frustration over to your mind. Your mind knows the questions to ask that will make sense of frustration. For example: When did the problem start? What events are tied to it? How have you handled similar frustrations in the past? When you see the connections and chronology, the source of your frustration can crystallize and you can respond.

- *Consultant #2: Your body.* You could hand your frustration over to your body. Frustration may result from thwarted desires, blocked energy, or lack of action. If you feel pent-up frustration, get your body moving. Work out or go for a walk. Or tune in to your body in a quieter way: sit, rest, meditate, breathe deeply, or notice where you feel tense or clenched. If the frustration results because action is needed, your body can swing into action: speaking your piece, righting wrongs, and moving on.

- *Consultant #3: Your heart.* You could take your frustration back to its source: your heart. Ask your body and mind to stand down. Stop wondering *why* you feel as you do or what you should *do* about it. Just honor the feeling. If you sit with your frustration and observe it, your frustration will eventually deepen (which can spark insights or motivate you to act), ease, or give way to other feelings.

Sometimes the initial answer each consultant offers may not be the best one. For example, if you are lonely and your heart feels deprived, your body may try to help by doing what your body does when it feels deprived: eat. The problem is you end up with "emotional eating," a body solution to a heart problem. Your heart is indeed hungry, but what would feed it is emotional expression, not consumption. Ask yourself if there are more positive things the body could do to help. Exercising, taking a nap or a walk, writing in your journal, or seeing a heart-warming movie are all healthier alternatives than emotional eating.

Achieving Optimal Well-being

Healing expert Naomi Remen poses the question of how your life would be different if your body was unable to heal from physical wounds. For some, this is reality. People with illnesses like hemophilia or "brittle bone" disease know that making a mistake while slicing an apple or walking down stairs could kill them. Can you imagine how your life would change if you faced such an illness?

The deeper point Remen makes is that, although we normally take for granted our ability to heal physically, we may treat ourselves as emotional or mental hemophiliacs. We think our fears can kill us. We assume that we don't have what it takes to recover from loss—that our hearts and minds don't possess the same natural ability to heal as do our bodies.

You give yourself a profound vote of lack of confidence when you try to avoid loss because you think you can't handle it or recover from it. When you live in fear of your own feelings and thoughts, you tell yourself, *I'm insufficient*. This leaves you scrambling to reduce risks, change circumstances, deny or skirt around facts, and substitute losses. This is no way to live. You have the ability to heal and strengthen your heart and mind as well as your body. The model of physical fitness can be applied to mental and emotional fitness as well.

Just as failing to exercise or stretch can injure your muscles or cause atrophy, blocking or ignoring your feelings can weaken your emotional muscles. Just as repeating a painful movement can injure tendons or joints, repeating painful thought patterns can injure your mental health.

Emotional and mental fitness are achieved, as is physical fitness. Few of us would question that to run a marathon we'd have to start slowly and train extensively. When strong emotions arise, however, we think that we should be able to handle them with the facility we have for our tiniest feelings. It doesn't work that way. You increase your capacity to tolerate intense emotions by taking the opportunity to experience the smaller feelings that come along.

We often view our emotions as static objects—things that fill an internal reservoir and at a certain point we flush out. If you choke down your feelings or save them for later, you are forfeiting an opportunity to grow. In addition, it's insulting to your heart to keep feelings locked up, letting them out only when you can't hold any more.

In physical workouts, you build conditioning by interval training in which you vary your exertion level. Similarly, from time to time, push your mental and emotional envelope. Seek experiences that you have historically avoided. Instead of sticking with familiar styles of literature, art, and music, expose yourself to those about which you "haven't a clue" and notice your thoughts and reactions. Consider new viewpoints and perspectives, particularly ones you wouldn't normally consider. Approach underdeveloped emotional areas as if you were building up your abs. It may take time. Neither physical nor emotional muscles tone overnight.

In the relationship realm, look for lopsided areas. Are you relationally muscle-bound in terms of keeping your distance? Perhaps it's time to work on intimacy and vulnerability. Conversely, do you focus on pleasing others at your own expense? Balance the scales by taking more time for yourself.

As with any exercise program, it may initially feel awkward. Your mental or emotional "muscles" may feel a little sore. We expect this with a physical workout. If you feel mentally tired or emotionally sore, instead of taking this as a sign that you've done something wrong, it may just be that you've exercised your mind and heart.

You are given a mind. Expand it. You are given a body. Strengthen it. You are given a heart. Express it.

If You'd Like To Go Deeper: Learning the Languages of Your Mind, Body, and Heart

The following questions can deepen your awareness of your mental, physical, and emotional lives.

1. Among your mind, body, and heart, which:

   • Do you most identify with?

   • Is least utilized?

   • Is overused?

   • Is most undiscovered?

   • Is least nourished?

2. How well do you trust your mind? Body? Heart?

3. Do you feel confused or betrayed by one or more?

4. How well do your mind, body, and heart each trust you?

5. If trust is lacking in either direction, how might you reestablish it?

Summary of Part Four: Unearthing the Treasures You Keep from Yourself

1. Fear and denial, through your inner characters and Subterranean Accountant, tend to obscure your desires and values. Don't let them.

2. You can move beyond fear by identifying the core desires that match your fears and then pursuing those desires.

3. Selective self-acceptance tends to be self-defeating. Get to know and embrace as many aspects of yourself as you can.

4. You can either focus on survival and try to reduce life's risks, or focus on growth and empower yourself to face life's risks.

5. Whether you acknowledge it or not, you're innately worthy and able regardless of external factors.

6. When you feel powerless or undeserving, remember who holds the power to convince you of that.

7. To know what matters and to live based on it, use these tools:

   • Assess your choices and values with an end-of-life perspective.

   • Consult your three gifted children: your mind, body, and heart.

◆

Triumphing over Challenges and Adversity

If you don't break your ropes while you're alive,
do you think
ghosts will do it after?

—KABIR

Part Five will put everything we've covered to practical use. You'll learn several ways to enhance your balance and perspective, increase your motivation, and triumph over a wide range of challenges.

19

WHAT TO DO WHEN YOU'RE STUCK

We made too many wrong mistakes.

—YOGI BERRA

When you feel overwhelmed, confused, or uncertain, it helps to have a surefire way to anchor yourself. Here are seven ways to cut problems to manageable size:

1. Be specific: Describe *when, where,* and *how* the problem occurs.

2. Be precise: Identify the *conflict* that makes it a problem.

3. Be honest: Acknowledge *hidden* or *conflicting* priorities.

4. Be thorough: Articulate any problems *underneath* the obvious problem.

5. Be concrete: Identify the *direction* of change needed.

6. Be complete: Search for *mind, body,* and *heart* elements.

7. Be introspective: Use emotional distress as a *road map,* not a stop sign.

As you read on, you might keep in mind a challenge you are facing and try one or more of these approaches to see how you can cut your challenge down to size.

Be Specific

Describe when, where, and how the problem occurs

Begin by picking one specific instance of the problem. Notice or recall in as much detail as possible what happened. What did you think, do, and feel? What did others say or do? When did the problem begin? What triggered it? What was your most distressing thought or biggest concern?

For example, let's say you feel lonely. If you define your problem as *I feel lonely*, you have a huge problem: you are lonely, all the time, everywhere. Try to be more specific. Ask yourself: When are you most lonely? What are you lonely for? What are the thoughts and feelings that go with loneliness? On which days of the week are you most and least lonely? Are there times you don't feel lonely?

Perhaps you distill your problem to *I'm lonely, especially on Sunday afternoons, and would like to be with a group of people.* This is a more manageable problem. The solution: find activities on Sunday afternoons that put you in contact with others.

On the other hand, if you defined your problem as *I'm lonely a lot of the time and I miss my husband who died*, your solutions are different. Letting yourself mourn, talking with trusted friends, and perhaps seeing a counselor may be helpful. Immersing yourself in a Sunday afternoon group activity, by contrast, might even make you feel more lonely.

Be Precise

Identify the conflict that makes it a problem

Problems exist in conjunction, not isolation. A feeling or thought by itself isn't a problem. Take the statement, *I'm unhappy in my job.* That may be true, but it's not the whole story. When you thoroughly describe a problem you'll usually articulate a conflict with at least one "but" or "and." For example: *I'm unhappy in my job BUT I need to earn money AND I don't feel qualified for any other job, the job market is tight, and I don't want to relocate.*

Problems are unsettled conflicts. Identifying the "but" or "and" clauses clarifies what is at conflict. In the example above, the conflict is between sacrificing income to be happier versus sacrificing happiness to maintain your income.

Once you've clarified the conflict, take each conjunctive clause one at a time. Assess the importance each part plays in the bigger problem. Then think of possible solutions to that part. For example:

Clause #1: I'm unhappy in my job. If you are unhappy at work, is there anything you can do to make it more palatable? Is there a specific situation at work that, if addressed, would increase your happiness?

Clause #2: BUT I need to earn money. What other sources of income can you tap? Do you have opportunities you aren't pursuing? Can you trim spending?

Clause #3: AND I don't feel qualified for any other job, the job market is tight, and I don't want to relocate. Are your concerns about your qualifications and the job market accurate? What could you do to increase your qualifications? How do the financial and emotional costs of relocating compare with the price you'll pay if you stay put and remain unhappy?

Be Honest

Acknowledge hidden or conflicting priorities

When you have a goal that is not being achieved, you may have conflicting priorities that you're unaware of or not acknowledging. Consciously or not, you are always setting priorities. Denial obscures your priorities.

For example, suppose your mate complains that you work too much. You respond, "But we need the money." On further reflection you realize that, although more money could make your life more comfortable, it's a want, not a need. Perhaps the truth is that you work long hours because you love your job. Or perhaps you work long hours to avoid a dissatisfying home life. Whatever the reason, not acknowledging the truth will leave you and your mate shadowboxing. The problem isn't lack of money. The problem is that in your hierarchy of priorities work is higher than spending time with your mate while your mate's hierarchy of priorities is the opposite.

Sometimes priorities are obvious. If you're stranded without food, you may be uncomfortable, but you won't have a life-threatening problem for several days. If you're without water, you have no more than two or three days to get it. But if you're without air, then water and food are unimportant. You have two or three minutes to live unless you find oxygen.

In everyday problems, your hierarchy of priorities may be less obvious than with air, water, and food. However, once you clarify the priorities in conflict and identify which among them you value most highly, solutions may naturally suggest themselves.

Be Thorough

Articulate any problem underneath the obvious problem

The more thoroughly you identify the heart of any problem, the more satisfied you are likely to be with the solution. When you identify only part of a problem or focus just on a symptom, you may generate ineffective solutions.

For example, if you are perpetually late to work, is being late the core problem? If it is, there are numerous ways you can motivate yourself to get to work on time. But being late to work may be a symptom of a deeper problem. Perhaps you dislike your job, are anxious about your performance, or hate feeling pressured but are afraid to protest this directly. Each of these problems has different solutions. Getting to work on time won't solve any of them.

You may not know what the core problem is until you address some of the problems that stem from it. Look for underlying issues. Ask yourself, "What's the problem?" and "Why is that a problem?" Keep asking until you get to the core.

Chuck, fifty-four, has been in recovery from alcoholism for ten years. He took his first drink at age sixteen to soothe his loneliness and escape his abusive family situation. At age forty-four he went to Alcoholics Anonymous, sought therapy, and devoted his energies to a one-day-at-a-time fight against the urge to drink. His central focus became his recovery from alcoholism. With time, he was successful. His drinking-related problems ceased and the quality of his life improved.

About six years into his recovery, Chuck admitted that he had another addiction. He was obsessed with sex, often visiting X-rated massage parlors. He sought therapy and attended another twelve-step program, Sex- and Love-Addicts Anonymous. He restrained his sexual compulsions and once again saw an improvement in his quality of life.

Three years later, Chuck faced a stunning realization. The heart of his problem was not drinking or sexual compulsions, it was escapism.

Even as a child, Chuck had spent most of his days "checked out," doing anything to avoid being present to the pains of daily life. Although Chuck overcame his drinking and sexual compulsions, he still engaged in other behaviors to avoid being present, for example compulsively talking, fantasizing, surfing the Web, or watching television.

When the problem was defined as alcoholism, the solution was not to drink. Chuck solved that problem. When the problem was defined as sexual compulsions, the solution was to bring balance to his sexual life. Chuck solved that problem. In both cases, he reaped benefits from creating a sober and more responsible lifestyle. Recognizing the problem underneath both addictions led Chuck to redefine his challenge as that of conquering his escapism. To overcome escapism, Chuck set a goal of being present to the here and now, whatever it may bring, as well as not using alcohol or sex to escape. That has opened the way for Chuck to be happier than ever.

An evolution like Chuck's is common. By solving one problem, you may see an underlying issue.

Useful questions to point you toward the heart of a problem include:

- What do I spend the most time worrying about?
- What takes the most energy or upsets me the most?
- What one thing would I change about my life?

Be Concrete

Identify the direction of change needed

The world is three-dimensional, but problems tend to be two-dimensional. Problems generally involve either *excess* or *scarcity*. For example, you have either too much or too little, you're too close or too far, or it's too soon or too late. When you identify the excess or scarcity, you identify the direction of change needed to solve your problem. You have a clear yardstick by which to measure potential solutions.

For example, when your thoughts, feelings, or events have gone too far in one direction, one solution is to move back toward center. If you feel flighty, seek to ground yourself. If you're weighed down, let some burdens go. If you feel crowded, seek solitude. If you feel lonely, seek companionship. If you're bored, find something worth doing. If you have too much time on your hands, take on some compelling, worthwhile activities. If you are overwhelmed with too much to do, eliminate one or more of your least-compelling or least-worthwhile regular activities.

When you feel stressed, determine what is out of balance. Too many demands? Not enough pleasurable activities? An impending event? A long absence of your partner? Each of these imbalances has a different remedy.

Be Complete

Search for mind, body, and heart elements

Problems are collections of thoughts, circumstances, and feelings. For example, let's say that you are concerned about your weight. Identify the thoughts, circumstances, and feelings that concern you. Perhaps you think *I'm unattractive* or *I have no discipline.* Perhaps your weight is diminishing your health or keeping you from activities you love. Perhaps you feel frustrated, hopeless, or deprived.

Ask yourself whether your problem is primarily an *attitude, external situation,* or *feeling.* Determine which component—thoughts, circumstances, or feelings—is most painful. In so doing, you clarify whether the needed solution will be aimed at changing attitudes, situations, or feelings.

In the example of *I'm unhappy with my weight* you'd want to determine what is most pressing:

1. Your self-criticism and concerns about how others might view you? (Attitude)

2. The physical limitations imposed by your weight? (Situation)

3. Your feelings of unhappiness? (Feeling)

Which of the these components would make the biggest difference if it changed? If your weight stayed the same but you accepted and stopped judging yourself, would that solve or ease the problem? If your weight stayed the same and you still had negative thoughts but you learned not to feel as upset, would that be a viable solution? Or would actually changing your weight be the most rewarding solution?

Sometimes your thoughts, behaviors, and feelings may be in such turmoil that *each* could be seen as the primary problem. In such cases, pick one place to start: mind, body, or heart. It doesn't matter which, since they're interconnected.

Be Introspective

Use emotional distress as a road map, not a stop sign

The personal challenges that most concern us tend to be those which diminish our sense of self. Emotional distress tends to result from one or more of five dilemmas. You feel:

- *Stuck* and unable to motivate yourself, initiate action, or escape

- *Confused* about what the problem is or how to solve it

- *Overwhelmed* by too many or excessively intense thoughts, circumstances, or feelings

- *Underwhelmed* by a lack of desire, options, knowledge, awareness, or resources

- *Torn* by competing desires, choices, or priorities

Keeping this S-C-O-U-T framework in mind is an easy way to remind yourself to "scout" the nature of challenges. You might take a moment and think of a problem or concern in your present life. Which of these five forms of distress is present? Which best characterizes the heart of your problem? By identifying the nature of your distress, you orient yourself toward applicable solutions. For example, if you're stuck, you may need perspectives and actions that will get you moving. If you're confused, you need clarity before acting. If you're overwhelmed, you need to slow down and seek less stimulation. If you're underwhelmed, you need to tune in to find ways to bolster or expand your desires, options, or resources. If you're torn, you need to fully and carefully weigh both sides.

The following table illustrates these seven approaches to defining problems.

Cutting Problems Down to Size

Approach	What to do	Result
Be specific: Describe when, where, and how the problem occurs	• Pick a specific instance of the problem • Dissect that instance for the nub of the problem	Makes the problem finite
Be precise: Identify the conflict that makes it a problem	• Describe the problem fully, then take each conjunctive clause and brainstorm solutions • Weigh the pros and cons of each solution	Highlights the central conflict that needs resolution
Be honest: Acknowledge hidden or conflicting priorities	• Assess all relevant priorities • Act based on your highest priorities or change priorities	Clarifies your hierarchy of priorities
Be thorough: Articulate any problems underneath the obvious problem	• Search for underlying issues • Choose a solution aimed at the deepest aspect of the problem	Focuses on the heart of the problem not just its symptoms
Be concrete: Identify the direction of change needed	• Address the imbalance by increasing or decreasing amount, distance, size, pace, etc.	Provides a yardstick for measuring success
Be complete: Search for mind, body, and heart elements	• Decide whether a change in attitude, circumstance, or feeling would make the biggest difference	Identifies the nature of the solution needed

Approach	What to do	Result
Be introspective: Use emotional distress as a road map, not a stop sign	• Determine whether your predominant concern is that of feeling stuck, confused, overwhelmed, underwhelmed, or torn • Fashion a solution aimed primarily at getting unstuck, finding clarity, regaining perspective, increasing initiative, or resolving a dilemma	Highlights the key concern your solution must address

Here are some examples of how you can use these approaches with life challenges.

Audrey: "I Get Distracted So Easily"

Audrey finds it hard to stay focused on conversations for more than a few minutes before her attention wanders. At work, she takes a half-dozen coffee breaks a day. Audrey feels bewildered and defensive and wonders if something is wrong with her.

Be Specific: Describe When, Where, and How the Problem Occurs

Audrey needs to recall one or more specific situations in which she was most distracted and then search for patterns. For example, does her attention tend to wander more in the morning, afternoon, or evening? Does she feel most distractible in work situations, during conversations with friends or family, while interacting with strangers, or when she is alone? Does she become more distractible when she is hungry, tired, or stressed? Has she always had this problem or did it develop recently? Are there situations in which she rarely gets distracted?

If Audrey notices situations in which she rarely gets distracted, she would want to determine what is unique about these situations. If she doesn't get distracted when she is doing a favorite activity, that might suggest that her distractibility is stress-related, since it goes away when she feels relaxed, happy, or confident. On the other hand, if she has always been distractible and finds few situations in which she does not get distracted, this might suggest an overarching condition, possibly with a physiological basis as in attention deficit disorder. In such a case, she would want to consult a physician.

If Audrey finds that she is most distractible when she is tired, hungry, or stressed, her wandering focus may be relatively normal. This knowledge could reassure her. One solution would be to pay more attention to eating, sleeping, and managing stress. In particular, she would want to prepare for important situations by being well fed and well rested.

Be Precise: Identify the Conflict That Makes It a Problem

By itself, distractibility isn't necessarily a problem. What makes it a problem for Audrey? Is she unable to recover once she gets distracted? Are her distractions so pleasant that she finds it difficult to return to reality? Or is Audrey's primary concern that others don't like it when she spaces out?

If she feels unable to stop herself from getting distracted, Audrey would be wise to pinpoint any contributing physiological factors and lifestyle habits.

If she doesn't want to let go of pleasurable distractions, Audrey might look for ways to increase pleasure and relaxation in her life. This could ease her unhappiness deficit and make it easier to stay focused when she needs to.

On the other hand, if the heart of her problem is others' reactions to her distractibility, then Audrey could speak candidly with her friends about her difficulties in maintaining focus so that they could understand her better and offer support.

Be Complete: Search for Mind, Body, and Heart Elements

Audrey could determine what bothers her most:

1. The attitudes and thought processes she generates when distracted

2. The actions she takes when distracted

3. The emotions that are kindled by being distracted

When her attention wanders, Audrey would want to notice whether her mind seems to drift or race. Does she feel happy, mellow, or hyper? What does she do about it? Does she engage in multiple activities or slow down and do little? Does she have a cigarette or caffeine, either of which could worsen her distractibility after their initial effects wear off?

If attitudes are her prime concern, she could identify the fear-thoughts or survival rules that are intruding. Then she could reality-test them and regain perspective.

If behavior is her prime concern, she could try behavior modification, for example by substituting a walk or meditation for coffee or cigarettes.

If emotions are her prime concern, she could pinpoint her core fears and transcend them.

Harold: "When Someone Close to Me Gets Upset, I Feel as if I Have to Fix It"

You may remember Harold and his wife, Maggie, from chapter 1. Harold found Maggie's emotions threatening and responded by trying to fix them, leaving Maggie feeling frustrated. Harold and Maggie could make their problem more manageable in several ways:

Be Thorough: Articulate any Problems Underneath the Obvious Problem

Troubling patterns in close relationships can stem from personal issues that date to childhood. Maggie is distressed by feeling not heard or seen by her husband. Her childhood with a disengaged father and hypercritical mother left her frequently feeling misunderstood or ignored. It isn't that Maggie doesn't want Harold to offer any solutions; in fact, at times his suggestions have been helpful. In recognizing this, Maggie could avoid dragging in older, deeper feelings that may be out of proportion to the situation at hand.

By the same token, Harold needs to acknowledge that the problem is not that Maggie is emotionally out of control but that he himself fears feeling out of control. Trying to hush Maggie with quick fixes will do nothing to conquer Harold's fear of losing control. Instead, perhaps with the help of a therapist, Harold could understand and work with the fears and needs that drive him to control emotions around him.

Be Concrete: Identify the Direction of Change Needed

Harold needs to determine what change would make the biggest difference. Does he desire less stress? More intimacy? Greater emotional stability? Though he may want all three, the paths to each are different. Pursuing greater intimacy may increase stress—at least at times. On the other hand, seeking greater stability may not necessarily include more intimacy. Couples who avoid talking about their problems may reduce their daily emotional ups and downs but lose aliveness and engagement in their connection.

For her part, Maggie needs to determine what change is most important to her. Does she want Harold to listen longer without rushing in? Understand her better? Display more compassionate behavior, by giving her hugs, for example? Once she determines what she wants, she can seek a solution for achieving that change.

Be Honest: Acknowledge Hidden or Conflicting Priorities

Harold needs to determine his priorities. Assuming he can't have both, which is more important: emotionally supporting Maggie or feeling less upset? If it's most important to feel less upset, Harold's best option may indeed be to pull back, at least temporarily, to avoid getting stressed out. If it's more important to support Maggie, Harold needs to realize that Maggie emotionally supports him in ways that may not be easy or comfortable for her. Seeing this may increase his motivation and willingness to support Maggie emotionally in the ways she needs even when it is stressful for him.

Angelica: "I'm Not Happy Even Though I've Achieved Much of What I Wanted"

Angelica is searching for meaning in her personal life. The fifty-one-year-old lawyer is successful, financially stable, and happy in her marriage, yet lacks a sense of purpose.

Angelica could:

Be Introspective: Use Emotional Distress as a Road Map, Not a Stop Sign

If Angelica were to SCOUT her problem, she'd most likely identify it as *underwhelm*. Angelica isn't troubled by what she has, she's troubled by what's missing. When you feel underwhelmed it often helps to return to your core desires. Achieving goals can be a hollow experience when you've lost touch with the guiding vision behind your goals. Angelica might think about what first motivated her to be a lawyer. Was it a desire for acclaim, power, or financial rewards? A desire to stretch her abilities or do something she loves? A desire to do something that matters or contribute to others?

By returning to her initial vision, Angelica could determine whether she has strayed from that vision. Perhaps Angelica needs to take on different kinds of legal cases or approach her job differently. Angelica could then capture the substance of her dreams, not just their form. Perhaps Angelica's ennui at the top of the professional ladder comes because she climbed the ladder based on a *should* or an attempt to please someone. Achieving life goals that don't come from your heart is generally unsatisfying. Angelica might ask herself whether she chose to be a lawyer primarily based on a love for the law or based on something else, maybe a desire to gain peer or family approval and respect. By honestly squaring her choices with her values, Angelica might discover that she yearns for a new career even if it means starting up a new ladder.

Be Concrete: Identify the Direction of Change Needed

When you lack meaningful goals and activities, you may inflate insignificant tasks or issues to keep busy. Perhaps Angelica's life has become too easy, lacking challenges. She may have lost sight of her unique abilities. She may need to rediscover her best self. In doing so, Angelica could become inspired by her capabilities and motivated to take on more meaningful challenges. It may also be that Angelica feels dissatisfied because she's not meeting her needs. When you have a deficit of self-nurturing, you may find it more difficult to derive meaning from even your favorite activities or relationships. Perhaps Angelica needs to increase her emotional self-care through activities that she loves.

A Reminder about Problem Solving

All solutions have advantages and disadvantages. Every solution brings losses and gains. Resist the urge to seek a solution guaranteed to avoid all loss. Following that urge may have led to the problem you're now facing.

20

CREATING WAKE-UP CALLS BY DESIGN

Don't be afraid to go out on a limb. That's where the fruit is.

—H. JACKSON BROWNE

When you're wrestling with a challenge and feel outmatched, it is generally because the challenge seems too big and/or your motivation and resources feel too little. The solution is to reverse the imbalance: cut your problems down to size, and enhance your motivation and sense of self.

This is an intuitive process. You've done it thousands of times in your life. Even so, it helps to have a reference guide when you're stuck, confused, or seeking a resource to increase your awareness. The following "Wake-up-call Generator," which covers the book's major points, can serve as just such a reference guide.

You can start anywhere. If the first point doesn't do it, pick another one. There is rarely only one way to solve problems. Think of the Wake-up-call Generator as a "break glass in case of emergency" resource or an "emergency rescue disc."

Wake-up-call Generator
Part 1: Recognize Signs of Self-sabotage

Are you experiencing any of the following:

☐ *Behavior that:*

- Seeks to solve a conflict with no loss whatsoever (p. 43)
- Is based on an unrealistic assessment of likely losses (p. 43)

- Is reactive, not chosen (p. 16)
- Arises from not seeing all your options (p. 16)

☐ *Inaccurate and negative self-definitions (p. 12)*

☐ *Any litmus-test behaviors of self-deception*

- Misleading, distracting, overpowering, or abandoning yourself (p. 32)

☐ *Negative influences of inner characters*

- Moviemaker, Indulger, Persuader, Dr. No, Mini-Me, Capt. Superior, Escape Artist, King Kong, and Dramateer (p. 79)

☐ *Animallike overreactions*

- Immobility, withdrawal, submission, or defensive aggression (p. 63)

☐ *Childlike reactions*

- Blaming, pretending, throwing a tantrum, hiding, or changing the subject (p. 68)

☐ *Self-handicapping fight-or-flight reactions*

- Confusing a thought, feeling, or situation with "you" and reacting as if your survival is at stake (p. 109)

☐ *Unhealthy attachment to expectations*

- Using expectations from one area of your life to make up for what is missing in other areas (p. 113)

☐ *Reactions or behavior based on the Subterranean Accountant's fuzzy math*

- Unquestioned but false assumptions (p. 56)
- Either-or thinking (p. 56)
- Exaggerating possible benefits while downplaying costs (p. 52)
- Self-undermining "win by losing" logic (p. 54)

☐ *Fear-thoughts or survival rules*

- Fear-thoughts: "What-if" worst-case scenarios (p. 129)
- Survival rules: "Or-else" assumptions you must follow (p. 129)

☐ *Usual suspects*

- Characteristic thoughts, behaviors, or feelings that are designed to camouflage, procrastinate, assuage guilt, preempt loss, feel bigger, or take the focus off you (p. 72)

☐ *Survival-based or growth-based living*

- *Survival-based:* Organizing your actions, feelings, and thoughts around anticipating, bargaining with, denying, rationalizing, avoiding, or escaping risk (p. 183)
- *Growth-based:* Building your resources, awareness, flexibility, and support systems so that you can face whatever comes up and grow from the process (p. 183)

☐ *Mind-body-heart imbalance in which your mind, body, or heart:*

- Hijacks its siblings or bosses them around (p. 209)
- Feels left out or ignored (p. 209)
- Gets confused about its identity (p. 209)
- Forgets that it's a member of a family (p. 209)

☐ *Signs of emotional distress*

- Stuck, confused, overwhelmed, underwhelmed, or torn (p. 225)

Part 2: Cut Challenges Down to Size

Do one or more of the following:

☐ *See through the Subterranean Accountant's bad math*

- Identify the Accountant's ill-founded but unquestioned rules and assumptions (p. 55)
- Identify the costs and benefits of your actions, then choose the best course (p. 58)

☐ *If you're emotionally over-attached, reevaluate what you define as "you" (p. 108)*

☐ *Calm your fight-or-flight reactions*

- Remember that you can transcend your animal origins with higher brain functions like perspective, reason, and reflection (p. 111)

☐ *Gain perspective about loss*

- Recognize any role played by developmental or existential issues (p. 116)
- Let go of the illusion that it's possible to avoid loss entirely (p. 43)

☐ *Challenge and dissolve denial*

- Notice potential benefits of your actions (p. 124)
- Notice what is being avoided or obscured by your actions (p. 124)

☐ *Remember the nature of fear*

- It is only one of many possible futures (p. 129)
- It highlights worst-case scenarios without regard to their likelihood (p. 128)
- It tends to diminish when you restart the mental movie and realize that what you dread will pass (p. 135)

☐ *Identify mind FITs*

- If you're assuming that a situation is *forever, innate,* or *total,* look for evidence of the situation's *temporary, external,* and *limited* nature (p. 131)

☐ *Challenge fear-thoughts and survival rules by asking yourself:*

- OK, if what I dread did occur, *then what?* (p. 136)
- What would it *mean* if what I fear took place? (p. 136)
- I must follow this rule *or else what?* (p. 136)

☐ *Look for core fears underlying the situation*

- Flawed, unworthy, empty, fragmented, weak, bad, out of control, trapped, alone, deprived, dominated, rejected, hurting, unsafe, and hurtful (p. 138)
- Remember that you've faced each of these fears before (p. 142)
- Recall how you have defeated the current fear in past situations (p. 142)

☐ *Observe how your core fears translate into action*

- Complete this statement: I am avoiding *(specific action or situation)* by *(method of avoidance)* because I don't want to feel *(core fear)* (p. 143)

☐ *Determine whether you're using counterproductive methods of avoiding core fears*

- For example, numbing out, overachieving, or denying your desires (p. 144)
- Then ask yourself, "How else might I respond?"

☐ *Demystify core fears by going beneath them*

- When weeding out fears, go for the roots by recognizing feelings driven by emotions from decades earlier (p. 162)
- Determine which of your feelings are based in the actual situation at hand and which arise more from a fear of loss, limitations, or not getting what you want (p. 112)
- Ask yourself, "What am I afraid that I lack and how can I supply it?" (p. 157)

☐ *Reality-test fears*

- Call fear's bluff by asking yourself:
  1. How likely is it that my actual, physical survival is at stake? (p. 159)
  2. What are my options for action? (p. 159)
  3. What have I done in similar situations in the past? (p. 159)
  4. What other outcomes are possible? (p. 159)

- Lay bare the contradictions inherent in fear (p. 160)
- Reality-test fear's assumptions (p. 160)
- Tackle fear's emotional reasoning (p. 161)
- Look beyond fear's oversimplifications (p. 161)
- Do the math: Weigh the pros and cons (p. 162)
- Consider fear's track record (p. 163)
- Ask proactive questions (p. 164)

☐ *Pick one or more ways to define the problem and cut it down to size*

- Be specific: Describe when, where, and how the problem occurs (p. 220)
- Be precise: Identify the conflict that makes it a problem (p. 220)
- Be honest: Acknowledge hidden or conflicting priorities (p. 221)
- Be thorough: Articulate any problems underneath the obvious problem (p. 222)
- Be concrete: Identify the direction of change needed (p. 223)

- Be complete: Search for mind, body, and heart elements (p. 224)
- Be introspective: Use emotional distress as a road map, not a stop sign (p. 225)

Part 3: Increase Your Motivation and Enhance Your Sense of Self

---

Do one or more of the following:

☐ *Remember your core desires and cherished values*

- The desire to feel valid, worthy, complete, whole, strong, good, stable, independent, connected, fulfilled, accepted, happy, safe, generous, and creative (p. 174)

☐ *Idenfity the core desires inherent in your behavior*

- I want (*result you're seeking*) and am trying to get it by (*your efforts or contemplated action*) because, more than anything, I value (*core desires or values*) (p. 178)

☐ *Identify the corresponding core desires inherent in your fears (p. 176)*

☐ *Choose actions based on core desires*

- I want (*core desire*) so I will seek (*specific result*) by (*actions to be taken*) (p. 178)
- Ask yourself, "If I were motivated by my desire rather than my fears, what would I do right now?" (p. 179)

☐ *When you recognize a core fear, look for the perceived deficit and remind yourself:*

- You're the one who says whether or not you're deficient (p. 195)
- You're the one who says whether you possess the ability to overcome deficits (p. 185)

☐ *Identify under-actualized desires*

- Ask yourself: What do I want but am convinced I cannot have, do, or be? (p. 173)

☐ *If you're struggling with limitations:*

- Remember that you have both limitations and potential (p. 184)
- Do the "Acknowledging your accomplishments" exercise (p. 196)

☐ *Identify and embrace hidden self aspects that may be influencing you*

- Qualities you dislike in others may be aspects of yourself that you are trying to hide, cast out, or fight (p. 188)
- Qualities you admire in others may indicate positive parts of yourself that you are unwittingly overlooking or downplaying (p. 190)

☐ *Determine what matters most*

- Review your "Life is an open-book exam" answers (p. 203)
- Consult your unique core desires (p. 174)
- Remember that you generally have several ways to solve problems (p. 226)

☐ *Seek balance through mind-body-heart teamwork*

- Improve mental and emotional fitness as well as physical (p. 213)
- Turn to each "consultant" for insight and advice (p. 212)

☐ *Remember:*

- You have the ability to define yourself at any time (p. 12)
- The extraordinary within (p. 23)
- Your thoughts and feelings are only part of you, not the whole of who you are (p. 186)
- You are CEO of your life (p. 187)

Let's see how to apply the Wake-up-call Generator in a range of challenging situations:

- A woman facing the dilemma of following her father's dream or finding her own path

- A couple fearing they are headed for the rocks because of increasing arguments

- A woman who gives so much to others that she has nothing to give herself

- A woman who lost her mother and lover and turned her grief inward, blaming herself

- A man struggling to get off the treadmill of his gambling addiction

Each example illustrates several possible ways to cut problems down to size, increase motivation, and enhance sense of self. There is rarely only one way to solve your problems. Recognizing that you have an abundance of possible solutions to your challenges can help you pursue growth-based living over survival-based loss-avoidance.

Pam: "Whose Dream Is It, Anyway?"

Pam, a twenty-seven-year-old investment-banker, has been on a financial fast track since age four when her dad taught her to read stock prices in the newspaper. "I remember how happy it made him once I learned to read the stock tables," Pam recalls. "My grandfather had lost everything in the stock market in the Depression just before my father was to go to college." As a result, her father worked as a butcher at the A&P for forty-five years before retiring.

Pam remembers visiting her father after school and seeing him tote huge slabs of beef on his back. Over the years her father suffered painful back problems and surgeries. During his working days, her father avidly followed the stock market and put what few discretionary dollars he had into stocks. By the time Pam finished high school, her father's investments were enough to pay for her college tuition.

"I don't know that I ever considered anything other than a career in the financial field," Pam says. "I think I decided at age four, looking at my father's pride in teaching me to read stock tables, that this was what he wanted me to do and this was what I would do. Knowing that his every dollar was saved to pay my tuition pretty much sealed my choice of a career." Pam majored in economics and earned an MBA.

In an unspoken, intergenerational pact, Pam picked up her father's own shattered dreams of college and a financial career and hefted them on her back much like the slabs of beef he carried. The problem is that Pam's heart has never been in finance. She feels diminished by many aspects of the male-dominated investment-banking culture and finds few opportunities to express her creativity.

As a girl, Pam loved to dance. If she could have chosen any career she would have been a dancer. She loves travel, art, and literature but says that finding kindred spirits among her fellow investment bankers is "as likely as finding ice cubes in the Sahara."

Pam is driven to excel and routinely works fourteen-hour days. She's usually too busy to think about her unhappiness, but her feelings have begun to intensify, especially on Sunday afternoons. "I'll be looking over reports for Monday morning, and I'll see people leaving Broadway matinees, having dinner, or strolling through the park. I think about how my weekend is already over and how I'll be at work within a few hours. My heart sinks," Pam says.

Pam feels trapped. She can't imagine easing back at work. At the same time, she fears her father would be devastated if she were to change careers.

How Pam Could Cut Her Problem Down to Size

Solution #1

When you feel trapped, it helps to inspect the trap. If you were caught in a physical trap, you'd look for the trap's mode of operation and weak points. When you're mentally or emotionally trapped, you free yourself in the same way. With mental and emotional traps, the weak points tend to be unfounded assumptions and overstated fears.

Pam keeps flashing on a mental image of telling her father she wants to change careers, seeing his crestfallen face, and then feeling like an ungrateful daughter. Her core fears are of feeling bad, hurtful, and unworthy. In reality, Pam's father never said he wanted her to go into finance. He put no conditions on how she used her college tuition. Nor has Pam ever explicitly asked her father if he had such feelings, In addition, despite her worry of being ungrateful, Pam is anything but ungrateful to her father. She has honored his sacrifice for her with sacrifices of her own. She needs to remind herself that, far from being a bad, ungrateful daughter, much of her reluctance to do what's best for her stems from the well-meaning sense of loyalty and love of a four-year-old daughter for her father.

At the very least, Pam owes it to herself to talk with her father about the subject. If she assumes that she knows what her father wants without finding out, she'll live her father's unlived dreams while forfeiting her own. That isn't in the best interests of either Pam or her father. (*Solution: Identify core fears and reality-test them.*)

Solution #2

Even if Pam's instincts are correct and her father would be upset if she were to change careers, what then? Pam is not allowing herself to go past the time-halting mental image of her father's disappointed look. In actuality, that moment would pass. Pam and her father would have many options and a great deal of time to work through their feelings. As time passed, feelings could change. *(Solution: Restart fear's frozen horror movie.)*

Solution #3

Pam might examine her assumptions. For example, is it really true that her father, no matter how much he is proud of her career choice, would want Pam to suffer? This doesn't add up. She could find many other ways to give to her father and show her love for him. *(Solution: Identify fuzzy math and recalculate it.)*

Solution #4

Pam has voiced a sobering realization: Out of her love and loyalty for her father, at least in part, she chose a career that has become a burden to her. The reluctance to take responsibility for this may be at the heart of her confusion. In retrospect, she has dishonored and hurt herself. *(Solution: Challenge denial and recognize self-inflicted wounds.)*

Solution #5

Pam faces disconcerting questions. Does she continue in investment banking knowing that it isn't what she wants? Does she muster the courage to consider a career change and face her father's disapproval when she breaks the news? Pam fears that her current day-in, day-out emptiness would be nothing compared to the disloyalty and guilt she would feel were she to disappoint her father. Yet she must risk something if she is to move on. *(Solution: Identify efforts to solve problems with no loss whatsoever.)*

Solution #6

By working as hard as she does, Pam distracts herself from facing the problem. By dismissing her musings when they surface, she tries to escape her disquieting realizations. In recognizing that her distracting and abandoning behaviors are not in her best interests, Pam could stay with these uncomfortable questions until she finds answers. *(Solution: Apply the litmus test for self-sabotage's four behaviors.)*

How Pam Could Increase Her Motivation and Enhance Her Sense of Self

Solution #1

Pam is cheating herself. She is so much in "do" mode that she rarely has time to be present, appreciate what is happening around her, or feel her emotions. She loves dance, theater, and literature but rarely savors these loves. Her body feels increasingly burdened, yet she ignores such warning signs as carpal tunnel syndrome from hours at the keyboard. In a sense, Pam didn't listen to her heart's desire about her career long ago. Now her body is increasingly sending her wake-up calls that she missed something. *(Solution: Use the mind-body-heart metaphor to clarify confusing situations.)*

Solution #2

In recognizing her lack of balance, Pam could devote her considerable self-discipline to building more body- and heart-nurturing activities into her life. She could set specific goals for cultural and physically nurturing activities and track them as religiously as she does the market. She could finally take that dance class she keeps thinking about. She could reach outside her work circle to find kindred spirits and visit museums, galleries, and theaters. She could stop ignoring her physical complaints and see a physician or physical therapist. There's a clinic on her block, and her health plan has generous coverage. Pam simply needs to give herself permission. *(Solution: Cut the problem down to size by identifying the direction of change needed.)*

Solution #3

Pam's desire for fulfillment is legitimate. She needs to recognize that all of us, herself included, deserve to find ways to do what we love. Not only will she benefit, but those around her will as well. *(Solution: Identify and embrace core desires.)*

Carlyle and Roger: "How Can We Recapture the Closeness?"

Carlyle and Roger have been together for seven years. Both are concerned about their lack of closeness and trouble communicating. Carlyle feels starved for physical affection and intimate conversation. Roger seems disengaged from the relationship. Recently, the two have begun having heated arguments followed by days of icy avoidance.

How Carlyle and Roger Could Cut Their Problem Down to Size

Solution #1

When reality doesn't match your expectations, it helps to:

- Reassess your expectations to see if they are useful and realistic.

- Check your perceptions of reality to see if they are accurate.

Romantic relationships often contain unrealistic assumptions and expectations. Among the tacit beliefs Roger and Carlyle hold:

- Relationships cannot endure too much disappointment.

- Other people can make us whole.

- Love is a feeling.

Unrealistic assumption #1: Relationships cannot endure too much disappointment. In a sense, romantic relationships start in earnest with the first disappointment. The staying power of a relationship isn't formed when you first meet your mate, fall in love, or are at the peak of attraction. Staying power is built at the moment following your first disappointment and can deepen following each subsequent disappointment. How you handle disappointments can determine the quality of your relationship. Bringing a relationship "back from the dead" after mentally writing it off is a key skill in long-term relationships.

Unrealistic assumption #2: Other people can make us whole. A common but self-defeating expectation is that others can give you worth, goodness, wholeness, and stability when you lack it within yourself. A helpful reminder about fulfilling your basic needs is *Self first, then the other*. You have to nurture your relationship with yourself in order to give to and receive from others. This is not being selfish. It means developing a healthy sense of self and realizing that it is up to you to meet your internal needs to feel worthy, whole, and strong. Though having a strong love connection is important, love cannot fill all your needs for companionship nor erase feelings of personal emptiness. If you can't hold on to yourself in an intimate relationship, you risk not being able to hold on to the relationship. As Pearl Bailey said, "You cannot belong to anyone else until you belong to yourself."

Unrealistic assumption #3: Love is a feeling. We often view love as something that happens to us, a place we "fall" into, or a feeling another person does *to* us. More accurately, love is a choice to have a feeling. Loving is a choice you let unfold, deepen, and continue, or not. When love is experienced as a choice to have a feeling, it can live as a creation that is not dependent on what the other person does nor upon your feelings at any given moment. *(Solution: Identify the Subterranean Accountant's faulty assumptions and let them go.)*

Solution #2

Although Carlyle and Roger are troubled by the iciness following their arguments, they have a choice about tolerating or continuing it. It's not unusual at times to feel a lack of intimacy or even civility with a mate. Though such feelings are real, they may not be entirely true. Notice how quickly your tone of voice changes in the middle of an argument if you stop to answer the phone. Notice how you can control your dysfunctional behavior when you're in public or in the presence of your boss, in-laws, or children.

Carlyle and Roger could both ask themselves, "If God (or Oprah, the Pope, Katharine Hepburn, Michael Jordan, or whomever you most admire) materialized right now and suggested that you act differently, what would you do?" You can't control what you feel, but you can choose your actions. Although you may sometimes have trouble tolerating a loved one's emotions, you do not have to act on your feelings in such destructive ways as ignoring, ridiculing, minimizing, or denying your partner's emotions and stature. *(Solution: Reality-test assumptions by finding exceptions.)*

Solution #3

Carlyle fears being alone and rejected. Carlyle might focus on building an emotional home inside her where she can seek sanctuary whether Roger is detached or not. She could deepen her relationships with other people. She could recognize Roger's defensiveness as *his* problem and not take it personally. She could ascribe it as Roger temporarily suffering from Mute Male Syndrome, something that isn't permanent.

Carlyle could also recognize that she, not Roger, holds the solutions to her fear of being alone. *(Solution: Seek alternative explanations.)*

Solution #4

Roger fears feeling trapped and out of control. Though he fears feeling trapped, in truth he is not. He chose to be in the relationship, and he can choose to leave. In addition, Roger is capable of feeling both autonomous and connected. One does not exclude the other. When Roger feels guilty for wanting emotional distance, he could remind himself that wanting emotional space from time to time is a healthy sign in relationships. By the same token, when Roger feels crowded by Carlyle's desire for intimacy, he could remind himself that she is not the enemy. The enemy is his overblown fear of being trapped, unworthy, and weak. Carlyle can be his ally in facing these fears. *(Solution: Challenge denial and reality-test fears by identifying either-or thinking.)*

How Carlyle and Roger Could Increase Their Motivation and Enhance Their Sense of Self

Solution #1

Carlyle and Roger may each be adding to the problem in ways they don't readily see. Carlyle is frustrated by Roger's withdrawal. We often feel frustrated when a partner clams up verbally or emotionally. We may respond by asking "What are you thinking?" or making accusatory statements like "You never talk about what is really important." Although being with an uncommunicative partner can be frustrating, your reactions to it can cause more distress than your partner's lack of communication. *(Solution: Identify overreactions or childlike behavior.)*

Solution #2

A question Carlyle might ask is, "How can I soothe myself?" Carlyle could focus on taking care of herself rather than on changing Roger. Paradoxically, such a shift can lead an uncommunicative partner to open up. In any event, no matter how Roger responds, Carlyle would gain the benefits of self-soothing. Another useful question for each of them might be, "Why is this making me so upset right *now*?" (*Solution: Ask the right questions.*)

Solution #3

Several core desires are inherent in Roger's and Carlyle's fears. Carlyle fears rejection and being alone, in part because she also desires acceptance, love, and connection. Roger fears feeling trapped and out of control, in part because he values self-reliance and stability. In recognizing these core desires, Carlyle and Roger could shift their focus to reaching for their desires rather than avoiding their fears.

Carlyle could work to increase both her self-acceptance and her acceptance of Roger. She could cherish the good parts of their connection and reach out to Roger on his level. Roger could build his self-reliance and emotional stability—goals he seeks not just in the relationship but in his life as a whole, by using the relationship as the perfect place to work on those issues. Roger's job is to recognize when he is letting his fears control him, and gradually begin to share those fears with Carlyle, rather than shutting her out. (*Solution: Identify core desires inherent in fears.*)

Dianne: "My Kids Think I'm Supermom"

Dianne, a forty-six-year-old real-estate agent and mother of three, cannot recall a time in the past year when she's taken time to relax and put her feet up. She's been the top seller in her real estate office for six years. She's highly involved in her children's schools as well as community groups. Two years ago, Dianne moved her ailing eighty-six-year-old mother from back East to a house three blocks away. Within a year her mother will likely need twenty-four-hour home care. Dianne characterizes her marriage to husband Tom, also a real estate agent, as "stable." She says the marriage lacks the romance of earlier years, and the couple is generally too busy or tired to make love.

Dianne's two closest female friends moved away in the past year. Since then Dianne feels as if nobody sees her as she really is. Part of this, she acknowledges, is because she tends to take care of everyone around her and ask little for herself.

"I love my family dearly, but my husband expects me to have dinner on the table no matter when he or the kids come home," Dianne says. "My kids think I'm Supermom. My mom doesn't understand how much time my job takes. She wants me to be there any time she is lonely. My boss expects me to list and sell more homes every year. I can't remember the last time somebody said 'Mom' or 'Honey, what do you need? What do you want?'"

She finds dwindling enjoyment in her job and has no time to do things for herself like reading, which she dearly loves. "In many ways I have everything I always wanted, but it doesn't feel like I thought it would. I feel isolated and empty, and then I feel self-critical for not being happier," she says.

How Dianne Could Cut Her Problem Down to Size

Solution #1

Dianne is caring for so many others that she's neglected to nurture her relationship with herself. Feeling overwhelmed is like being trapped in a room with a large, expanding balloon that is steadily crowding you into a corner. One way out is to pop the balloon. Dianne needs to let some air out of her demanding lifestyle and give herself breathing room to honor her needs. *(Solution: Identify what's out of balance.)*

Solution #2

Dianne might identify emotional over-attachments. For example, Dianne is wedded to such beliefs as, "If I don't take care of my family, no one else will," "If I focus too much on my own needs, my family will suffer," and "If I were to neglect any one of my responsibilities, I'd feel like a bad person." Dianne has come to think of her family's needs as part of who she is, and she commits to filling every need. Dianne could step back and realize that a better mix of her needs and her family's needs is in everybody's interests. *(Solution: Recognize over-attachments arising from confusing your identity with external circumstances.)*

Solution #3

If Dianne were to state her problem in one sentence it would be something like, "I want to care for my family and be successful at work, *but* doing so leaves me inadequate time to care for myself, *and* that makes me feel empty, alone, and upset with myself." She could take each clause and look more deeply.

1. *"I want to care for my family and be successful at work."* This doesn't seem to be Dianne's problem. She appears to be doing this quite well. If she thinks she isn't, she may be overly demanding of herself.

2. *"Doing so leaves me inadequate time to care for myself."* Dianne could ask herself how she can create adequate time to care for herself. Is time what she really wants, or would certain well-chosen activities be intensely nurturing even if done for short periods?

3. *"That makes me feel empty, alone, and upset with myself."* Feeling empty and alone are core fears. Dianne responds to her core fears by being upset with herself. She denies and ridicules her feelings rather than having compassion for her suffering.

The conflict at the heart of her problem is that Dianne is a caring person but she is not caring for herself. Her self-blaming only adds to her pain. *(Solution: Identify the conflict that makes it a problem.)*

Solution #4

She could reality-test her fear-thoughts by identifying exceptions, exaggerations, and contradictions. For example:

• Although Dianne fears letting anyone in the family down, she's currently letting herself down. This obvious contradiction isn't good for Dianne or her family.

• Though Dianne fears being hurtful, in reality she is anything but hurtful to those she loves. She needs to recognize this as a fear, not a reality, and treat it as such.

• Though Dianne fears focusing "too much" on her own needs, this doesn't mean she can't focus more on her needs. Self-care is not either-or, it is a matter of degree. By the same token, just because Dianne would do anything for her children, it doesn't mean that she must do *everything* for them.

Though she fears that she is the only one who can take care of her family, in truth her husband and children are capable of carrying their share. Dianne hasn't asked them to do more. As a result, the entire family has fallen into the habit of expecting Dianne to do whatever is needed. Though she hesitates to do so, Dianne needs to ask for help. She could ask her children to do more chores at home. She and Tom have the resources to afford a sitter. The couple could designate at least one night a week as "date night" and rekindle their romance. They could pay someone to prepare and deliver evening meals that they could reheat. (*Solution: Reality-test fears.*)

Solution #5

Dianne needs to confront and acknowledge the losses, stress, and diminished energy she is suffering. She lost her two best friends, added more job and family responsibilities, and gained an ailing mother in her immediate environment. Yet she keeps giving and doesn't seek replenishment. Is it possible that this one-sided exchange avoids or protects something for Dianne? Perhaps she fills her life to skirt an emptiness or loneliness she feels within. Or perhaps she derives emotional payoffs from being seen as a Supermom. Or perhaps she believes that, to be worthy or loved, she must give endlessly. In any case, looking beneath her behavior will allow her to confront the root cause squarely. (*Solution: Challenge denial and see what is being avoided.*)

How Dianne Could Increase Her Motivation and Enhance Her Sense of Self

Solution #1

Dianne has lost touch with her original motivation for being such a good real-estate agent, mother, wife, caretaker, and community supporter. As a result, her many activities lack meaning. Dianne sought her job because she wanted to help people realize their housing dreams. She cares about making her community a nurturing place to live. She moved her elderly mother close by because she wants her mother's final years to be as comfortable as possible. She and Tom once had a passionate

connection, and the fact that she misses it shows that she is still a passionate person. All of these are evidence of how much Dianne wants to
love and contribute to others. When she does contribute, as long as her
life has reasonable balance, she feels fulfilled. *(Solution: Determine what
matters most.)*

Solution #2

Dianne might call her two best friends for advice about her
dilemma. It is likely they'd tell her that she has the right to be loved and
contributed to by others rather than sacrificing herself for others' needs.
(Solution: Seek alternative perspectives.)

Solution #3

Dianne might be happier if she honored her desire to value herself
as much as she honors others. She could start a reading group or join a
book club. She could give herself one night a week with friends. She
could ask that her family cook dinner for her one night a week. She
could reassure her mother of her love but candidly share about her
many demands in hopes of greater understanding on her mother's part.
If her mother cannot be understanding, Dianne may need to set boundaries with her mother in a firm but loving way. *(Solution: Embrace and
promote core desires.)*

Solution #4

If Dianne is thinking that she rarely hears others ask her "What
do you want," why isn't she voicing this? She has the right to ask this
of her husband, children, boss, coworkers, and friends. She deserves
this just as much as those she is giving to. *(Solution: Ask proactive
questions.)*

Solution #5

To improve the situation, Dianne could acknowledge and take
advantage of her abilities and resourcefulness. She is a highly effective
salesperson. That means she already has blueprints for setting goals,
achieving them, persuading others, and facilitating projects. She could
use this expertise to provide herself with more self-nurturing. She
could persuade herself that honoring her own needs is a worthy and

necessary cause. She could speak to those close to her about how the lack of balance in her life is not in either Dianne's or their long-term interests, and get them on board doing more of their share. (*Solution: Seek a more accurate self-image by acknowledging strengths.*)

Greta: "Even Though I Was the One Rejected, I Feel as Though It Was My Fault"

Greta, a thirty-three-year-old teacher, lost her mother to cancer a year ago. A year prior to that, her lover of eight years, Bonnie, left and reunited with a previous lover. In the two years since Bonnie left, Greta has felt depressed and anxious. She rarely visits her gym where she formerly worked out six days a week. She has turned down invitations from friends to socialize. She worries that Bonnie left because of some basic flaw in Greta. She struggles with her regrets that she didn't spend more time with her mother in her twenties when Greta lived out of the country for six years pursuing a graduate degree and performing as a violinist.

"I have no enthusiasm for starting another relationship. I can't believe I was so naive that I never saw Bonnie's departure coming. I don't know if I can trust my instincts now," Greta says. "I know it sounds pitiful but even though I was the one rejected, I feel as though it was my fault."

How Greta Could Cut Her Problem Down to Size

Solution #1

Greta's dilemma is that a part of her wants to look to the future but another part is firmly planted in the past. One of the hardest parts of coping with grief and loss is finding a balance between taking adequate time to mourn and eventually encouraging yourself to move on. When part of you holds back following an emotional loss, even when you think it's time to move forward, sometimes that part is trying to tell you that you've missed a step.

Perhaps Greta has not allowed herself to face her heartbreak. Grieving major losses takes time. Rushing through or leaving out parts of the normal phases of grieving can cause problems down the road. She lost the two women in her life within two years. Perhaps her heart is trying to get her attention by upping the volume of her guilt and shame. (*Solution: Consult mind, body, and heart.*)

Solution #2

Although Greta is not dating, she does miss deeper connections. In part, she is succumbing to fear-thoughts that she could not survive another heartbreak. With fear-thoughts of her "survival" at stake, it will be hard for Greta to find sufficient motivation to overcome her fears. Greta could ask herself: "If I were to love and lose again, would I survive?" Losing another love might be devastating but it would not be deadly. By taking survival out of the equation, Greta could fashion a more accurate formulation of her situation. She may not want another heartbreak, but that is far different from being unable to survive another heartbreak. Wanting is a choice. When survival is at stake, you have no choice. (*Solution: When fear plays the survival card, call its bluff.*)

Solution #3

With a trusted friend or therapist, Greta might explore her assumptions, expectations, and desires about romantic love. Perhaps Greta needs to look more deeply at what she wants and needs from a partner. Though she blames herself for Bonnie's departure, Bonnie's actions were her own. Bonnie's leaving may indicate long-standing duplicity or lack of self-awareness on her part. Having such insights might free Greta to be more forgiving of herself, a significant healing step. In any case, her actions would be based on self-awareness and conscious choice in contrast to her current status of feeling neither desire nor choice. (*Solution: Recalculate the Accountant's math.*)

Solution #4

Greta could ask herself what her torrents of self-criticism accomplish. Does she feel that by attacking herself, she'll preempt others' judgments of her? Does she fear that if she lets up on her internal tirade, she'll discover bigger "flaws" in herself? Does she worry that if her mental self-punching stops, she won't know what to do next? Does she feel guilty for not having been around for several years while her mother was alive, and is now punishing herself by not moving on emotionally? Are her self-criticisms driven by fears of feeling bad, unsafe, or flawed?

These questions can help Greta weigh the costs and benefits of her actions and choose healthier patterns. One solution might lie in building nurturing connections with others as well as connecting to her best self. With a trusted friend or therapist, she may want to work on gradually giving herself increased positive feedback, especially in new situations or when she feels uncertain. In terms of her concern that being blindsided by Bonnie's departure means that Greta cannot trust her judgment in future relationships, Greta could see a therapist, join a self-help group, or read about relationships, mate selection, and self-awareness. (*Solution: Challenge denial and see the costs, payoffs, and what is being avoided.*)

Solution #5

Greta's stream of criticism has her on the ropes. As she recovers from one mental blow, another lands. Greta lives in a reactive, defensive posture. Such excessive self-criticism can be a usual suspect. In seeing this, Greta could recognize that her problem isn't the "flaws" her inner critic harps on, but the inner critic itself and her habit of listening to it. Habits can be changed more easily than innate characteristics. Greta could try behavior-modification techniques like mentally yelling "Stop," physically putting her foot down, or snapping a rubber band on her wrist each time she notices a self-critical thought. By interrupting the habit, then replacing the thought with a positive one, she could moderate her self-criticism. (*Solution: Round up usual suspects.*)

Solution #6

Greta might ask herself what troubles her most. Is it her lack of enthusiasm? That's a heart problem, needing an emotional solution. Is it her thought that she "should" want or have a new relationship? That's a mind problem, needing reality-testing and exploration of her assumptions. Or is it that she really does want a new relationship but is unsure how to move forward? That's a problem of action, needing a body solution, a specific plan to meet people, for example. (*Solution: Identify the conflict that makes it a problem.*)

How Greta Could Increase Her Motivation and Enhance Her Sense of Self

Solution #1

On the one hand, Greta's heart suffers from too much feeling in the form of the shame and guilt that overwhelm her. On the other hand, she suffers from not enough feeling in that she isn't allowing herself to grieve her losses. Her shame and guilt are so powerful that they take her focus away from the one emotion it might be best to let herself have: grief. To lose a treasured connection with her lover out of the blue and then to have her mother stricken by a fast-moving cancer posed deep losses. Mourning losses like these takes time. Grief moves at its healthiest pace when you honor instead of pressure yourself. *(Solution: Recognize mind-body-heart imbalance.)*

Solution #2

To deal with her grief and regret over not having spent more time with her mother, Greta might create a mourning ritual, like visiting her mother's gravesite or writing a letter to her mother. She might seek help from friends or in counseling. She could volunteer at a grief-counseling center. By helping others face the issues that challenge her, Greta might gain perspective and strength. *(Solution: Cut the problem down to size by identifying the direction of change needed.)*

Aaron: "I Can't Seem to Handle My Finances"

Aaron, a twenty-nine-year-old salesman, is deeply in debt. He has student loans on which he has yet to pay back any principal. His credit cards are maxed. His rent is a month late. Feeling desperate, Aaron drove two hours to a casino. He initially won fifty dollars at blackjack but lost most of it playing slots. With gas and food, his trip was a net loss.

How Aaron Could Cut His Problem Down to Size

Solution #1

Aaron is entranced by the Escape Artist and King Kong. He needs to ask himself what these characters are helping him avoid. For example, the Escape Artist generally seeks to avoid feeling trapped. What trap does Aaron fear? Does he fear the limits of sticking within a budget? Does he fear admitting that he may not have the discipline to quit gambling? In either case, getting those fears on the table would allow him to reality-test and disarm them, get help, or accept them and turn his attention to things he can change.

King Kong's worst fear is boredom. In being seduced by the thrill of gambling and the risks of mounting debt, Aaron is anything but bored. There is always the possibility, at least from the inner character's perspective, that he could hit the jackpot at any time.

If Aaron were to be candid with himself, he'd see that his characters do little to keep away what he fears. The Escape Artist keeps his options open so that he'll avoid feeling trapped, yet he is trapped by his debts. King Kong seeks to generate intensity with the thrill of gambling, but Aaron's consistent lack of financial self-discipline has become a steady grind that is anything but exciting. *(Solution: Recognize inner characters.)*

Solution #2

Instead of admitting that *he* places each bet, Aaron lives as if something bigger than him forces him to gamble. Instead of acknowledging that he is concerned and upset about his plummeting credit rating, he lets it pass and hopes that time will solve the problem. Aaron loves to gamble and make expensive purchases yet responds angrily when anyone suggests he is financially irresponsible. When you mentally and emotionally drift into confusion for too long, you risk becoming anesthetized to your problems and their costs. Aaron needs to shake up his denial by asking himself about his motives, no matter how uncomfortable this may be. *(Solution: Challenge his denial.)*

Solution #3

Aaron needs to take an honest look at the pros and cons of his current course. He could list the benefits he derives from his gambling and financially irresponsible patterns (excitement, avoiding responsibility) and then list the costs (anxiety, loss of self-respect, narrowing of his options). He might ask himself what is the likely outcome of his current course and write down where he sees himself in one or two years. Then, he might ask himself where he would likely be if he changed course, got help, and worked to overcome his habits. By honestly looking at the two possible "future Aarons," he might increase his motivation to make changes for the better. *(Solution: Do a cost-benefit analysis.)*

Solution #4

Aaron's denial is helped by mind FITs. Aaron thinks his irresponsible financial habits will last forever, are part of his innate nature, and are so total that they can't be overcome. These are exaggerations that ignore Aaron's power to alter the scenario. Aaron could regain perspective by remembering that his worries about being unable to stop gambling or earn more money are colored by fear-thoughts. Fear-thoughts show worst-case scenarios but the actual experience may be less painful than he imagines. In addition, he needs to remind himself that even if he fails, he can get up, dust himself off, and try again. This is a perspective we frequently forget when in the grip of fear-thoughts. *(Solution: Identify mind FITs.)*

Solution #5

Aaron is unable to control his behavior consistently. He tries to quit gambling but can't keep at it. He sees his debts but sits on his hands. It's not that Aaron is dull, stupid, or immature. In fact, he is quite creative and intelligent. He is not using his powers of observation to look beyond his routine patterns and habits. Aaron could ask himself what he feels just before he places a bet or makes an expensive purchase. When he considers not betting or making a smaller bet, what happens? Does he distract himself? If so, how? Answering these questions can bring him face to face with the deeper reasons driving his behavior. *(Solution: Describe when, where, and how the problem occurs.)*

How Aaron Could Increase His Motivation and Enhance His Sense of Self

Solution #1

The solution to unwanted debt is to earn more than you spend and set aside the extra earnings to pay debts. Since Aaron is capable of earning enough to pay his debts but consistently fails to, he may be denying a deeper reality. Perhaps Aaron should ask himself about his tacit beliefs. Does he believe that he shouldn't have to pay debts? Does he really expect that he'll somehow come into a windfall, like from an inheritance or winning the lottery? Such beliefs can be Persuader or Moviemaker characters. They may make Aaron feel better, but they won't solve his problem. He has to decide whether the illusion-based stress-relief of his characters outweighs the real-world consequences. *(Solution: Weigh pros and cons of inner characters' behavior.)*

Solution #2

Aaron is not being realistic in expecting his problems to change magically without reducing his gambling or earning more money. He needs a realistic and thorough plan if he is going to change. He needs to identify how he can generate more income, where he can cut costs, and set up a schedule with meaningful rewards and consequences to achieve both goals. Aaron fears the process of facing his creditors. One solution might be to seek financial counseling and come forward with his best plan for renegotiating the debt. Though this process may be uncomfortable in the short term, a revised payment plan could reduce Aaron's stress and improve his longer-term financial picture. *(Solution: Identify the direction of change needed.)*

Solution #3

Aaron needs to be honest about what most concerns him. If it is that he is spending more than he is making, he needs behavioral interventions that will reverse this. If his greatest concern is his distress over his situation, he may need to seek emotional support and help as well as look for ways to achieve emotional fulfillment without gambling. On the other hand, perhaps his emotional distress is caused by a secret he is keeping from himself. If, for example, Aaron has no intention of paying off his debts, his solution may be to stop being confused or beating himself up and accept whatever consequences that ensue from defaulting on his debts so he can move forward. *(Solution: Identify hidden priorities.)*

A Final Task: Making Peace with Your Self-defeats

If you haven't forgiven yourself something, how can you forgive others?

—DOLORES HUERTA

When you take stock of your unnecessary losses, some truisms generally emerge:

1. If you'd seen the warning signs earlier . . .

2. If you'd better understood the internal forces leading you into self-defeat . . .

3. If you had accepted yourself more deeply . . .

. . . the outcome might have been different.

In any given situation, you can choose to either sabotage or enhance your life. That's free will. If you choose to self-sabotage, you will find ways to do so. Neither your choice nor the outcome means that you are a bad or flawed person. Give yourself a break. Excessive expectations or harsh self-judgments about your past self-defeats are simply more self-sabotage. Remember, self-sabotage is innate, has payoffs, takes countless forms, and is protected by powerful defenses. It is unrealistic to expect that you will always overcome these factors.

Instead, when you deliberately undermine yourself, recognize that at least you've made a conscious choice. This is better than an unconscious choice. When you find yourself on an undermining course but don't want to deviate, it may help to recognize that this is one of your *chosen* self-defeats. Accept it. You don't have to always do the "right" thing. Forego guilt and take the pressure off yourself.

At times, we worry that if we undermine ourselves in a current situation, we may never be able to stop self-sabotaging. In my experience, self-sabotage persists more from resistance to acknowledging it than from accepting it. If you want to undermine yourself, go ahead. Sometimes you just have to let yourself do so. When you are ready, you will return to what is in your best interests. You are trustworthy and capable. You carry the extraordinary within.

Similarly, when you're in a quandary and don't want to make a choice, develop a guilt-free shorthand way of signifying that. Post an imaginary or virtual "Out to Lunch" or "Gone Fishing" notice. Rather than trying to hold back the tide, acknowledge that you're in the dark or just along for the ride for a time. Choose it. Let it happen. Don't judge yourself harshly.

Remember, recognizing how you've hurt yourself is the first step to stopping counterproductive behavior. Rather than looking at past oversights as evidence that you're bad or flawed, look at them with compassion. Remind yourself that your past mistakes may make sense, given the benefits that often come with self-sabotage. There is no point in denying that you've inflicted suffering upon yourself. Use the past to help you take better care of yourself from now on.

It is also possible that sometimes what looks like a self-sabotaging action may turn out to be for the best. Perhaps there are factors you don't see. Perhaps you are being guided by instinct or wisdom you don't fully recognize. In any case, once you've assessed a situation and made a choice, you have done all you can.

Summary of Part Five: Triumphing over Challenges and Adversity

1. When you're stuck, it is because your problems seem too big and your abilities seem too small. Reverse the ratio. Cut the problem down to size and enhance your sense of self.

2. You generally have more than one viable solution to your problems.

LIVING FROM YOUR BEST SELF

You got to have a dream. If you don't have a dream, how you gonna have a dream come true?

—BLOODY MARY IN THE MUSICAL
SOUTH PACIFIC

Looking for the keys to life? Any of this chapter's seven approaches can add significant growth and fulfillment to your life.

The Goliath Principle

If you don't risk anything, you risk even more.

—ERICA JONG

Every day, do something you fear or resist. Even better, do so the first thing each day. In the morning, identify a task or problem that saps your energy just to think about. Then, like the biblical David, pick up your slingshot. When you pick the biggest, most-resisted problem or task of your day and do it first, your day will zoom. Once you set off to battle, you are no longer passive, hoping the battle will pass you by or waiting for the ax to fall. When you set your sights on a resisted task, even if you do nothing else all day, you will feel a stronger sense of self.

One way to get started is simply to begin doing what you've been avoiding and keep at it for at least fifteen minutes. You'll find that you can tolerate pretty much anything for fifteen minutes. Furthermore, you'll often find that fifteen minutes of doing what you had been resisting is enough to dispel many paralyzing thoughts and feelings. If after fifteen minutes you want to quit, fine. You're still ahead of where you were when you started.

Remember that things you resist are unlikely to feel good, at least at first. That's why you resist them. The first step is often the hardest and can take far more effort than later steps. By way of analogy, the space shuttle uses nearly three-quarters of its fuel to ascend only one-quarter of the way to orbit. If you begin with the promise to yourself that you will do a task you resist for at least fifteen minutes no matter what it feels like, you may find that your prior anxieties will soon appear as tiny and far away as the launch pad appears from a space-craft once in orbit.

You can use the Goliath Principle to conquer long-standing fears as well as everyday problems. You might take a day that holds meaning for you—your birthday, the new year, or other holiday—and, on that day, look for a major challenge or fear that is shaping your life in negative ways. Pick something that symbolically has your feet nailed to the floor. Then create a plan for overcoming it within the next year, step by step, using the Goliath Principle each day.

One of the biggest fears Bette, a forty-three-year-old therapist, had carried since childhood was of not being able to defend herself if physically attacked. But at age forty, she took a self-defense course in which a large, extensively padded staff member stages an "attack" on each participant. The participants' job was to use the simple defense techniques they'd been taught. The promise of the course was: "You'll be capable of defending yourself against a single attacker of any size." Since the course, Bette has walked straighter, stopped cowering physically and emotionally, and felt a confidence she'd lacked. She let go of a lifelong burden of hiding from bullies. She found it easier to deal with emotional confrontations as well.

As Eleanor Roosevelt said, "You gain strength, courage, and confidence by every experience in which you really stop and look fear in the face. You are able to say to yourself, 'I lived through this horror. I can take the next thing that comes along.' You must do the thing you think you cannot do."

Benefit of the Goliath Principle: Promotes action.

Don't Take It Personally

It's not a slam at you when people are rude—it's a slam at the people they've met before.

—F. SCOTT FITZGERALD

When someone criticizes, slights, or tries to demean you, remind yourself that their actions and motivations are primarily about them, not you. For example, a coworker who labels you "self-centered" may be revealing something about herself. Perhaps she observes your healthy habits and would like to do the same but hasn't been able to. Perhaps she is trying to bring you down a notch so she won't feel as bad about herself. Or perhaps she has unrealistic expectations of you. When you don't "feed" her expectations, even if you are acting appropriately, she may attack to cover her disappointment.

When someone accuses you of something, remember: They are often symbolically talking about themselves. This recognition can free you from taking on unwanted projections and uninvited problems. This doesn't mean you should turn a deaf ear to constructive criticism. Part of being responsible is an openness to seeing better ways of doing things. It's important to make a distinction about responsibility. Responsibility is not blame or fault. Blame and fault are useful in legal settings but thinking about blame and fault confuses the issue if your goal is growth and fulfillment. Keep in mind:

- You are *not* responsible for what others do.

- You *are* responsible for what you do.

Reminding yourself of these principles can help you sidestep two common obstacles to growth and self-improvement:

1. Overfocusing on things not in your control, like what *others* do or don't do.

2. Underfocusing on things within your control, like what *you* do or don't do.

When you have a clear sense of responsibility, you can weather criticism more readily. You can assess whether another's comments are truly about you and whether you need to do anything in response. Taking responsibility empowers you. Personalizing and blaming do not.

Benefit of not taking it personally: Promotes perspective.

Live Beyond Comparison

We are here and it is now. Further than that, all knowledge is moonshine.

—H. L. MENCKEN

Much suffering in life comes from comparing, judging, expecting, assuming, and other mental functions related to the past or future. These functions can be valuable but they have limits. To compare is to conceive of two or more things in two or more points of time and judge them. Without comparisons there are no judgments. Your inner characters are based on comparing and judging. At the core of all negative comparisons and judgments is some version of one fundamental thought: *I don't like this reality. I want a different one.*

A common saying in twelve-step recovery programs is "Don't compare your insides with others' outsides." It's a nice phrase that captures what nearly all of us tend to do. When you observe others, you see only their visible, external selves. You know nothing of their mental and emotional states. Though you cannot hear others' self-doubts, you are acutely aware of your insecurities. You may assume yourself to be inferior while thinking that others feel confident and worthy. Your feelings and actions follow your mental comparisons, and you may become intimidated, disappointed, or defer to others in self-defeating ways.

All comparisons are judgments. Unless you're a film critic or quality-control expert getting paid to judge and compare, comparing can work against you. For example, have you ever taken a day off and gone to the beach or lake, only to spend so much of your day comparing that you rarely enjoyed the setting? Perhaps you compared the person you were with to someone you wished you were with instead. Perhaps you compared how you felt to how you expected to feel or "should" have felt. Or you compared your mood with other people's. Or you compared the weather to that of other days, or to how the weather should have been at that time of year, or to the weather forecast. Maybe you compared this ocean or lake with others; this day off with other days off; today with tomorrow or yesterday.

Comparing takes you out of the *now*. You can't enjoy the *present* when you're not in it. Although our most-cherished moments can only occur in the now, we so often live *not now*. Writer Eckhart Tolle warned of the "compulsion to live almost exclusively through memory and anticipation." When you experience the day, the water, your mood, and everything else as one of a kind, you're in the now. All else is an alternative reality.

Benefit of living beyond comparison: Promotes living in the now.

Listen Deeply

Wisdom is the reward you get for a lifetime of listening when you would have preferred to talk.

—DOUG LARSON

Listening has been described as an art, a science, entertainment, and a necessity. In my view, listening to another person is an opportunity to commune with the best in you and others. When you listen to others without trying to change what they are saying, you receive and offer a rare gift. To listen deeply, all you have to do is try to imagine what it would be like if you were having the feelings or experiences the person is expressing. There is something magical about deep listening. Time no longer matters, distractions fade, and you connect with another.

Sometimes it seems as if people are talking just to fill space, making much ado about nothing, or repeating the same old story. In such cases, try to remind yourself that other people want to communicate something of value just as you do. You can find value in their communication if you listen. For example, when someone seems to be talking just to fill the space, he may be communicating that he is anxious, bored, or not at ease. What if you heard *that* message instead of his chatter? Would you respond differently? *Me too*, you might say. *Don't be nervous, I won't bite*, you might console. Perhaps you'd ask, *Is something worrying you that you'd like to talk about?*

People repeat stories for a reason. When people tell you about their hospital operation, pet peeve, or ancient resentment, they are searching for a way to move forward. Whether we know it or not, telling of our traumas is an attempt to regain the loss of control that comes with trauma. What can make the difference is someone who is willing to listen. Just like you, people want to be heard. When someone really hears you, it can lift your concerns.

People who tell stories that irritate you are generally not trying to dominate you. They don't need you to agree with them or fix anything. All you have to do is listen. Put aside your agendas, fears, and shoulds. Perhaps ask questions that deepen. When you react primarily to what others' words set off in you, you lose sight of both your and the other person's extraordinary nature. When others are complaining, it is easy to forget that they are just as capable as you. When another person is hurting, it can be hard to simply be with him as he talks or cries.

When you listen, you address the bigness in people, not the smallness. If you had a life where you did nothing else but search for and speak to the bigness of people, you would have a great life. Listen to people you've been ignoring. Instead of avoiding people's stories of trauma or fixation, listen. Imagine what it's like to be that person. Listen as though it is the most important, fascinating thing in the world.

Benefit of listening deeply: Promotes connection.

Live as Though You Make a Difference

You must be the change you wish to see in the world.

—MAHATMA GANDHI

During my years working as a journalist, I was fortunate to meet and observe a number of well-known people. I've met the Pope, three U.S. presidents, several Fortune 500 CEOs, and many political, sports, and entertainment legends. One thing I noticed is that many of them seemed to possess a sense of purpose that ordered their lives. They lived as though whatever they did mattered.

These women and men were not larger than life or fundamentally different from you or me. However, by taking their job or mission in life seriously, they pursued commitments so big and compelling that they had little time to get bogged down in meaningless details or waste time on matters that were not priorities. This sense of purpose comes from being committed to a cause you believe is noble. Living as though you make a difference is available to anyone: a bank teller, street sweeper, or a ten-year-old.

Any time you see a successful venture, relationship, family, or creative work, you know that someone chose to take a risk for something that mattered. If you are looking for inspiration, ask yourself questions like "What do I love most?" "What do I most admire in others?" and "What could I do all day and never tire of?" Such questions connect you to your passions. From your passions will flow your goals and actions.

Crispness of action comes from having a purpose that matters. A purpose that matters is different from having a lot to do. Having a lot to do may simply mean you're busy or overwhelmed. When what you do is important to you, you'll find yourself moving and speaking with a directness that is life-enhancing. It is possible to live as though you make a difference. You do.

Benefit of living as though you make a difference: Promotes courage.

Live as You Breathe

There are only two ways to live your life. One is as though nothing is a miracle. The other is as though everything is a miracle.

—ALBERT EINSTEIN

When you breathe, both inhaling and exhaling serve a nurturing purpose. Breathing in gathers fresh air. Breathing out expels the by-products of metabolism. Inhaling is an expansion and exhaling is a letting go.

We sometimes hold our breath psychologically or emotionally. The longer you hold on psychologically, the shallower your psyche's breathing will become. For example, think of a time when you feared losing control. Control is a state that eats anything in its path. The need for excessive control is like a drug. Control becomes your oxygen line. We often seek control, because we confuse *losing* control with *letting go* of control. The way out of excessive control is to let go. Letting go takes faith, courage, and trust.

Your breathing can serve as a model for how to let go mentally or emotionally. When you exhale, you're not worried about losing control of that breath. You have faith that a new breath will follow. You simply let it go. Doing so cleanses and makes room for the next breath, for growth, and for healing. As with your breathing, your life is a flow. In the flow of your life, notice when you are mentally, physically, or emotionally holding your breath in the face of a troubling or frightening thought, feeling, or situation. Rather than trying to hold on, *let go.*

Contraction and expansion are part of life. At each moment, your sense of self is either expanding or contracting. If you want to experience this phenomenon, try an experiment: Think of a time you felt belittled or incompetent. As you think about the incident, notice what happens in your body. Does your breathing change? Does your energy level rise or fall? Does your gut tighten or your jaw clench?

Then, think of a moment of triumph or great passion. Now notice what happens in your body. Do your posture or breathing change? Do you feel expansive? Where does the sense of expansion seem to come from? Your heart? Chest?

When you recognize signs of contraction, you have the opportunity to change course. You can't expand endlessly but you can choose between contraction and expansion in any given moment. To identify contraction, use the indicators we've already seen such as inner characters, childlike and animallike responses, and denial. When you see yourself contracting, find ways to release the tightening.

By the same token, notice when you are expanding. Whatever you're doing, it's working. You are creating blueprints for future successes. Just as with doing push-ups, each time you expand, you increase your ability to expand further.

Benefit of living as you breathe: Promotes awareness.

Practice Gratitude

Gratitude is heaven itself.

—WILLIAM BLAKE

Gratitude can be an antidote to virtually any dysfunctional feeling state. When you appreciate anything—your mate's smile, a sea breeze, a child's gentle breathing, the color periwinkle—you create acceptance and inner peace. Gratitude soothes the soul.

Fear often gets in the way of experiencing or expressing gratitude. Psychoanalyst Robert Karen wrote, "There are so many reasons not to feel gratitude. It means letting go of resentment, that dependable source of power, that old friend, that symbol of loyalty to our childhood hurts and the people who inflicted them. Gratitude opens wounds. It reawakens us to our heartbreaks."

With practice, you'll find that you can access gratitude even when you feel afraid or stressed. You might invest at least a couple minutes each day and notice who and what you appreciate. As you do so, notice what happens in your body. Does your stomach unclench? Do you feel more energy? Feeling grateful can dissolve negativity. It celebrates both you and others. You don't necessarily have to express gratitude verbally or even reciprocate for that which you are grateful, although doing so is usually a rich experience. The right to feel grateful is inherent in being human. Practice it every chance you get.

Benefit of practicing gratitude: Promotes acceptance.

If You'd Like to Go Deeper: Living from Your Best Self Starting Today

As an experiment, take a moment right now and try one of the seven approaches. Do one each day for a week. Monday, for example, start your week by felling the Goliath of your schedule. Then designate each successive day as the day you:

- Don't take something personally that you normally would have.

- Catch yourself making at least one comparison and then let it pass, accepting the situation just as it is

- Listen to someone you normally would avoid

- Have a conversation, do a chore, or take a trip in which everything you do matters

- Notice a situation in which you're contracting and then emotionally or psychologically let go, making room for expansion

- Pause and notice something for which you are grateful

ACKNOWLEDGMENTS

My profound thanks and appreciation to the brilliant and patient souls who volunteered to read drafts and contributed so many unique and valuable suggestions: Kelly Baker; Beth Carmody; Lori Hurwitz; Larry Kassin; Merrily Milmoe; Lucy Perkins, M.D.; Moddie Stone; Nicole Young; and Tom Zephyrs.

A special thank you to Marly Perkins, Ph.D., whose input in the formative stages of this book was extraordinarily insightful.

I thank the courageous pioneers who volunteered to be interviewed for this book. Their stories and contributions will help others make meaning of their lives.

I'm indebted to my editor, Diane Reverand, who believed in this book from the start, and through her wise vision and guiding hand helped me craft a book that extends well beyond my original conception. I also appreciate the remarkable staff at St. Martin's Press, especially Arun K. Das, Mark Steven Long, Vicky Hartman, and David Baldeosingh Rotstein. I'm particularly grateful to Regina Scarpa and Melissa Contreras for their attention to detail and tireless commitment to keep things running smoothly.

My agent, Patti Breitman, never flagged in her enthusiasm for this project and found the best possible home for this book.

For inspiration and support, I thank: Walter Anderson; Bonnie Brose; Mary Clayton; Brent Cox, M.D.; Joan Cox; Rick Hanson, Ph.D.; Lucy Scott, Ph.D.; Julia Serebrinsky; Shannon Tullius and the staff and volunteers of the Maui Writer's Conference; David Wallin, Ph.D.; Audrey Webb; and Miles White.

My deepest gratitude to the members of my steadfast men's group: Scott Cameron, Ph.D.; David Frankel, Ph.D.; Scott Lines, Ph.D.; Mike Shuell, Ph.D.; and Robert Wynne, Ph.D.

My thanks to Sandy the wonderdog for offering unconditional love and unlimited play, and to three sweet spirits who lit up my life and opened my heart: Tanja, Julia, and Lisa.

Finally, my heartfelt thanks and love to my family: A.J., Dani, Jan, Joseph, Loretta, and Al. I could not have done this without you.

NOTES

1. Who Are You When You're Not Being Yourself?

25 percent of high school students . . . 83 percent of college students . . .
94 percent of university professors . . .
   From Thomas Gilovich, *How We Know What Isn't So* (New York: Macmillan, 1991).
80 percent of drivers . . . Individual investors at one conference . . .
   From Brian O'Reilly, "Why Johnny Can't Invest," *Fortune*, Nov. 9, 1998.
85 percent of people rate their own manners . . .
   From "Oh Please!" *USA Today*, Dec. 4, 2001.
Our aversion to economic loss leads us to value . . .
   From Steven Pearlstein, "And the New Thinking About Money Is That Your Irrationality Is Predictable," *The Washington Post*, Jan. 27, 2002.
Social psychology researchers call this phenomenon counterfactual thinking . . .
   From Neal Roese and James Olson, *What Might Have Been: The Social Psychology of Counterfactual Thinking* (Mahwah, N.J.: Lawrence Erlbaum, 1995); and from Thomas Gilovich, *How We Know What Isn't So* (New York: Macmillan, 1991).

3. Why We Get in Our Own Way

. . . traumatic incidents appear to be imprinted in our brains differently than other events . . .
   From Antonio Damasio, *The Feeling of What Happens* (New York: Harcourt Brace, 1999); and from Joseph LeDoux, *The Emotional Brain* (New York: Touchstone, 1996).
"Losing money feels twice as bad as making money feels good," economist Richard Thaler said . . . On a behavioral level, we weigh now much differently than later . . .

From Brian O'Reilly, "Why Johnny Can't Invest," *Fortune*, Nov. 9, 1998.

. . . instead of measuring our lives in years added since birth . . .

From Daniel Levinson, with C. N. Darrow, E. B. Klein, M. H. Levinson, and B. McKee, *The Seasons of a Man's Life*. New York: Ballantine, 1978; and from Osherson, Sam. *Holding On or Letting Go: Men and Career Change in Midlife* (New York: The Free Press, 1980).

This shift can trigger midlife reevaluations . . .

From Murray Stein, *In Midlife* (Dallas: Spring Publications, 1983); from R. L. Gould, "The Phases of Adult Life: A Study in Developmental Psychology," *American Journal of Psychiatry* 127:521–531, 1972; and from C. G. Jung, *Modern Man in Search of a Soul* (San Diego: Harcourt Brace Jovanovich, 1933).

5. Taming the Beasts Within

When an animal is threatened or startled . . .

From Isaac Marks, *Fears, Phobias, and Rituals: Panic, Anxiety and Their Disorders* (New York: Oxford University Press, 1987).

. . . the freeze response . . .

From Joseph LeDoux, *The Emotional Brain* (New York: Touchstone, 1996).

9. The Facts of Life

The estimated 100 billion humans who have walked this planet . . .

From the Population Reference Bureau, *Historical Estimates of World Population* (Washington, D.C.: 2000).

11. The Truth About Fear

This Forever-Innate-Total combination is seen in panic attacks . . .

From Aaron Beck and Gary Emery, *Anxiety Disorders and Phobias* (New York: Basic, 1985); and from Martin Seligman, *Learned Optimism* (New York: Knopf, 1991).

12. Going to the Heart of Your Fears

Sigmund Freud, for example, acknowledged that one of his worst fears was feeling helpless.

From Ernest Becker, *The Denial of Death* (New York: Free Press, 1973).

16. Emerging from the Shadows

We know from cognitive therapy . . .

From Aaron Beck, with John Rush, Brian Shaw, and Gary Emery, *Cognitive Therapy of Depression* (New York: Guilford Press, 1979).

18. Decoding the Languages of Your Mind, Body, and Heart

. . . rhythmic movements can release chemicals that soothe the mind and calm the body . . .

From Barry Jacobs, "Serotonin and Behavior: Emphasis on Motor Control," *Journal of Clinical Psychiatry* 51 (12 suppl.).

. . . a rise in testosterone levels, further elevating your mood.

From P. Bernhardt, J. Dabbs, J. Fielden, D. Lutter, "Testosterone changes during vicarious experiences of winning and losing among fans at sporting events," *Physiology and Behavior,* Aug. 1998 65(1):59–62.

BIBLIOGRAPHY

Albom, Mitch. *Tuesdays with Morrie*. New York: Doubleday, 1997.

Baldwin, Martha. *Self-Sabotage*. New York: Time Warner, 1987.

Beck, Aaron, and Gary Emery. *Anxiety Disorders and Phobias*. New York: Basic, 1985.

Beck, Aaron, with John Rush, Brian Shaw, and Gary Emery. *Cognitive Therapy of Depression*. New York: Guilford Press, 1979.

Becker, Ernest. *The Denial of Death*. New York: Free Press, 1973.

Bernhardt, P., J. Dabbs, J. Fielden, and D. Lutter. "Testosterone Changes During Vicarious Experiences of Winning and Losing Among Fans at Sporting Events." *Physiology and Behavior* 65, no. 1 (Aug 1998): 59–62.

Bolles, Richard Nelson. *What Color Is Your Parachute?* Berkeley: Ten Speed Press, 2002.

Brody, Jane. "Ancient Tool of Survival Is Deadly for the Heart." *The New York Times*, May 21, 2002.

Burns, David. *Feeling Good: The New Mood Therapy*. New York: Morrow, 1980.

Burnham, Terry, and Jay Phelan. *Mean Genes: From Sex to Money to Food: Taming Our Primal Instincts*. Cambridge, Mass.: Perseus Publishing, 2000.

Cushnir, Howard Raphael. *Unconditional Bliss: Finding Happiness in the Face of Hardship*. Wheaton, Ill.: Quest Books, 2000.

Damasio, Antonio. *The Feeling of What Happens*. New York: Harcourt Brace, 1999.

Fingarette, Herbert. *Self-Deception*. Berkeley: University of California Press, 2000.

Gilovich, Thomas. *How We Know What Isn't So*. New York: Macmillan, 1991.

Goleman, Daniel. *Emotional Intelligence*. New York: Bantam, 1995.

Gould, R. L. "The Phases of Adult Life: A Study in Developmental Psychology." *American Journal of Psychiatry* 127 (1972): 521–531.

Jacobs, Barry. "Serotonin and Behavior: Emphasis on Motor Control." *Journal of Clinical Psychiatry* 52, no. 12 (Suppl.) (1991).

Johnson, Spencer. *One Minute for Myself*. New York: Avon, 1987.

Jung, C. G. *Modern Man in Search of a Soul*. San Diego: Harcourt Brace Jovanovich, 1933.

Karen, Robert. *The Forgiving Self: The Road from Resentment to Connection*. New York: Doubleday, 2001.

Kindlon, Dan, and Michael Thomson. *Raising Cain: Protecting the Emotional Life of Boys*. New York: Ballantine, 1999.

LeDoux, Joseph. *The Emotional Brain*. New York: Touchstone, 1996.

Levinson, Daniel, with C. N. Darrow, E. B. Klein, M. H. Levinson, and B. McKee. *The Seasons of a Man's Life*. New York: Ballantine, 1978.

Marks, Isaac. *Fears, Phobias, and Rituals: Panic, Anxiety and Their Disorders*. New York: Oxford University Press, 1987.

National Center for Health Statistics. "United States Life Table." Washington, D.C.: 2000.

"Oh, please!" *USA Today* (graphic), Dec. 4, 2001.

O'Reilly, Brian. "Why Johnny Can't Invest." *Fortune*, Nov. 9, 1998.

Osherson, Sam. *Holding On or Letting Go: Men and Career Change in Midlife*. New York: The Free Press, 1980.

Pearlstein, Steven. "And the New Thinking About Money Is That Your Irrationality Is Predictable." *The Washington Post*, Jan. 27, 2002.

Pipher, Mary. *Another Country: Navigating the Emotional Terrain of Our Elders*. New York: Riverhead, 1999.

Pittman, Frank. *Grow Up! How Taking Responsibility Can Make You a Happy Adult*. New York: St. Martin's Griffin, 1998.

Population Reference Bureau. "Historical Estimates of World Population." Washington, D.C.: 2000.

Remen, Rachel N. *Kitchen Table Wisdom: Stories That Heal*. New York: Riverhead, 1997.

Roese, Neal and James Olson. *What Might Have Been: The Social Psychology of Counterfactual Thinking*. Mahwah, N.J.: Lawrence Erlbaum, 1995.

Ruiz, Don Miguel. *The Four Agreements*. San Rafael, Calif.: Amber-Allen, 1997.

Seligman, Martin. *Learned Optimism*. New York: Knopf, 1991.

Stein, Murray. *In Midlife*. Dallas: Spring Publications, 1983.

Tolle, Eckhart. *The Power of Now*. San Rafael, Calif.: New World Library, 1999.

Viorst, Judith. *Necessary Losses*. New York: Ballantine, 1986.

Wolpe, David. *Making Loss Matter: Creating Meaning in Difficult Times*. New York: Riverhead, 1999.

INDEX

ABOUT THE AUTHOR

Dan Neuharth, Ph.D., is a psychotherapist and bestselling author. He has appeared extensively on national TV shows, including *Oprah, Good Morning America,* and CNN's *Talkback Live.*

Neuharth holds a Ph.D. in clinical psychology and has twelve years' experience as a licensed marriage and family therapist in the San Francisco Bay area. An award-winning journalist, Neuharth has taught at five universities and worked as a print and broadcast reporter, radio talk show host, and advice columnist.

He is the author of *If You Had Controlling Parents: How to Make Peace with Your Past and Take Your Place in the World* (HarperCollins Publishers, 1998).

Visit the author's Web site at **www.SecretsWeKeep.com.**